Regionalism and the Pacific Northwest

Regionalism
and the Pacific Northwest

Edited by William G. Robbins
Robert J. Frank
Richard E. Ross

OREGON STATE UNIVERSITY PRESS
Corvallis, Oregon

The paper in this book meets the guidelines for permanence and durability of the Committee on Production Guidelines for Book Longevity of the Council on Library Resources.

Library of Congress Cataloging in Publication Data
Main entry under title:

Regionalism and the Pacific Northwest.

    1. Northwest, Pacific—Civilization—Addresses, essays, lectures. 2. Regionalism—Northwest, Pacific—Addresses, essays, lectures. I. Robbins, William G., 1935- . II. Frank, Robert J. (Robert Joseph), 1939- . III. Ross, Richard E. (Richard Everett), 1932- .
F852.2.R43 1983   979.5   83-2416
ISBN 0-87071-337-X

This book is for our children:

Andy
Aubrey
Jennifer
Jody
John
Kelly
Kirsten
Larry
Serena

PREFACE

The essays included in this book were read at a symposium on Pacific Northwest regionalism held at Oregon State University on October 29, 30, and 31, 1981. The symposium was sponsored by the Humanities Development Program with assistance from the Office of Undergraduate Studies, University Convocations and Lectures, the Office of Research, the departments of Anthropology, English, and History, the College of Liberal Arts, and the schools of Home Economics and Forestry—all at Oregon State University. The Beekman Professorship of Northwest and Pacific History at the University of Oregon also provided support.

The purpose of the symposium was to offer a "state of the art" forum for research and writing about the Pacific Northwest. Our ambition was to raise questions about the concept of "region" and to investigate the Pacific Northwest as a geographical, economic, political and cultural entity. The conference organizers also wanted the gathering to serve as a vehicle for examining the Northwest in relation to the national culture and as a state of mind. In arranging sessions and selecting presenters, we decided to include informed citizens as well as academic specialists to make this symposium truly a public one. The content of this volume suggests the degree to which our expectations were fulfilled.

We hope that the diversity of these essays will contribute to a better understanding of the past and present condition of regional thought. In this way we can learn more about ourselves and our world, so that each of us can develop a reasoned vision of a truly human regional community.

William G. Robbins
Robert J. Frank
Richard E. Ross

CONTENTS

Introduction

William G. Robbins

Although the study of regionalism in the United States dates at least to the writings of Frederick Jackson Turner, most of the published literature is fraught with contradiction and ambiguity. This intellectual disarray may well be a lasting condition, because regionalism by definition—with its many hues and shades of meaning—is largely a mental construction. But it is a phenomenon based, in part, on physiological fact. A region can be defined as a geographically homogenous entity and usually is associated with loyalty to and sense of place. As such, it is a useful reference point for examining the way in which people identify with their environment. Understanding the contradictions and limitations of regional studies offers a perspective from which to probe the broader dynamics and cohesiveness of human communities. Regionalism also implies a broadly based common perception of social reality which, while not simply and lucidly defined, directs attention to the shared particularisms of one's roots, values, and sense of purpose.

The best of regional expression, whether literary fiction, sociological treatise, or historical analysis, is grounded in social reality— the world of human aspiration and struggle, of greed and exploitation, of selfless accomplishment and tragedy. Social conditions, after all, reflect and shape attitudes toward home, community and work, and these necessarily involve a collective and wider regional consciousness. And great variety. Some communities, as on the American frontier, can be transitory with few constraints on individual action; under these circumstances identification with place, collective responsibility, and sense of rootedness are muted.

1

Despite these limitations, people have identified themselves with regions throughout the American past. They have referred to themselves as Northerners, Southerners, New Englanders, Plains dwellers, Southwesterners—and Pacific Northwesterners. These regional references took root in British imperial administration of its North American colonies, and geography, economic development, social tradition, and administrative need have perpetuated and elaborated the distinctions. Moreover, these distinctions have endured in an expanding and increasingly centralized nation-state. Although many of these regional entities provide the boundaries for federal administrative jurisdictions, they also serve as an antidote to cultural homogenization and economic centralization in a market- and commodity-oriented world.

The essence of regionalism poses a number of important questions. Do we hustle headlong into the future mindless of the centralizing and sometimes irrational demands of the modern age, or do we look more closely at our surroundings and try to understand the meaning and value of our own communities? These are the important issues and considerations to address. Paul Olson, a Nebraskan who is concerned that the ecology of the Great Plains will be permanently damaged through the heedless exploitation of its resources, refers to these concerns as the basic ingredients for regional survival. That struggle, he hints, will be against heavy odds, because the Plains, like other regions, has less control over its destiny with each passing day.

Regions are communities in a broad geographic sense with common cultural features and economic orientation. They are also the basic physical reality by which people define themselves, because human beings are both the beginning and the essence of region. Regional communities, therefore, involve mythologies and precedents which combine to forge those particularities that we associate with sense of place. Both myth and reality, the imagined and the real, shape people's consciousness of the world about them; each transforms and alters the other and thereby gives essential meaning to regionalism. Still, there are physical definitions which can circumscribe discussions of regions.

Although there is general agreement that the Pacific Northwest has certain geographic characteristics, there is great confusion as to whether the region is a distinctive entity in an economic and cultural sense. The essays in this volume reflect these ambiguities. The Northwest *is* a definitive geographic area comprising the states of Oregon, Washington, Idaho (and for those of a more generous persuasion, northern California, the mountain counties of western Montana, and southern British Columbia). It also has well-defined climatic and topographic features—a marine climate to the west of the Cascade Range and a subhumid continental climate to the east.

The region fronts the world community in two directions. From the Cascade Range east to the Rocky Mountains, aridity, dust, distance, and wind prevail and human populations have been forced to conform to these rhythms. Here the struggle centered on coping with extremes, and the effort did not always succeed. Rube Long, who lived in the Fort Rock country in eastern Oregon, characterized the high desert as a place where humidity is measured by the amount of sand in the air and where lack of moisture causes sagebrush to go looking for dogs. Long also gave testimony to the human tragedy that took place when people attempted to farm in the absence of water: "It usually took five years for a man to arrive, build a house, fence some land, break it, put in a crop, wait in vain to harvest it, lose his money, get tired of jackrabbit stew, and leave." But sensitive observers also pointed to the ennobling features of the sparse and barren eastern country. The late Supreme Court Justice William O. Douglas, who was reared in Washington's Yakima Valley, insisted that the poverty of nature east of the Cascades sharpened perception: "Even a minute violet quickened the heart when one has walked far or climbed high to find it. Where nature is more bountiful, even the tender bitterroot might go unnoticed."

But the dominating front of the Pacific Northwest and its most heavily populated area looks west to the Pacific Ocean and the international community beyond. This subregion also provides great continuity between the past and the present. Human settlement patterns, both during the Indian period and after, have been concentrated in the wet lowlands west of the Cascade Range.

Sixty-five percent of Washington's population inhabits the Puget Sound area, and more than two-thirds of the people in Oregon live within 100 miles of Portland. As if to emphasize this concentration in settlement, outsiders always have identified the green lands west of the mountains as the real heart and center of the region. When America's imperial spokesmen began casting covetous glances towards the Northwest in the 1830s and 1840s, the object of their interest centered on the lush farming country of the Willamette Valley (and later the Puget lowlands). Today people beyond the region still identify the Pacific Northwest in this way.

All of this raises important questions about the integrity of the region as a coherently defined geographic area. How does the ungainly and sometimes disparate state of Idaho fit within this framework? Are the loyalties and cultural ties of northern Idahoans directed south to the state's capitol at Boise or west to the commercial link with Spokane and the Inland Empire? And what do people living along the great stretch of the Snake River in southern Idaho have in common with the population west of the Cascade Range? Are their affinities, as Earl Pomeroy suggested nearly 20 years ago, directed to Salt Lake City and the Great Basin country? Whatever the answers, it is important that these issues are raised.

And there are other realities to consider. People living west of the Cascade Range in Oregon and Washington share more in common than those who live on opposite sides of the mountains. Residents of Brookings and Astoria in Oregon and Gray's Harbor and Port Townsend in Washington are more akin than the denizens of Eugene and Pendleton, Oregon. Within each of these two climatic zones, economic life, topographic features, and the distribution of rainfall influence human activity in different ways. It is the rich mix of these contrasting but challenging and dramatic landscapes that provides much of the stimulus for the descriptive literature of the region.

But still the Pacific Northwest does have certain physiographic features that pull the region together and function in a unifying way. The Columbia River is the most significant; it was *the* important transportation and communications arterial in Indian times and continues to work as a major regionalizing influence today. The Columbia draws the two distinct climatic areas east and west of the Cascades together. Long before the Euro-Americans arrived, native peoples traded goods through the great river corridor; today the Columbia waterway, with its tentacles reaching far into the interior, is still the great trading nexus between the Inland Empire wheat country and Pacific Rim markets. And the river's hydroelectric grid system is a superimposed physical tie linking the region together.

There are many other elements that give unity to the Pacific Northwest. The region's economy, both east and west of the mountains, has centered for the past 200 years on one or more of the region's extractive resources: furs, fishing, mining, farming, and lumbering. Such activities underscore a fundamental reality—this is a region valued for its land and resource abundance. No section of the continent was more ballyhooed as the "New Eden" than the Oregon Country in the 1840s and 1850s. These qualities have attracted newcomers and capital to the Northwest in the past—and likely will continue to do so in the future.

There is considerable controversy about the benefits the region has reaped as a consequence of turning its resources into market commodities. A good argument can be made that most of the wealth accrued through the exploitation of that abundance has gone out of the region. Dorothy Johansen, long-time history professor at Reed College, once likened the region to a cow whose feeding end was in the Pacific Northwest but whose milking apparatus was located on Wall Street.

When we turn from considerations of geography to cultural developments or discussions about the political economy, there is little agreement. But these are quarrels of the mind. Undoubtedly, as Bernard DeVoto claimed many years ago, there always existed western moods that were counter-productive to community building—a predatory belief "of letting my neighbor go his way" so that I can better jump his claim. Excessive mobility and the urge to move on to the next main chance were constant factors in undermining the substance of community. Yet there was cohesion and cooperative effort in much of the western experience. There existed in the Pacific Northwest a feeling of area-kinship, which some of the essays in this volume make evident—a distinctive way of looking at the world and a tenacity to cling to old attachments. Writers beyond the Pacific Northwest have persistently lent credibility to these qualities.

In fact, outsiders (sometimes with an abundance of uninformed self-assurance) always have been willing to speak authoritatively about the region. When the English freebooter and sea captain, Sir Francis Drake, sailed into North Pacific waters in 1579, he described a land "where the rain was an unnatural congealed substance," followed by the "most vile, thicke and stinking fogges." At the peak of the "Oregon Fever" in the 1840s, descriptions of the region defied imagination. According to Bostonian Hall Jackson Kelly, this was a land whose mountains were "peculiarly sublime and conspicuous"; it enjoyed a "salubrious" climate, was "well watered, nourished by a rich soil, and warmed by a congenial heat," and "exactly accommodated to the interests of its future cultivators." Kelly, sometimes called the "Oregon Prophet," had not yet visited the region at the time he wrote the pamphlet.

Other propagandists, railroad promoters, and political expansionists even improved Kelly's descriptions of the country. But the abundant promotional and travel literature about the Northwest points to a fundamental truth about the region—it is a land of extremes. This is evident both from the great variety of serious writing and from the grandiose accounts of polemicists who have exaggerated the region's qualities for pecuniary reasons.

There are still other intangibles that influence the regionality and distinctiveness of the Pacific Northwest. It could be argued with some conviction (at least until the Great Depression) that population mobility and the newness of community building in the region was not conducive to indigenous cultural development; the region seemed to lack the perspective of time and sense of pace necessary to produce good writers and a literature that reflected its unique qualities. But the contributions to literature of people like H. L. Davis, James Stevens, Don Berry, Ken Kesey, Richard Hugo, and most recently, Ivan Doig, suggest the existence—at least since the 1930s—of a distinctly regional style of writing. And artists like Mark Tobey, Morris Graves, Guy Anderson and Kenneth Callahan represent a genre steeped in regional symbols and signs of place. The artistic expression of these people represents a mixture of praise for the region with a healthy eye for its rough underside and provincialisms. Novelists, poets, and writers of history, in particular, have been less indulgent and more critical in their appraisal of the Pacific Northwest in the past several decades. The major piece that marks the break with the older sentimental tradition is H. L. Davis' Pulitzer Prize-winning novel, *Honey In The Horn,* published in 1935. And the name of Joseph Kinsey Howard, who so poignantly told the story of Montana's economic plight in the 1930s and 1940s, must be added to the list of those who looked realistically at the region.

But there may be danger ahead. The corporatization and homogenization of culture in our present age threatens to inhibit and suppress localized and unique creative expression. What passes for mass culture in our time is too often an assault on the cultural particularisms of place. Whether the critical tradition established by Davis and others will survive depends, in part, on the ability of the region to shape its own future.

The essays in this volume portray two attitudes about the region: that of an older era of optimism with an emphasis on "development," and a more recent tendency to question and to assess more critically the world around us. Those who share the latter view are less confident about the future. There *are,* according to John McClelland, "Fewer Acres of Clams," and there *is* the awesome fact, as Jarold Ramsey points out, that the explosion of the atomic bomb over Hiroshima in 1945 suddenly pushed the rural Northwest headlong into the international community. Northwesterners are vividly aware that they are part of a broader political culture, as fluctuating interest rates, MX missile proposals, and other schemes coming from outside the region make apparent. Congressional passage of the Northwest Power Planning and Conservation Act in 1980 is but one example of legislation that gives coherence to the Northwest at the same time it erodes the region's autonomy.

The contributors to this book reveal great diversity of thought on the issue of regionalism. Robin Winks draws upon his broad international experience to show the variety of regional particularisms that are manifested in symbol and myth. His global and continental view suggests both the complexity and ambiguity of regional definitions. By contrast, Judith Austin points to specific geographical and historical realities that unite the Northwest. There are, she suggests, truly *western* qualities of the Pacific Northwest that exist primarily in its *eastern*-most parts. Desert and sagebrush as well as rainclouds, she argues, have shaped the land and its people; the present need is for a reasoned and fair assessment of the region.

The Austin and Winks essays address similar issues—the symbols, landforms, and cultural exhibitions that identify distinct and unique qualities of a region. More comprehensive is Richard Maxwell Brown's extended discussion of western/northwestern literature, cinema, art and architecture. Brown examines previous tendencies toward regionalist thinking and provides convincing evidence of resurging interest in regional particularities in the Pacific Northwest and elsewhere in recent years. Left unanswered in his wide-ranging discussion are the underlying reasons for the emergence and popularity of magazines and other publications with a decidedly regional focus. Certainly the sales appeal of books like Ernest Callenbach's *Ecotopia* should be attributed, in part, to the troubled times of the 1970s and 1980s.

In other times the Pacific Northwest also has produced writing of real literary merit that reflected the tensions and ambiguities of the region. The region, Edwin Bingham contends, was "something more than backdrop"; the best Northwest writers and poets always found sustenance for their creative work in an environment that was limited and local. Jarold Ramsey's "New Era" essay provides a striking example. Growing up in the stark, high country of eastern Oregon, Ramsey's reminiscence captures a slice of life that was unique to its time and place. But an increasingly mobile population and the postwar housing boom destroyed this distinctive cultural milieu, as the Deschutes River country was turned into a recreational playground.

Human cultures with widely differing values have shaped the Pacific Northwest landscape, with the most dramatic alterations to the river, forest and prairie environment occurring over the past 150 years. Today, as Richard Ross and David Brauner point out, international boundaries circumscribe the borders of these cultural regions. Before white penetration of the area, however, environmental conditions and geographical features shaped aboriginal peoples' adaptation, and a cultural homogeneity developed that extended well beyond present geopolitical boundaries. All of the cultural systems that existed on this Pacific edge of the continent, Richard White tells us, have altered the regional landscape, but the most extensive changes are very recent. White suggests that the consequences of these predominantly capitalist economic drives do not bode well for the future of the Northwest environment.

The nation's economic problems, which have grown steadily more serious over the past few years, have bred a verbal divisiveness between the different sections of the United States. David Sarasohn explores the symbolic differences between the Frost Belt, Sun Belt, and Rain Belt (Northwest) states over issues such as energy policy and population. Although he ignores the possiblility that these differences may be rooted in historical antecedents related to capital movement and profit flow, one can discern that there are major forces underlying the present drift toward sectionalist sentiment that he identifies.

PERSPECTIVES ON
REGIONALISM

Regionalism
In Comparative Perspective

Robin W. Winks

Not too many months ago a number of students of regionalism were gathered at the University of Mississippi to discuss "Regionalism in America." Some participants were amused to discover that the presentations by one person created little knots of anger at each session in which he appeared. The person was Raymond D. Gastil, author of *Cultural Regions of the United States,* and the sources of anger and annoyance were never precisely focused.[1] As a relative newcomer (and historian) amongst a body dominated by folklorists and sociologists, I found much to disagree with in Gastil's presentation, though I was far more interested in the reaction to his views. What was it about his argument that so irritated the *cognescenti?* Some were offended by Gastil's identification of an area he called "The Mormon Region"; others thought him methodologically unsound to equate a state (Alaska) with an entire region; others found the use of homicide rates, educational performance, white infant mortality, and other sociological indicators inappropriate or insufficient to define regional boundaries. I decided that Gastil's principal sin, however, was to attempt what his title said he would attempt—cultural (as opposed to demographic or physical) definitions of region.

Overwhelmingly we Americans have chosen to define regions through geography. I do not mean that we have been simple-minded geographical determinists. I mean that, in common with most settler societies, we have engaged in a long-standing love affair with our landscapes. We are enamoured with the idea of movement, and unless that movement reveals some substantive difference, movement has lost its meaning. We are unwilling to accept what the untutored eye might see—similarity so vast that dozens of states reveal no fundamental differences. This view (particularly common in *New Yorker* cartoons) produces one of our most pervasive mental maps, which unites the self-consciously intellectual denizens of both coasts. This map shows "the bit in between" as one vast cultural desert, with Iowa indistinguishable from Indiana and both Dakotas equally foresquare.

To combat the suspicion that everything between the Alleghanies and the Sierras is one long dial tone, Americans have tended to boast of our size, of our diversity, and of a sense of healthy competition between the regions. (When the competition is unhealthy we have called it sectionalism.) Using geography, with particular emphasis on rainfall, modes of production, and self-conscious self-perceptions, we have traditionally recognized no fewer than four regions in our historiography and in our university curriculae. When the American Historical Association was producing its excellent series of pamphlets for teachers of history, it recognized the customary four regions: New England, the South, the West (which until recently embraced all land beyond the Mississippi), and the part that was leftover—the Middle West. In 1951, when Merrill Jensen edited *Regionalism in America*[2] (still possibly the most influential book on the subject), these were the regions of conventional wisdom, though Jensen recognized agriculture, technology, and modes of production as factors in regional identity by including essays on the Tennessee Valley Authority, the Great Lakes cutover region, and the Pacific Northwest.

I have no quarrel with either of these approaches. Common sense and my own love affair with the American landscape make me comfortable with the conventional definitions of region. On the other hand, my travel in all 50 states, my ear for accent and language, and my close study of economic imperialism make Gastil's definitions seem reasonably compatible. I find I can work with either set of definitions, with any number of working models, and enjoy the contradictions between them without suffering mental indigestion over their ambiguities. Nor do I assume that Jensen was the first, or Gastil the last, word.

Rather, what has always intrigued me in Jensen, Gastil, and the range of books that fall between them, is their insularity. Though regionalism is meant to be a door into national as well as regional character, we seldom use our arguments about regionalism to ask questions about the nation as a whole. To be sure, Frederick Jackson Turner, Walter Prescott Webb, David M. Potter, and C. Vann Woodward have used arguments about regions to illuminate the nation's history, but they are exceptions, both in being giants and in using the region as a microcosm for the whole. Most regional history in the United States looks inward, not outward, and becomes a slightly expanded version of local history. Authors tell us how split-rail fences in Missouri differ from those in Vermont; we discover how technology, the breed of sheep, and the distance to market led to different types of barbed wire in place x as opposed to place y; and we learn that Canadians, State of Mainers, and a few others pronounce vowels in the Scottish manner. Our terror and love for our vast continent leads us to think it so large that one cannot reasonably look outside it for insights. Though all settler societies have developed in stages marked by fundamental changes in life style, regionalists in the United States (except for comparative frontier scholars) have refused to ask whether arguments about regionalism in Australia, Canada, the Soviet Union, South Africa, Great Britain, or among the *annalistes* of France might have anything to tell us about ourselves. Neither Jensen nor Gastil contains a single reference to any of these nations or their historiographies.

I share the belief that there are deep differences between the people of, say, California, Indiana, and Vermont. I also share the belief that much of the dynamism of this society has sprung from these differences; generations of Americans believed that if they did not like the values of one place, or if they were unsuccessful, unfulfilled, or just plain bored, they could strike out for new territory to find new freedom, a second chance, a different game. I see this tension between the regions as largely desirable, even aesthetically beautiful, like the "divine tension" admired by students of Greek sculpture. I deplore the national tendency toward homogeneity and remain fascinated with the minutiae of difference—

whether a yellow center line tells one to pass or not to pass, whether one may marry at 15 or 18, or whether the state kills its criminals by drug injection, firing squad, hangman's noose, electric chair, or simple neglect. Nothing is so culturally deadening as a centralized nation.

Yet I suspect that much of this is my own nostalgic romanticism. There are markedly few lands of beginning again in a great depression, and since the New Deal our nation has moved ever closer toward a common set of expectations. Denver and New York are one region in a nuclear war, both targets. Phoenix and Boston are one region in an energy-depleted nation, one needing cool air and the other hot air for comfort. A sense of regional pride survives, though too often couched in terms of an adversarial relationship to Washington (as in the alleged Sagebrush Rebellion), and less often in terms of pride in some positive characteristic unique to the self-defined region.

The definitions of region supplied by Jensen and his authors have been swept aside by Depression, New Deal, War, and the New Immigration.

Regions still survive in the United States, and they can best be studied from a comparative perspective. They were shaped historically by many factors, though four require emphasis above all others. These four factors are cultural, geographic, economic, and situational; they are not mutually exclusive, since the situational grows in part from the geographic, and what I describe as economic is, at least in part, the product of the cultural.

These four factors can be reduced for purposes of simplicity to four questions. What was the nature of the people who came to occupy a particular landscape? What about the geography of that landscape, in its location, configuration, natural resources, and amenability to the prevailing technology, made it particular? What was the nature of the interaction between those people, on that landscape, with other people on the fringes of the landscape and with the indigenous people found there? What controlling influences continued to be exercised from a distance upon the people, the landscape, and the interactions? While these questions are capable of normative historical answers, one must add a fifth question, since all true history is the history of thought: what did the people perceive to be true of their situation, how did they transmit those perceptions, and what is the prevailing coventional wisdom about the history of the region? For as all historians know, what really matters in understanding human motivation and pride is not what actually happened but what people believe about what they think happened.

Regional Perspectives in Literature

Let us begin with the last point, for it is at the core of my argument. What, for example, did the conventionally wise believe about the West as a region (and in particular about the literature of the West as an indicator of the region), when they first began to teach about the West as a place, a process, and a state of mind in American life?

One of the earliest scholarly works to deal with western literature was the product, in 1900, of Barrett Wendell of Harvard. He referred to the "relaxed inexperience" of Westerners who were "the lower sort of Americans"; the Westerner was inclined to "revert to the ancestrally extinct," he thought, and western writing reflected an "obnoxious materialistic" bent. As Wendell surveyed the "great confused west," he found only three writers whom he thought might one day be taken seriously: George Horatio Derby, Charles Farrar Browne, and David Ross Locke (the last two just recognizable as Artemus Ward and Petroleum B. Nasby). Five years later another survey of American literature by Alfonso Newcomer told its readers that one must be prepared in reading materials from the West for "altered standards."

Yet were Wendell and Newcomer necessarily so wrong? What is at issue here is the West's evolving definition of itself and its literature. As Henry Nash Smith argued so persuasively in *Virgin Land* over 30 years ago, the place, process, and state of mind one may divine from Beadle's Dime Novels tells us much about the American consciousness. Smith also told us a good bit about the problem of defining literatures, especially regional literatures, in terms of elite authors. Genuine regionalism often must rest, to be recognizably regional, upon elements of the formulaic. One need not accept all the formulaic elements singled out by John Cawelti in his analysis of the *Six-Gun Mystique* to recognize the artistic line between a Remington, a Theodore Roosevelt, and an Owen Wister. A sense of place is essential to regional awareness, and a commonality of place does tend toward the formulaic. Even the highly regarded regional literature of the South has its formulae; compare *Intruder in the Dust* with *Reflections in a Golden Eye*.

John Steinbeck, Walter Clark, Robinson Jeffers, and Willa Cather wrote of far more complex themes than Wendell or Newcomer ever dreamed. These writers understood that a region is a place, a process, and a state of mind; they saw intuitively what Frederick Jackson Turner, David Potter, Vann Woodward, and the entire range of historians who have sought to identify regionality have told us. They understood the American Adam even before R.W.B. Lewis wrote of him. They understood the power of the arrival scene—the immigrant from another regional culture confronting for the first time a new landscape which was a metaphor of the new life.

Best of all, the far western writer could see the connection between the apparently eastern-rooted work of a James Fenimore Cooper and that of a Raymond Chandler. Through dangerous eastern forests, as down these mean streets, a man must walk. The movement from Natty Bumppo to A. B. Guthrie is clear for all to see; with a little closer look, the movement from Cooper's *The American Democrat* to the detective fiction of Hammett, Chandler, and Ross Macdonald can be seen as plainly. For what is the modern, urban-California detective thriller but the older, formulaic fiction of Zane Grey brought up to date? Today the cowboy has come down from the hills, down off his mustang, and has climbed into his Mustang to take to the freeways of the modern condition. The West is at once the land of beginning again and the land of ultimate continuity; though streetscapes may be of a certain place, the themes are as universal as sour soil and acid rain.[3]

A sense of place is essential to history and to literature, but the best of both uses that sense of place as the base for a universal human credibility. Surely no one thinks of Steinbeck as a regional author. Yet so skilled a writer as Walter Van Tilburg Clark continues to be seen in a western regional context, even though *The Oxbow Incident* is as powerful in its examination of guilt and its public perception as Hawthorne's *Scarlet Letter*. We recognize the universal content of *Moby Dick* and do not dismiss Melville as a mere regional novelist from the Massachusetts coast. Why, then, do we not see that Clark was attempting a western *Moby Dick* when he wrote *The Track of the Cat,* as obsessive in its pursuit of destiny and as careful in its examination of character (if not as magisterial in prose) as Melville's work?

The literary establishment continues to categorize books through mental maps that thrust upon the deserts and mountains of the West the expectations of another region. In 1945 Edmund Wilson found the literature of the West (by which he meant Steinbeck and Clark!) "too easy going and good natured . . . always dissolving into an even sunshine . . ."[4] Can Wilson possibly have been reading the Clark who wrote of the great black cat that moved through men's souls, or the Steinbeck who wrote of the grapes of wrath harvested by those who believed in the dream of a better life to be found beyond the borders of the conventional mental maps of the time?

Geographic Perspectives

But let us not engage in the old game of defending western writers against the Eastern establishment. After all, there is not even agreement on how many regions there are in the United States. Raymond Gastil found 13. The National Park Service has decided there are 6. Merrill Jensen implied there were 7. Most university curriculae, replicating the mistake of organizing historical study in terms of national identities, admit to 4. None of this is very helpful, and when definitions of region are so solidified as to place Missouri in the Middle West, Arkansas in the South, and eastern Colorado in the West, we ought to know that we are in trouble. The problem with most definitions is that they reveal the principal bias of their orginator more clearly than they tell the scholar who keeps an icicle in his eye how to organize data for analysis.

In one sense we are engaged, to the extent that we are seeking definitions of region, in a game both fruitless and foolish. The risks are parallel to those that arise from organizing historical or social inquiry in terms of national identities. Most American universities, after all, offer courses in the history of France, the history of England, the history of China, etc.

To organize the study of history in this way is to encourage students in a subtle Whig bias, that history is about the rise of the nation-state and that once Italy or Germany have been created, something triumphant about human identity has been asserted. Of course history is about the rise of the nation-state, but only partially; it is also about problems—imperialism, the Industrial Revolution, the Protestant Reformation, socialism, capitalism—that cut across national boundaries. Nonetheless we continue to imply that capitalism in x or y must be different from capitalism in a or b when we fragment its study into national receptacles. Not only does this practice encourage students in dangerous provincialism and the assertive chauvinistic assumption that the history of the United States is unique, but it encourages all the biases inherent in the principle of exceptionalism. Stated this way, we can see that the nation-state is not the only or best receptacle for collecting and analyzing data about the human condition. For the same reasons, we should look closely at the basic assumptions of those who want to further fragment the possibilities for comparative analysis by teaching regional studies or something called Texas History or New Jersey History.

Americans are victims—in our literature, our history, and our foreclosed options—of our mental maps. A few years ago two British scholars looked at the mental maps of American university students in five locations, four in the North and West and one in the deep South. A few of their examples are sufficient to make their central point clear. The Minnesota Viewpoint, as they labeled it, was based on a study of the perceptions of regional identity in relation to spatial location as reported by university-educated individuals at the University of Minnesota. I quote: "A local dome of desirability forms the primary peak of the surface over Minnesota, but there is also a high ridge of desirability along the west coast reaching out from a secondary peak in California . . . the Utah Basin and Colorado High are quite distinct, and the steepest gradient on the entire surface is west to the Dakota Sinkhole. The Southern Trough is the lowest area . . ."

For North Dakotans, just next door, the Denver area and the Pacific Coast were thought to be the most desirable locations in the United States, higher even than North Dakota itself (counter to the perception everywhere else that anyplace other than home was a bit lower on the scale of acceptability). No wonder, then, that the Dakotas have been a persistent area of outward migration.

Texans, however, had quite a different perception of space, for they saw California as quite near (because it was both large and desirable, as was Texas), and they measured Florida, Utah, Connecticut, and Missouri as equidistant from Texas. Off the scale of acceptability was Alabama, with Rhode Island orbiting roughly in the position of Pluto. So far as Texans perceived human geography in terms of similar cultural environments, the region of which they were the center consisted of themselves and California.

The same phenomenon can be observed in other nations. In Aberystwyth, Wales, all of Scotland appears beyond the Pale, though London and the southeast of England are roughly on a par culturally. A few miles north, in Bangor, Wales, Aberystwyth is seen as similar to the Scottish Lowlands, and Lancastershire is perceived as one of the few areas more desirable. In Australia, Sydneysiders see themselves as closer to San Francisco than to Perth, so deep is the regional division fostered in part by separate colonial status until 1901. In South Africa, the Orange Free State is, in name and in language, closer to the Netherlands than to the neighboring state at Cape Town.[5]

Economic Perspectives

The commonest definitions of region used in the United States are at once emotional and economic. We contend that ours has been an economy of abundance and that we have been, in David Potter's words, a "people of plenty." Yet most regions tend to define themselves in negative terms in relation to this perception of our national character. The South has always seen poverty as part of its identity; the West has argued that it was the victim of exploitation by Wall Street, or the eastern railroads, or the federal government; and New England clutches to its bosom the notion of prudence, the rural poor, and antique decay as central to its aristocratic yet genteel poverty. Someone else is always to blame for these economic realities, of course.

The grievance collectors in these regions may well be right in their analysis of negative regionalism, though they are in no sense unique. Were they to look abroad to the larger question of world poverty and exploitation, they might wish to reformulate their arguments. On the whole I hold with P. T. Bauer of the London School of Economics that economic differences are primarily the result of individual capacities and motivations and are not the fault of social organization (though obviously the way a society is organized may circumscribe what is desirable in the individual).

Just as different academic disciplines view the world differently because they are asking different questions, regions perceive themselves differently in part because their environment and economies make them different, and in even greater part because they have attracted individuals whose definitions of freedom, or success, or self-identity differ. The end result is, on a large scale, somewhat akin to Irving Goffman and Clifford Geertz's idea of the "focused gathering"—a body of people who achieve their focus (and thus their inner coherence) because they share common attitudes toward values of central importance to them. Geertz calls this "deep play" and argues that even in our games and recreation we reveal what we expect of each other, our neighbors, the state, the past, and the future.

Historical Perspectives

Consider these intriguing indications of different conceptions of history (and, thus, of self-identity and pride). In the United States we mark what we call "historic sites"—that is, places where events deemed to have historical significance occurred. It does not matter whether a vestige of the original site has survived; a plaque on the wall of a high-rise building in New York City will tell you that Henry James once lived there. In England, on the other hand, only sites not substantially altered are regarded as historic. In the United States we focus on the role of the individual (often the heroic individual). Of the 326 units in our National Parks System (of which the great majority are historic, rather than scenic or natural), 5 are devoted to Theodore Roosevelt. In Britain, Claverton Manor is preserved because it is architecturally significant; it was Americans who placed a plaque on the building denoting the place where Winston Churchill gave his maiden political speech. In Canada, nearly 50 percent of National Historic Sites are subtly about war, defense, and the establishment of an identity separate from the United States; that is, they are covertly anti-American.

Canadians learn by reading a plaque erected in Windsor by the Historic Sites Board of Ontario that "here, under the Lion's paw, the fugitive slave found freedom," clearly reinforcing Canada's belief in its moral superiority to the United States. No plaque anywhere tells that slavery was legal in Canada until 1833.

One may expect historical awareness to be manipulated to national ends, perhaps, and one ought not be surprised to find the same within a single nation. Visit Andersonville, Georgia. There, in the great cemetery where so many of the Union dead are buried, is a monument erected by the federal government (that is, by the victor) that remarks on the harsh treatment meted out to prisoners by the camp commandant. In the center of the village stands a statue, paid for by the grateful citizens of the village, that honors the commandant as a hero, maligned and innocent.

Why, one wonders does New Mexico provide the passing motorist with a place to park, and read at leisure of the history encountered along the highway, while Pennsylvania and Virginia erect signs too small to read along the busiest highways without advance warning or parking place? Obviously one state has more room than the other, but it also has more regard for history and more awareness that public historiography is a contribution to education, statement of ideology, and an assertion of pride. One wonders whether these attitudes are paralleled in school texts, local museums, and political speeches.

Not long ago, I presided over hearings to consider new nominations to the list of National Historic Landmarks. The nominees included Bear Butte, the most sacred mountain of the Cheyenne Indians (in South Dakota), Thorstein Veblen's farmstead and the Peavy-Haglin Experimental Concrete Grain Elevator (both in Minnesota), and Little Rock Central High School (in Arkansas). As the discussion developed, I thought about how regions revealed themselves through their sense of why their history was to be commemorated.

No region cares to memorialize those aspects of its history which now stand condemned. Consider the South. To many, slavery was central to a separate Southern identity; to many others, slavery was a deviation from the central core of that identity. Two of the South's most noted historians, Potter and Woodward, sought out identifying characteristics other than slavery. Potter pointed to the family, concern for the soil, and the agrarian tradition, while Woodward emphasized the impact of the South's defeat and military occupations. A New England regional historian might be forgiven for concluding that the characteristics singled out by Potter and Woodward took on special meaning because of slavery. Neither position would be wholly wrong or right, though each position speaks eloquently of the way in which a region needs to perceive itself.

If one drives through Scottsboro, Alabama today, one finds four state historical markers around the tidy courthouse square. One marks the oldest opera house in northeast Alabama; none commemorates that single event by which most of us know Scottsboro. Traveling through the small Connecticut River villages of Vermont, one may read of local hero Jacob Bayley, who sought to hold Vermont to the new United States in 1791, when the majority of its leaders seriously considered reuniting with Canada and the British Empire. Nowhere will one encounter a plaque that openly admits that Vermont (the 14th state) voted its pocketbook and, playing both sides of the Revolution, held aloof until long after the Peace of Paris of 1783.

Bias, do we say, or simply a different regional perception of what events mean? "Tell the truth, and tell it slant," Emily Dickinson wrote, and this is what much regional history does (and perhaps ought to do). The nomination of Little Rock Central High School as a national landmark offered in justification the fact that the high school had gone undefeated for many years in football and that the structure was widely regarded as one of the most beautiful in the state; somewhat incidentally it mentioned that the school was where the federal government first enforced the Supreme Court's school desegregation decision. To the national historian surely the last is the high school's only claim to fame; yet, to the regionalist, may not the beauty of its architecture and the pride of its athletic tradition be as significant? How do we compare these two perceptions of reality?

In any case, almost never does the regionally oriented historian, as revealed through the roadside plaques, see the regional event in larger perspective; he shrinks rather than expands the event and the region in which it occurred. Beecher's Island or Wounded Knee are about far more than Colorado or South Dakota, though we would not know it to visit the sites. "The frontiers are not east or west, north or south, but wherever a man fronts a fact," as Henry Thoreau saw in his week on the Concord and Merrimack rivers.

One of the problems in perceiving a region's history arises from the plain fact that history (especially historical preservation and public historiography) is the special interest of the literate upper middle class. Visit the Museum of the Plains Indian, a federal institution in the midst of the Blackfeet reservation, and see how regional history is depicted there. The so-called traditional costumes are those of the late 19th century, the time to which the thousands of white tourist visitors can best relate—a time when Indian culture was already deeply influenced by the encroaching whites. Read the labels: "The arrival of the White Man and his trade goods . . . served to revolutionize Native American cultures, providing the tribes with miraculous new tools. The Plains Indian culture blossomed and became the classic American Indian culture which we are familiar with today." Horses and guns "vastly improved" the Indian's method of hunting buffalo. Indian chiefs who joined forces with the whites were "wise," while those who turned to war dances were "superstitious."[6] It is little wonder that the Blackfeet seldom visit "their" museum, for it is not theirs; it is a testimonial to the needs of the western regional culture to convince itself that the white man helped the Indian rise to the moment of his greatest glory.

Let me disavow any intention here to argue that either southern or western regional identities are imbued with racism. They may be, though this is not the thrust of my argument. I do not contest the fact that the victor writes the history, and that the story of Indian-white settler conflict will, for most persons, be seen through the eyes of the settlers.

The story of the defeat of the Indian is the old story of empire—the impact of a high technology culture on a lesser technology. In asserting that the United States had and has an empire, I am simply asserting a fact about technologies, power, and the movement of people. Britain had an empire, as did France, Germany, Spain, Portugal, and the United States. Yet western regional historians, bent upon resisting the fact of American imperialism (they prefer the term "expansionism"), cut themselves off from the hard-eyed studies of other empires in Canada, Australia, Kenya, or Rhodesia, by which they might have learned much about how other high-technology societies deal with more primitive native societies.

Cultural Perspectives

The new regionalism of the 1970s and 1980s arises from a variety of factors: from new senses of grievance and new sources of strength; from new encouragements by the National Endowment for the Humanities (or, perhaps in negative ways, by the Department of the Interior); and from new types of scholars and writers who construct their worlds in regional terms (that is, from a renewed or persistent sense of place).

We hunger for this sense of place in our architecture, music, films, food, and whatever linguistic, demographic, and economic realities the cliometricians may point to. In the end Ivan Doig, John McPhee, Larry McMurtry, John Updike, and K. C. Constantine are writing about a domestic sociology that emerges from the particularity of place.

The main indicators of regional identity must at root be emotional. There must be a broadly common body of opinion, a set of regional symbols (perhaps regional sounds and songs which are the counterpart to a national anthem). Certainly there will be regional heroes, regional shrines, and a regional literature. The last, being the most accessible, will be the most studied: chairbound scholars or those whose values are essentially bookish will measure the maturity and distinction of a region from its literature. This may be a mistake.

For the region, like the nation, draws upon the oldest and most primitive feelings of mankind—the need for security achieved through social groups. Hans Kohn's fine phrase used to explain nationalism is equally applicable to regionalism: "The immense power of habitude" leads one to take pride in native characteristics, whether in any objective sense they are worthy of pride or not. The more primitive, or insecure, or assailed a people are, the more they will bolster their sense of identity through what Kohn calls "vital lies"—commonly held beliefs which, even though they may be proved false, are so widely and tenaciously held that they serve the function of truth. Nathan Hale never said he regretted that he had but one life to give for his country; not all who live in Seattle are laid back; and not all long-distance runners live in Eugene. But continue to hold to these lies, for they are vital to a sense of worth, a sense of place, and, most important, a sense of separation and distance from others. Regionalism is the history of ideas, for regional identity is an operable truth. Myths have a way of perpetuating themselves and of becoming real, if not true.

Thus a region may see itself as created by nature, by God, or by some ill-defined mystical force often called Providence or History. Hard-headed practitioners of the regional craft will discover that it has been determined by soil, natural boundaries, perhaps even by blood. Self-concious regionalism will be the product of the self-aware and reasonably articulate. Invariably there will be a presumption of a commonly shared struggle for existence, against environment, against the tyranny of distance (to use a happy Australian phrase), against Wall Street, Bay Street, Bloor Street, or Lombard Street. The region may be unified within and separated from others by common speech, though this seems to me much less important in a mobile society than Raymond Gastil has argued. There will certainly be an assumption of a common historical past, so that evolutionary arguments will come into play. The passwords and high-signs, intonations and rhythms, the badges of identity in custom and tradition, will be learned quickly by those who seek to belong to the region. Negatively or positively, there will be the equivalent of the Hegelian dialectical notion of a "living and active corporate will."

How, then, will this sense of corporate will be communicated? Social communications are exceptionally complex, and for every integrative process one may theoretically identify at work within a broadly defined geographical area, there will be fissiparous tendencies equally at work on the fringes. Cultural learning and unlearning, a sense of mutual responsiveness between identities, even mutual interdependence, may lead to self-conscious role playing by a group of people, who (as in Canada today) see themselves as defenders of the national rather than a regional identity.

The range of activities across which social transactions transpire is enormous. Karl W. Deutsch, a political scientist, listed measures of communication that he felt contributed to the development of a sense of separate identity. His proposed inventory is helpful in the sense that it is, at the least, inclusive and orderly. Let us recall for a moment those measures of social communication Deutsch felt most significant to the creation of a self-conscious identity.

Regions are, in part, identified by political realities. There no longer is a solid South and not every western state is Republican, but there are shared attitudes toward legislative and electoral functions, toward the role of the judiciary, and toward administrative and appointive powers. That is, we do define democracy differently, or we would not continue to debate gun laws, abortion, and the ERA. Whether as product or cause, there are noticeable differences in regional perceptions of both public and private finance; some of us close our universities and shut down schools before we block off our thruways. Approaches to the capital market, to interest rates, to investment probabilities and to the ethos of saving for the rainy day differ, to the extent that federal regulations permit.

Even in the distributioin of commodities—that is, in our definitions of the good life and of appropriate modes of production—there are clear regional differences. Capital goods, basic foods, basic clothing, housing, services, and the prevailing definition of what comprises a luxury as opposed to a necessity are balanced in quite different ways even from state to state. These elements may appear to be a statement about economics, though in fact what is significant is the debate—the intellectual history of the manipulation of these factors—over the meaning of these values.

There are, too, more obviously nonmaterial issues involved in regional differentiation. Personal mobility is important both to stabilizing a broad region and to bringing change within the region. Migration patterns, the nature of the labor market, travel, educational residence, and even athletic rivalries play significant roles in determining, sustaining, and expressing regional loyalties. So, too, do literary rates, health rates, distribution of religious affiliations, the quality and content of newspapers, the parochial nature of local periodicals, and how local radio and television stations define news. Indirect and informal communications reinforce self-identity (and the reverse side of the coin, insularity), whether through fashion, language, idiom, rumor, preferences in styles of leadership, definitions of imitation and freedom, or more subtly, through ideologies. The mental maps that result define what British sociologist Alan Shuttleworth calls "humane centers"—places which comfortably define for us our own sense of our humanity.[7] The result is the creation of idols for our tribe.[8] As the distinguished folklorist Barre Toelken has remarked in an essay on Northwest regional folklore, "local lies allow local people to focus on the emotional and personal factors of their environment . . ."[9] Lies are no less vital for being local and heroes no less heroic for being unknown four counties away.

Comparative Approaches to Regionalism

Comparative studies have passed through a peak of fashionability. The fact that many so-called comparative inquiries have been found wanting does not render the technique invalid, at least as a descriptive and interpretive art, if not an analytical one. Too often allegedly comparative work has merely consisted of a series of parallel studies, with the reader left to draw his own conclusions. Of course peasants in Japan and Turkey have certain characteristics in common which help us define the concept "peasant"; of course the cultural surroundings of peasants in Japan and Turkey are so different as to render all but the broadest generalizations misleading. The lumpers amongst us are content with the broadest of generalizations and the splitters will have none of even the lowest level of generality, so comparative studies are unlikely to please many. Social science seeks for generalization and history for individualization. Yet if the historian has any hypotheses—and clearly he does, since no one really believes that history is simply the record of one damn thing after another—then generalizations must be used. Comparing regions is no more difficult than any other comparative task, and comparing approaches to regionalism within different nations is simply one more step removed from particularization.

What one needs is a set of firm definitions of concepts so that data may be homogenized sufficiently to allow for comparison. Obviously one must compare the comparable: regions of arid settlement in Australia, South Africa, or the United States; regions of tropical agriculture in the southeast United States, Malaya, Queensland, or Natal. Most comparisons fail if one insists—as a scientist properly should—on strictly comparable sets of data, for such will seldom exist. Amongst the sillier errors attributable to the controversial work of Fogel and Engerman in their analysis of the anatomy of exploitation was their conclusion that slaves in the South in 1860 actually enjoyed a higher level of caloric intake than did the white population in the nation in 1879. For one thing, Fogel and Engermann had no way to take into account work loads, or the relative price of peas, or the fact that their nutritional analyses were based on present knowledge, which differs from the knowledge of plantation owners in 1860. Although they engaged in some clever work on milk production and showed that sweet potatoes (which blacks ate) contained more calories than white potatoes (which whites ate), they had no way to compare class, aesthetic, or ancillary disease issues. Most important, they compared the caloric intake of slaves in 1860, at the top of a curve of improved food supplies for slaves in the face of vigorous attacks from northern abolitionists, with the caloric intake of whites in 1879, at the bottom of a curve of food intake following the worst depression of the century.

Clearly there are dangers, and one ought not to claim for comparative studies any special scientific accuracy. The accuracy in the method is precisely the same as the accuracy in any historian's method; it is the accuracy of common sense, of probabilities, and of leaps of faith between data and conclusion.

For those who wish methodologies other than those customarily applied by the historian, I am prepared to assert the following propositions, though I have no expectation of proving them all here now (or some of them ever). Regions are customarily defined in economic, political, and demographic/land form terms; yet, regions may also be defined much as nations are, in terms of shared historical experiences. The theoretical literature on nationalism, as well as the theoretical literature on imperialism, is at least as applicable (and is certainly fresher) to regional studies as the literature we customarily employ. Obviously economics, politics, and geographical determinants play a role in shaping the historical experience, but there are also matters of history which either reach outside these limits or are more sharply limited. So, when one examines a region in terms of its self-conscious historical awareness, it emerges with quite different boundaries.

I believe one best understands how people conceive of themselves regionally by observing what they take collective pride in. And this, over time, is best measured by what they consciously choose to preserve from the culture (mythical or real) that they have historically defined for themselves through operable truths and vital lies. The Rocky Mountains and New England are obviously self-conscious regions in this sense, and the Rocky Mountain

Empire is real, not the creation of the Denver newspapers. In the same sense, there is a Vermont character which is distinct from the New England character.

Regional identities emerge with equal clarity when one asks how people seek to preserve the visible symbols of their invisible past. Cultural traits override economic and geographical realities, as the recent Iranian revolution surely proves. In the final analysis, the economists from the Chase Manhattan Bank are wrong; Canadians will lower their standard of living, if they must, in order to control their own natural resources. However compelling the logic of economics, Canadians are tired of being thought to be simply a regional culture within the North American commonality.

A Comparative Approach to History

What, then, must the comparativist do to avoid the kind of problem Fogel and Engerman created for themselves? For the historian, comparative study had best focus on two or more different regions within a single nation, rather than the cross-cultural comparisons between societies so dear to anthropologists. For one thing, the particularity of historical data makes it difficult to find instances where statistics have been kept in approximately similar ways in different societies. Furthermore, we compare regions in order to discover the relative representativeness of a cultural characteristic; to make such a judgment, we must know the cultures compared equally well. White settler societies offer a legitimate basis for comparison, so asking questions about regionalism in the United States, Canada, Australia, South Africa, and perhaps New Zealand makes sense. Asking the same questions about China would be useful only to dramatize differences.

The regional scholar in the United States who does not know the analogous literature in Australia does not truly know the literature to a grasp of the cultural differentials in his own region. On the other hand, the scholar who knows that the Inuit deal with death in one way while the Maori deal with it in another knows something about the varieties of human responses to death, but he has learned nothing about regions. Explicit comparison must be conducted in the middle distance, and this is precisely the distance which our mental maps generally reflect.

Australia and Canada are among the "regions of recent settlement," as defined by the economic historian Ragnar Nurkse. Massive transfers of North Atlantic people, technology, and capital created colonies that became nations while showing all the aspects of a regionally dependent economy. Just as Canada developed through a succession of staple dependencies, so Australia was a continuum of colony, nation, and region held together by the reality of economic dependency, compounded by the tyranny of distance. The intervention of nationalist historiographies has retarded an understanding of how recent settlement (in Nurkse's meaning of the phrase) created societies that were simultaneously nations and regions. For example, if one compares Canada and Argentina, one finds striking similarities in staple dependency, economic awareness, and conflicting sources of historical pride. One finds even more striking comparisons between Australia and Argentina, and equally valuable areas of comparability are apparent when one examines New Zealand and Uruguay (which in turn bear marked similarities to Montana).

The great comparative historian Marc Bloch argued that genuine comparative history requires a similarity between phenomena examined and a dissimilarity between the environments in which the events under examination occur. Political realities provide the dissimilarities, while the economic facts of recent settler conflicts with indigenous peoples, in relation to the three dominant factors upon which I have already touched, provide the similarities.

The United States, Argentina, and Australia offer this kind of comparative opportunity, for each involved substantial settlement in grasslands environments where a sturdy yeomanry based on homesteading provided a dependent population with both a sense of place and a sense of grievance. Regional realities developed in the United States partly on the basis of access to markets—that is, based on the pattern of the railways. This was also the case in Argentina, where the railways were regulated by the government. In Australia, however, the railways were built by governments, and market forces did not determine the pattern of growth. Thus the

Argentine Pampas became a coherent region expressive of rural capitalism, while the Australian Outback became a series of outlying dependencies by coastal cities in such a way as to render Australia effectively into a series of islands without genuine regional identities. The American upper Midwest represented a vital, if disgruntled, peripheral capitalism.

Each nation developed regions, and each identified the regions with different indicators. There was, to be sure, a Pampan literature, just as there would be a porteno literature; in the United States, there was a literature of the Middle Border, as there was a literature of the Burnt Over District earlier; in Australia, there was a literature of the city and a literature of the Outback, but not a literature of New South Wales as set against a literature of Victoria. Regions in the United States looked inward, while regions in Australia looked outward, back to Britain, and regions in Argentina looked to the sea, though not to Spain. The end result was three different conceptions of identity. By exploring the roots of those different conceptions, we may be able to grasp the nettle of class and caste in American regions to which such terms (usually reserved for John Dollard's southland) have not customarily been applied.

The argument here is complex, and I have oversimplified it gravely. The concept of "regions of recent settlement" and the surface differences between the societies under consideration, as well as interesting (though I believe misleading) observations about comparative studies, appear in John P. Fogarty's stimulating essay, "The Comparative Method and the Nineteenth Century Regions of Recent Settlement."[10]

Conclusion

When scholars organize a conference on regionalism, they communicate their sense of region on three levels. They seek to reinforce those who comprise the "focused gathering" of which Goffman and Geertz wrote—to say to each other, "this is the way we do things." They also seek to evangelize, to remind the outsider that he is from the outside. And they seek to project, almost as an act of theater, their own sense of values by which the message of that which is good in the region may be carried to others. By such subtle statements of self-value we are reminded just how important it is to the health of this nation that there continue to be genuine regional competition and sufficiently divergent value systems to offer our people true choices.

Defining a region is, it seems to me, a bit like defining a university. One may not know precisely what it is, though one does know what it is not. A university is not a supermarket, in which students and faculty select a variety of sustaining goodies from the shelf until they have consumed enough. A university is not a cruise ship, in which faculty and students voyage through a series of seas unknown, enjoying new views on life, until they reach some distant shore. A university is not a hospital, where the ills inflicted upon us are cured. The same must be said of any region, however we may define it; a region is not simply a collection of attractive idiosyncrasies that we can catalogue. A region is not simply a variety of handsomely different landscapes and architectural styles. A region is not a vehicle for curing the nation's ills or for meeting the individual's need to feel superior to those who lack the wisdom to live where one cannot see the air one breathes.

In the region of the mind, the lesser is never smaller than the whole. My favorite western poet, Thomas Hornsby Ferril, knew that landscape was simply "a static stage; it requires the movements of people, clouds, storms, the coming and going of vegetation, and most of all, human experience applied to these movements, if it is to be interesting in literature"—or, one might add, in history.[11]

This is any regionalist's agenda as he lets his mind wander over America: to balance myth and reality in regional identities.[12] We must seek out the particularities that make our regions diverse, but we must not turn those particularities into vital lies. If the eye looks closely enough, one finds that the canyons turn brown in early October, and so too do the forests of New England, and even in the deep South, the long year changes its skin at much the same pace.[13]

NOTES

[1] Raymond D. Gastil, *Cultural Regions of the United States* (Seattle: University of Washington Press, 1975).

[2] Merrill Jensen, *Regionalism in America*, reprinted. (Madison: University of Wisconsin Press, 1965).

[3] Robin W. Winks, *Modus Operandi: An Excursion into Detective Fiction* (Boston: Godine, 1981).

[4] Wilson O. Clough, *The Necessary Earth: Nature and Solitude in American Literature* (Austin: University of Texas Press, 1964), 151-52.

[5] Peter Gould and Rodney White, *Mental Maps* (Hammondsworth: Penguin, 1974), 97, 105-07, 74-76. The Australian and South African observations are my own. On South Africa, see Howard Lamar and Leonard Thompson, eds., *The Frontier in History: North America and Southern Africa Compared* (New Haven: Yale University Press, 1981), especially chapters 1 and 2.

[6] Barbara L. Kellerman, *New York Times,* 27 Nov. 1980.

[7] Alan Shuttleworth, *Two Working Papers in Cultural Studies,* Centre for Contemporary Cultural Studies, Occasional Papers no. 2 (Birmingham, England, 1966), 3.

[8] Harold R. Isaacs, *Idols of the Tribe: Group Identity and Political Change* (New York: Harper & Row, 1975).

[9] Edwin R. Bingham and Glen A. Love, eds., *Northwest Perspectives: Essays on the Culture of the Pacific Northwest* (Eugene: University of Oregon, and Seattle: University of Washington Press, 1979), 30.

[10] John P. Fogarty, "The Comparative Method and the Nineteenth Century Regions of Recent Settlement," *Historical Studies* XIX (April 1981): 412-29. But see also Donald Denoon, "Understanding Settler Societies," *Historical Studies* XVIII (July 1979): 511-27.

[11] As quoted in A. Thomas Trusky, *Thomas Hornsby Ferril,* Boise State College, Western Writers Series no. 6 (Boise, 1973), 21-22.

[12] Thomas Hornsby Ferril, *New and Selected Poems* (New York: Harper & Brothers, c1952), 153.

[13] With apologies for slight paraphrasing to Bill Hotchkiss, *Climb to the High Country: Poems* (New York: W. W. Norton & Co., 1978), 17.

The New Regionalism in America, 1970-1981

Richard Maxwell Brown

The Old Regionalism of the 1920s to 1940s

Regionalism of the 1920s to 1940s resulted from a coalition of academic, off-campus, and United States governmental efforts. To one of its protagonists, this surge in American cultural creativity was viewed as "the new regionalism."[1] And so it was in its own time, for its combination of regionally oriented academic and nonacademic activity was truly fresh and innovative.

There were some notable university centers of regionalism headed by Chapel Hill in North Carolina, Austin in Texas, and Nashville in Tennessee. At the University of North Carolina in Chapel Hill, sociologist Howard Odum headed a remarkable inter-disciplinary group of regionalists working for a revival of the South.[2] Texans came to revere a near holy trinity of southwestern regionalists composed of folklorist J. Frank Dobie, historian Walter Prescott Webb, and naturalist Roy Bedichek.[3] In Nashville, Vanderbilt University was the base of a movement of southern agrarians that included Robert Penn Warren and Donald Davidson in literature, Frank L. Owsley and Herman Nixon in history, and poets Allen Tate and John Crowe Ransom.[4]

Regionally focused scholarship also flourished at two great academic centers at opposite ends of the continent: Cambridge, Massachusetts, and Berkeley, California. California and the South-west were the focus of Herbert Bolton in history, George R. Stewart in literature, and Paul S. Taylor in labor economics.[5] The

New England cultural experience with its core in the colonial and early 19th century periods was the study of Samuel Eliot Morison in history, Kenneth Murdock and F. O. Matthiessen in literature, and Perry Miller in history and literature.[6]

There were other centers of regionalism on various campuses, but they had less intellectual impact than the ones thus far mentioned. Upper Midwest regionalism was vibrant in Madison[7], where the Turner tradition of reform-oriented regionalism was still vital, and in Minneapolis, where the region's deeply embedded Scandinavian-American culture attracted such efforts as T. C. Blegen's approach to "grassroots history."[8] In Lincoln, Nebraska, both Mari Sandoz and Everett L. Dick in the field of Great Plains studies were close to the University of Nebraska,[9] while at the University of Kansas in Lawrence James C. Malin's work on Great Plains history and ecology was one of the most original efforts at regionalism in the entire period.[10] In Montana the great regional editor, Harold G. Merriam, held forth in Missoula, while in Bozeman the very influential agricultural economist M. L. Wilson focused on the rural Great Plains.[11]

Paralleling the campus centers of regionalism (sometimes intermingling with them; sometimes eclipsing them) were many nonacademic regionalists throughout the United States. Many of these men and women were in the fields of journalism and literature. The South was a hotbed of regionalism in this sense; it is only necessary to mention the names of William Faulkner, Thomas Wolfe, Lillian Smith, Erskine Caldwell, and T. S. Stribling among others in fiction and such journalists as Jonathan Daniels, Virginius Dabney, and the unique Wilbur J. Cash, whose intellectual history of the South, *The Mind of the South,* was one of the great regional classics of the period.[12] Elsewhere, the profusion of regionally oriented nonacademic writers included Sinclair Lewis, Meridel Le Sueur, Ruth Suckow, August Derleth, Frederick Manfred, and Mari Sandoz for the Midwest and Great Plains; Wallace Stegner, Vardis Fisher, Joseph Kinsey Howard, and Bernard DeVoto for the Far West; John Steinbeck, William Saroyan, Carey McWilliams, Nathanael West, Horace McCoy, Dashiell Hammett, and Raymond Chandler for California; Lawrence C. Powell, Paul Horgan, Conrad Richter, Erna

Fergusson, and Oliver La Farge for the Southwest; and H. L. Davis, James Stevens, Stewart Holbrook, Richard Neuberger, and Robert Cantwell for the Pacific Northwest.

Closely related to academic and nonacademic regionalism were the great cultural programs and inventories conducted under private and federal auspices. The impact of the magnificent "American Guide Series" of the Federal Writers' Project[13] is still being felt. Although less oriented to regionalism *per se,* the Federal Theatre Project was organized on a regional basis with active centers of theatrical production in New York City, Chicago, Portland (Oregon), and Los Angeles, among other cities.[14] Aside from particular paintings by individual artists, the regional themes of the murals painted on the walls of post offices and other public buildings under the aegis of the Federal Art Project remain one of the great artistic treasures of our country.[15] In the realm of private publishing, two notable series were strongly regionalistic: the prolific "Rivers of America" series, in which virtually every volume was a classic,[16] and the "American Folkways" series of comparable scope and quality, with its own quota of classic books including *Southern California County* by Carey McWilliams and Meridel Le Sueur's *North Star Country.*[17]

Regional themes were also significant in art and music. Three of the greatest regionalists of the 1930s were the "American Scene" trio of Thomas Hart Benton, Grant Wood, and John Steuart Curry.[18] In his study of regionalism in American thought, Cornelius H. Sullivan sees the Social Realist painters (Ben Shahn, Hugo Gellert, William Gropper, Raphael and Moses Soyer) as representing a regional movement in their portrayal of the turbulent urban life and labor centered in the great industrial region of the Northeast.[19]

Genuinely indigenous regional musicians and composers included such figures as Woody Guthrie out of Oklahoma and Texas, who, initiated (with encouragement from regionally oriented musicologist Alan Lomax) the folksong movement of the 1930s and 1940s. Meanwhile in the southern Appalachians, the members of the Carter family and in Texas Bob Wills were protagonists in the rise of Country and Western music.[20] Some of our finest composers of the 1930s and 1940s—Virgil Thompson and Aaron Copland, especially—drew on regional themes and produced music for the regional revival of the period.[21]

Permeating the regionalism of the thirties and forties and at its intellectual center were a host of social scientists in universities and United States governmental bureaus. Some of the leaders (Odum and M. L. Wilson) have already been mentioned. Key contributions to this regionally based analysis and planning were made by political scientists, among them V. O. Key, with his work on Southern politics, and Charles McKinley of Reed College, with his work on local and regional planning and on the impact of the federal government in the Pacific Northwest.[22] Some of the more philosophically oriented academic regionalists were Odum at Chapel Hill and Donald Davidson at Vanderbilt (who were in basic disagreement on the significance of regionalism)[23] and an unduly neglected philosopher and educator, Baker Brownell, of Northwestern University. A former collaborator of Frank Lloyd Wright, Brownell was deeply affected by a study of small-town communities in Montana that he headed in 1944-1946.[24] As a result, Brownell produced a concept of the university as an institution of service to its area—a theory which he put into practice with remarkable success at Southern Ilinois University.

Enough mention has already been made of the federal government to underscore the point that, paradoxically, regionalism in the 1930s and 1940s drew much of its impetus from the center—that is, the federal government in Washington, D.C. Regionalism flourished in some great United States governmental action programs carried out as an integral part of the New Deal. President Franklin D. Roosevelt was, in effect, one of the great regionalists of the age. In his roles as a country squire on the Hudson and as a New York governor strongly committed to the public development of a great regional hydroelectric resource, Roosevelt easily and naturally thought in local and regional terms. It was significantly symbolic that his favorite song was a regional anthem, "Home on the Range," and it was characteristic of F.D.R. to advise a young New York college graduate to get a "real" education:

> Take a second-hand car, put on a flannel shirt, drive out to the (West) Coast by the northern route and come back by the southern route. Don't stop anywhere where you have to pay more than two dollars

for your room and bath. Don't talk to your banking friends or your chamber of commerce friends, but specialize in the gasoline station men, the small restaurant keeper, and farmers you meet by the wayside and your fellow automobile travelers.[25]

At the crux of F.D.R.'s advice to the young man was the mystique of the common people, which was one of the central features of 1920s-1940s regionalism. The great regional action programs of the federal government in the 1930s and 1940s were seen as a way of helping the common people, as well as a response to regional popular demand as exemplified by the protagonists of the public-power movement in the Pacific Northwest.[26] Both the Tennessee Valley Authority and the Bonneville Power Administration were viewed as primary agents of the economic and social revival of their respective regions, as were the shelter-belt concept of tree planting for the Great Plains and the Resettlement Administration charged with alleviating the plight of southern sharecroppers.[27]

Administrative regionalization in the federal government was one of the great motifs of the period. For example, the regional divisions of the Soil Conservation Service headed up the efforts to reverse the trend of soil erosion that plagued American agriculture north, south, east, and west in the 1930s. Another strong motif was that of governmental planning, but the premise of New Deal planning efforts was that planning emerged (or should emerge) from the local and regional grassroots, rather than coming from the top downward. Greatly oriented to this regionally based philosophy of planning was the National Resources Planning Board and its predecessors of the 1930s.[28]

The culmination of regionalism in the 1930s and 1940s seems to have been both a revolt against pre-1930 conditions and an effort to transcend those conditions. Thus, the ebullient regionalism of thirties, especially, was in part an insurgency from the southern and western outlands against the economic and cultural hegemony of the northeastern elites. Yet, the other side of regionalism was an attempt to transcend sectional divisions in the interest of a national revival. National transcendence through the accentuation of the region was the premise of 1920s-1940s regionalism whose goal, ethos, technique, and objective are also clear.

The goal, in a nation still significantly divided by the heritage of such regional rebellions as the Confederacy of the 1860s and the Populist movement of the 1890s, was to cut through all the animosities, contradictions, and confusions in order to find the real meaning of America.[29] The search for the meaning of America was a wide-ranging intellectual enterprise that produced a plethora of books and articles, best exemplifed by Louis Adamic's book, *My America*.[30] As William Stott has noted, the search-for-America writings produced the conclusion that America "was everything American. It couldn't be further analyzed or defined; one could only point to instances of it."[31] By and large, the instances identified were local and regional.

The ethos of regionalism was a species of cultural populism that both inspired and was reflected by the New Deal's emphasis on the common man. Without fresh, innovative expression, cultural populism is a cliche; what was distinctive about the regionalism of this period was the technique of "documentary expression" (to use Stott's phrase) by which the regionally focused cultural populism was conveyed. The mode of documentary expression was an original, exciting achievement in virtually all fields of art, letters, and scholarship: in fiction (John Steinbeck), in photography (Walker Evans and Dorothea Lange), in journalism (*Life* and *Look*), in reportage (John Spivak, Louis Adamic, and James Agee), in film (Pare Lorenz), and in social science (Helen and Robert Lynd, John Dollard, W. Lloyd Warner, and William F. Whyte).[32] These are only a few examples of the type of work that permeated the 1930s.

The objective and, indeed, the greatest theme of the Old Regionalism of the 1920s-1940s was reform. Whether explicit (*e.g.,* Odum, Walter Prescott Webb) or implicit, regionally oriented fiction, art, film, reportage, history, social science, and governmental action all had a strongly reformist motivation. Just as he was a great regionalist, the greatest reformer of them all was Franklin D. Roosevelt.

If the 1930s were the invigorating springtime and nurturing summertime of the Old Regionalism, the 1940s were the autumn that presaged the wintry demise of regionalism in the 1950s and 1960s. Although regionalists in the 1940s seemed not to sense that regionalism was on the wane, the mood of the period had autumnal qualities of complacency and near nostalgia. Some of the most important works of regionalism were published in the 1940s and on into the 1950s, but these were works that had their origins, intellectually and emotionally, in the regional vitality of the 1930s. Three works appearing in the forties and the early fifties typified the autumnal period of the 1940s: Bernard De Voto's historical trilogy, *Let Us Now Praise Famous Men* by James Agee and Walker Evans, and *Regionalism in America,* the collection of essays edited by Merrill Jensen.

We may forgive the emotional and scholarly flaws of De Voto's marvelous trilogy on the winning of the Far West—*The Year of Decision: 1846, Across the Wide Missouri,* and *The Course of Empire.*[33] With a narrative power that still entrances, De Voto wrote factual history in a critical spirit that had the effect of enhancing the myth of the West (which was soon to be subjected to the scathing critique of Henry Nash Smith). Although based near Harvard Yard in Cambridge, De Voto was western born and bred, and his youthful revolt against the cultural narrowness of the West gave way to a mature, even romantic appreciation of his native region. De Voto was one of the great regionalists of the period. He did not restrict his impact to the DeVoto fans who bought the books in his Far West trilogy; he used the influential platform of his "Easy Chair" column in *Harper's Magazine* as a powerful voice in behalf of conservation in the West during the 1940s and early 1950s.[34] By the time De Voto published *Across the Wide Missouri* in 1947 and *The Course of Empire* in 1952, the reformist regionalism of the 1930s was on the defensive in the West and elsewhere. It is obvious that De Voto's trilogy not only expressed his faith in America and the West but sustained him—as it did many western-ers—in the conservation battles of the forties and fifties. Inspiring in its own way, De Voto's historical trilogy was nonetheless part of the rear guard, rather than *avant garde,* of the Old Regionalism.

Warren I. Susman has proclaimed *Let Us Now Praise Famous Men* (a book written and photographed in the 1930s but not published until 1941) as the prototypical book of the 1930s. William Stott goes even further, contending that *Let Us Now Praise*

Famous Men not only climaxes the documentary expression of the 1930s, but at the same time "explodes it, surpasses it, shows it up."[35] With its combination of documentary reportage and photography dealing in a highly sympathetic way with a cluster of poverty-stricken tenant families in Alabama, the book is a strikingly typical example of the reformist regionalism of the 1930s.[36] As a work of unsurpassed emotional impact, the book is the apotheosis of thirties regionalism. Yet, Stott's conclusion that the book transcends the documentary approach (and, for us, the regional approach) is correct. Walker Evans' stark photographs transcend the sentimentality that characterized the photographs of southern poor whites by Margaret Bourke-White, another regionally oriented photographer of the period.[37] In rejecting the reformist ideology of Howard Odum and likeminded southern regionalists (in favor of a fatalistic Christian humanism) when confronting the tragically scarred lives of the poor tenants, Agee perhaps intuitively presaged the mood of the 1950s, which was to turn strongly away from reform and regionalism.

If *Let Us Now Praise Famous Men* was the climactic work of the Old Regionalism of the 1920s-1940s, *Regionalism in America* (1951) was the intellectual epitaph for the movement. More than 30 years later, *Regionalism in America* is still an impressive collection of interdisciplinary essays, with many of its pieces still useful today. But the book had a fatal flaw of which most of its contributors were understandably unaware; it looked to the future but was actually a work of the past. Howard Odum (whose academic sun had set at the University of North Carolina about ten years before) was one of the main contributors to the book, but his message had not changed since the 1930s. Nor did any of the other contributors present a new, original approach to regionalism. If anything, the book seemed more rooted in the past than many of its predecessor writings on regionalism in the 1930s. For the intellectual patron saint of *Regionalism in America* (mentioned reverently by Odum and again and again by others) was Frederick Jackson Turner.[38] Ironically, these invocations of Turner came at a time when the master's writings had never been under more devastating attack. By 1951 Odum and Turner, who dominated *Regionalism in America,* were ikons of American regionalism's past.

As the anachronism of *Regionalism in America* suggests, regionalism's hiatus came in the 1950s and 1960s. Regionalism was not actually dead but was quiescent during the 1950s, while in the 1960s the seeds of the New Regionalism of the 1970s and 1980s were quietly germinating beneath the surface of common observation.

On every side the decline of regionalism was evident. The regional approach in social science scholarship fell out of favor during the 1950s and 1960s. What happened at the nation's greatest citadel of academic regionalism, the University of North Carolina in Chapel Hill, was symptomatic. There, during the 1940s, an aging Odum stepped down as head of the Institute of Social Research, which he had founded and made the base of the Chapel Hill regionalists. Odum's successor turned the Institute completely away from the regional orientation, to an emphasis on functionalist social science scholarship that it retains to this day. And in Odum's home department of sociology, the turn was away from the almost entire emphasis on Southern regional sociology under Odum's influence to general sociology.[39]

The same period also witnessed the decline, disappearance, or change in the federal government's regionally oriented action programs. Both the Bonneville Power Administration and the Tennessee Valley Authority evolved away from the reformist spirit that motivated each in the thirties and forties toward an establishmentarian technologism that was far from the liberal idealism of J. D. Ross and George Norris. A significant new surge of governmental reform activity did come with the Great Society program of President Lyndon B. Johnson in the 1960s but, except for Appalachia, the regional emphasis was not revived. Instead, urban-oriented functionalist programs focused on poverty, education, environmental protection, historic preservation, and cultural uplift were the hallmarks of Johnsonian reform activity.

The demise of regionalism in social science and in government was also conjoined with its fall from favor on campus and in the general realm of art and letters. It was noteworthy that during the 1950s the fashionable new intellectual interdisciplinary movement of American Studies rose in esteem as regionalism fell. It is true, of course, that some of the leading regionalists of the thirties and forties were still active all through the 1950s and 1960s, while new regionalists also came on the scene. In literature Robert Frost reached the height of his popularity as an exemplar of the rockribbed eternal verities of the old New England culture, while Wallace Stegner was steadily productive at the highest level of his redoubtable creative power.[40] In history, C. Vann Woodward headed a remarkably vital and productive effort by historians of the South during the fifties and sixties and established himself in the eyes of many as the finest historian in the United States.[41]

Indeed, the regional impulse probably remained stronger in history than in any other field; studying American history in terms of regional subdivisions has always been (and no doubt always will be) a standard approach to our country's history. For example, a new generation of historians—Earl Pomeroy, Ray Allen Billington, Howard R. Lamar, Rodman W. Paul, Leonard Arrington, Willam Goetzmann, John W. Caughey, Vernon Carstenson, W. Eugene Hollon, Robert G. Athearn, Robert V. Hine, and W. Turrentine Jackson among them—were rewriting and expanding the history of the West during the fifties and sixties. New literary regionalists (for example, A. B. Guthrie for the West) also appeared on the scene, but literary regionalism was probably less vital than historical regionalism during this period of hiatus.

The eclipse of regionalism in the 1950s and 1960s was due to momentous changes in the material life of the nation and to the impact of vast homogenizing forces. Among the forces of homogenization, the impact of World War II was probably unexcelled. Not only did the enormous movement of military forces and civilian workers serve to dissolve regional barriers, but the war gave rise to great changes in the national economic structure which accelerated during the postwar fifties and sixties. The Northeast's long-term industrial and financial hegemony over the South and West came to an end in a wave of vast new industrial expansion in the former tributary regions. Discriminatory freight rates which had kept the South and West in economic bondage passed into limbo. In California the Giannini banking empire came to rival the financial bastions of Wall Street. The rise of Sun Belt industrialists and financiers in the 1950s and 1960s had enormous significance, marking as it did the decline of the economic sectionalism that had segmented the nation from 1800 to 1940.[42]

In a sense, regionalism waned in the 1950s and 1960s because it had succeeded. Southern and western regionalists in the 1930s (such as Walter Prescott Webb) had contended for the economic emancipation of the South and the West from the Northeast.[43] As the South and the West gained their economic freedom to a considerable extent, one result was the decline of aggressive southern and western regionalism. In spite of the skepticism of Donald Davidson and other southern agrarians, the regionalists of the 1930s had generally fallen into ranks behind Howard Odum's contention that regionalism (unlike political and economic sectionalism) produced national unity in diversity.[44] The history of the 1950s and 1960s shows that Odum and his regionalist colleagues were right; America's regions in the fifties and sixties did indeed exemplify unity in diversity. But going along with this was a loss in the mood of regional elan that had marked the thirties.

During the 1950s and 1960s there were three great homogenizers of national culture whose impact can hardly be exaggerated: interstate highways, jet airliners, and television. As Marshall McLuhan suggested, television made the whole nation an instant village; by jet airliner this national village could be traversed in no more than six hours. Interstate highways not only had a huge economic impact by creating the national long-distance trucking industry but had the culturally homogenizing effect of placing one or more Holiday Inns in virtually every community of 30,000 or more people.

By 1969 regionalism was largely out of fashion as a scholarly and cultural enterprise. Despite the homogenizing impact of interstate highways, jet airplanes, and television, however, regional distinctions had not perished, as the rise of a new breed of regionalists in the 1970s soon demonstrated.

The New Regionalism of the 1970s and 1980s

Origins of the New Regionalism

Eight factors outlined below have resulted in the new regional behavior and consciousness of the 1970s and 1980s. These factors have provided the basis and context for an indigenous revival of regionalism in academia, in the broader cultural life of the nation, and among a new generation of academic and nonacademic regionalists. Going along with this revival of regionalism are new approaches to regionalism as well as questions about the ultimate destiny of this new regionalism.

Persistence of regional identities. By the early 1970s there was a developing realization that the regions of America had not been swallowed up by overwhelming forces of national homogenization. Despite the great impact of the cultural homogenizers, the regions remained, altered but still in place. The South, which probably suffered during the 1950s and 1960s the strongest blows to its cultural identity, was still (as sociologist John Shelton Reed's study of 1972 established) "the enduring South."[45] What Reed referred to as regional "subcultural persistence in mass society" was demonstrated for America as a whole with the publication in 1975 of anthropologist Raymond D. Gastil's significant study of *Cultural Regions of the United States.*

Rise of the new local history. With occasional exceptions, professional academic historians had ignored the writing of local history in favor of a fixation with national political history. This long-standing neglect of local history (which had generally been left to the erratic efforts of amateur historians) began to change with the publication in 1959 of Merle Curti's massive study of a county in Wisconsin's frontier era. Also significant was the publication five years later of a study of the early industrial era of Newburyport, Massachussetts, by a brilliant young historian, Stephan Thernstrom.[47] As the 1960s wore on, younger historians caught the vision of giving depth to America's social and political history by studying it at the local level, and the local history boom was on. By the early 1970s, it was fashionable for precocious young graduate students to do their Ph.D. dissertations on local history topics.

Off-campus developments were also contributing to the rise of the new local history as a basis of the New Regionalism. A revitalization of state historical societies occurred, assisted by the efforts of the American Association for State and Local History based in

Nashville, Tennessee. New local historical societies appeared, while older ones became even more vigorous. State archives and libraries were also revitalized.

Public participation in the rise of the new local history was widespread. The unprecedented mass audience for the television series, "Roots," in early 1977 is a case in point; "Roots" traced the centuries-long history of a black family from Africa to Virginia to North Carolina to Tennessee. The enthusiastic public response to "Roots" was a measure of how families (white as well as black) were turning to family history in terms of locality and region for a heightened sense of personal identity in a nation where homogenizing forces were strong. The popular response to the new local history (and the New Regionalism) was also shown by the continuing success of James Michener's deeply researched historical novels on Hawaii, the Far West, and the Chesapeake Bay area.[48]

The surge in historic preservation. One of the keys to a continuing and revived regional consciousness is the preservation region-by-region of the nation's architectural and building heritage. For decades, systematic efforts at historic preservation on any significant scale had been largely restricted to New England and to such Atlantic Coast localities as Williamsburg and Charleston. A series of congressional enactments in the 1930s and 1940s helped but did not essentially alter the situation. Finally, two things occurred which led to a surge in historic preservation in the nation at large in the 1970s and on into the 1980s: (1) the postwar construction boom of the 1950s and 1960s led to the loss of innumerable architectural treasures (as Constance Greiff showed in her poignant two-volume work, *Lost America,* 1971-1972)[49] and caused a backlash of aroused public opinion, and (2) Congress enacted the crucial National Historic Preservation Act of 1966. These developments gave new vitality and scope to the key umbrella organization, the National Trust for Historic Preservation, established in 1947.[50] The National Trust's increasingly elegant magazine, *Historic Preservation,* has portrayed the achievements and challenges of historic preservation during the 1970s and 1980s. The millions of dollars that have poured into this movement from public and private coffers to help preserve numerous buildings from region to region form one of the most striking examples of the regional revival of the seventies and eighties.

Rise of the environmental preservation movement. This movement has proceeded in tandem with the surge in historic preservation. Here again the impetus came in the 1960s and has flourished in the 1970s and 1980s. With the filing of environmental impact statements now a standard procedure when alterations or additions to the landscape are proposed, the environmental preservation movement has done much to nurture the New Regionalism by its efforts to preserve unaltered regional landscapes.[51]

Rise of regionally oriented magazines. This phenomenon also goes back into the 1960s. From coast to coast, ambitious publishers began to realize that with booming urban populations there was a large potential market for a new type of local magazine. Typically these local and regional publications offer a combination of city promotion, local historical consciousness, entertainment and where-to-go features, coverage of local arts and letters, and treatments of community problems and public issues, [52] served up with a tone of easy sophistication and mild skepticism. The overall result has been a heightening of regional identification for their readers.

Impact of state humanities committees. While the role of the federal government in nurturing the New Regionalism has been much less than with the old regionalism, the federal impact has been none the less significant. This has already been indicated in connection with the surge in historic preservation, and it has been a major factor in environmental preservation as well. In regard to the New Regionalism, the key federal agency is the National Endowment for the Humanities. (I am presently unable to assess the impact of the National Endowment for the Arts.) Whether or not the volume of support provided by the N.E.H. for regionalism through its manifold programs is equal to the federal support for regionalism in the 1930s, the role of the N.E.H. has been great, and it is analogous to the programs of cultural support in the 1930s.

The New Regionalism has been enhanced by many of the nationally administered programs of the N.E.H., but its impact on regionalism has been most sustained and readily identifiable through the activities of the state humanities committees set up and financed by the N.E.H.[53] The remarkable film of a few years ago, *Northern Lights,* was a project supported by the North Dakota Committee for the Humanities. *Northern Lights* sensitively portrayed the human dimension of the Nonpartisan League, an early 20th-century movement of agrarian insurgency that swept over the upper Great Plains states; it not only gained the plaudits of film critics but was an important contribution to the historical consciousness of the upper Great Plains region. Similar in impact is the more recent N.E.H.-supported film, *Heartland,* dealing with frontier Wyoming. Closer to home, the Oregon Committee for the Humanities has during a ten-year period (1970-1980) supported a host of projects—films, plays, forums, local projects—that have a definite Pacific Northwest regional character.[54] Given their generally spontaneous nature, the regionally oriented projects of the state humanities committees are truly grassroots regionalism.

The States and the Nation Series. As a project for the national bicentennial observance of 1976, the N.E.H. provided funds for the publication of single-volume histories of all 50 states. The project was administered by the American Association for State and Local History, and the books were published by W. W. Norton & Company. Although not organized along regional lines, these volumes, taken as a whole, are one of the landmarks of the New Regionalism.[55] Although the books are much smaller in size, their common format and state-by-state coverage make them analogous to the state guidebooks published in the American Guide Series in the late 1930s and early 1940s under the auspices of the Federal Writers Project. The substantive achievement of the "States and the Nation" series in terms of state history alone is significant, for the result is that each state now has a one-volume history written by a competent authority—a condition that had not obtained until the completion of this project.

In our terms, the books are most significant contributions to the new regional consciousness, for each volume fits easily into the traditional divisions of regionalization in the United States. The volumes vary in quality but all are useful, and the best of them (e.g., Dodds on Oregon, Clark on Washington, Jensen on Illinois, Williams on West Virginia, Hamilton on Alabama) deal pointedly with state histories, cultures, issues, and problems that are regional in character.[56]

Intellectual recycling of the Old Regionalism into the New Regionalism. The 1950s and 1960s were a hiatus in American regionalism, but less significantly they were also a transitional period between the Old Regionalism of the 1920s-1940s and the New Regionalism of the 1970s and 1980s. The valuable heritage of the Old Regionalism has far from perished; it has been perpetuated through a process of intellectual recycling, in which the achievements of the Old Regionalism have been preserved through an ever-growing array of monographs and biographies that have appeared during the 1970s and 1980s. Among the books on the great regionally-oriented cultural programs of the Old Regionalism are: William Stott on documentary expression; Richard D. McKinzie on the Federal Art Project; Jerre Mangione and Monty N. Penkower on the Federal Writers' Project; Jane De Hart Mathews on the Federal Theatre Project; and various books on Lorena Hickok, Roy Emerson Stryker, Dorothea Lange, Walker Evans, and other documentary reporters and photographers of regional life for the New Deal action agencies.[57] Books on the regionally focused events and New Deal action programs of the 1930s include: Paul E. Mertz and Donald Holley on abortive New Deal efforts to aid the rural poor of the South; Donald Worster, Walter J. Stein, and Paul Bonnifield on the Dust-Bowl experience of the Great Plains; and Wilmon H. Droze on the shelterbelt program against wind erosion on the Great Plains.[58] A few of the numerous biographies and biographical studies of significant figures in the era of the Old Regionalism are: Richard H. King, Michael O'Brien, and Daniel Joseph Singal on the Southern Renaissance in history, literature, and social science; Joseph Blotner on William Faulkner; Joe Klein on Woody Guthrie; Wallace Stegner on Bernard De Voto; Gregory M. Tobin and Necah S. Furman on Walter Prescott Webb; Lon Tinkle on J. Frank Dobie; and John F. Bannon on Herbert Bolton.[59] Books on artists in particular include: Matthew Baigell, James M. Dennis, and Nancy Heller and Julia Williams on the American Scene painters (Benton, Wood, and Curry); and David Shapiro on the Social Realists.[60]

Rise of the New Regionalists of the 1970s and 1980s

There are too many new academic centers and programs of regionalism to name, but in the field of interdisciplinary curricular programs in colleges and universities, it is my impression that regional studies programs are on the rise while American Studies programs are holding. Just two examples of regional studies programs are the New England studies program at Boston University and the program in Pacific Northwest studies at Oregon State University.

There are also campus centers and institutes devoted to regional research and the publication of scholarly regionalism. Many of these centers and institutes also operate in conjunction with interdisciplinary regional studies programs such as those just mentioned. Of course, there is another dimension to regionalism on the campus; not all vital efforts in regionalism are formally organized. For example, in contrast to Howard Odum's Institute for Social Research at the University of North Carolina, there was no formally constituted institute or center of southwestern regionalism at the University of Texas in the era of Walter Prescott Webb and J. Frank Dobie. My own University of Oregon is in this category; although we have no formally organized regional institute, the tradition of West/Northwest regionalism—in terms of research resources, faculty regionalists, and Ph.D. and M.A. theses—has never been livelier than it is at present.[61] Somewhat the same can be said, I think, of the University of Washington, Washington State University, Portland State University, and, no doubt, many other universities across the nation.

Still, the formal institutes and centers have the capability (often realized) of greatly enhancing the impact of regionalism. Universities such as North Carolina (Chapel Hill), Vanderbilt (Nashville), Texas (Austin), and California (Berkeley) no longer lead in regionalism as they did in the 1930s, but since the middle 1970s three significant new centers of regionalism have arisen: the Center for Great Plains Studies (1976) at the University of Nebraska, the Center for the Study of Southern Culture (1977) at the University of Mississippi, and the Appalachian Center (1978) at the University of

Kentucky.[62] With a significant series of publications and conferences, the Great Plains center at Nebraska has already made an impressive impact, and vital programs are also underway at the University of Mississippi and University of Kentucky.

The names of many new academic regionalists are dotted through this paper. It would be redundant to rename them here. There are, indeed, hundreds of academic regionalists who have been publishing during the 1970s and 1980s, and there is no space or time to make even a start on citing them here.[63] With one exception, I think it is fair to say that none of the new academic regionalists has attained the stature or made the impact of such titans of the Old Regionalism as Odum, Webb, or Dobie. The one exception is Harry M. Caudill, who in recent years has been affiliated with the Appalachian Center at the University of Kentucky. Unlike Odum, Webb, and Dobie, Caudill did not establish himself as a regionalist while on a university campus; yet his first book, *Night Comes to the Cumberlands,* had the sort of impact for his region (the Southern Appalachians) that the best books of Odum, Webb, and Dobie had for theirs.[64]

There are many nonacademic New Regionalists. During the course of this paper I mention a significant sampling of the New Regionalists of the West and Northwest; there is no need to repeat their names here. But since I do not mention them elsewhere, let me at least cite a few significant southern regionalists who strive to explicate the meaning of the counter-classic South of the 1960s-1980s: publisher H. Brandt Ayers of Anniston, Alabama; journalist Marshall Frady, who is surely one of our finest writers of regional biography and reportage;[65] historian Hugh Davis Graham, whose subject has been the desegregating and desegregated South of our own time;[66] and novelist Walker Percy, whose South is not the traditional South but the booming, deracinated Sun-Belt South.[67]

New Approaches to Regionalism

The renewed vigor of regionalism is shown by the new approaches developed during the 1970s and 1980s: (1) new general interpretations of American regionalization; (2) studies that are multi-regional in scope; (3) studies of the political economy of the new regional reality; and (4) comparative and transnational studies of regionalism

New general interpretations. Among new general interpreters of American regionalization, the most significant conceptualizers are political scientist Daniel Elazar, anthropologist Raymond D. Gastil, and journalist Joel Garreau. Elazar has produced a complex framework of eight sections and three spheres (Northeast, South, and West), in which regional variations are based on settlement and migration patterns. These patterns in turn have resulted in three types of political culture that coexist in varying degrees from state to state and section to section: moralistic political culture, traditionalistic political culture, and individualistic political culture. Elazar sees the nation's politics *qua* national political system as a synthesis of regionally varying political cultures. Elazar had formulated his interpretation of regionalism by 1970 and has continued to apply it since.[68]

Gastil's 1975 book, *Cultural Regions of the United States,* was an innovative, impressive example of interdisciplinary scholarship.[69] Skillfully drawing together the most recent survey-research data, Gastil's study was a crucial work in the New Regionalism. However much specialists might quarrel with it, it convincingly demonstrated the persistence of regional identities in terms of Gastil's concept of culture areas. The impression that the homogenizing tendencies of television and a centralizing national economy were obliterating regional identities was destroyed by the profusion of hard evidence in Gastil's volume. Scholars who sensed that regional variations still mattered were bolstered by Gastil's book.

Gastil analyzed four specific cultural subjects (religion, politics, housing and settlement styles, dialect) in terms of regional variations, after having explored settlement patterns and the evolution of regional socio-economic patterns. He then took three common social indicators (homicide and violence, educational performance, white infant mortality) and showed their regional variations. The first half of Gastil's book was devoted to regional variations in selected topical subjects: the second half was devoted to brief profiles (in terms of population, regional borders, history and regional characteristics, districts and sociocultural divisions, and problems and potential) of his 13 regions:

New England	Upper Midwest	Pacific Southwest
New York Metro-	Central Midwest	Pacific Northwest
politan	Rocky Mountain	Alaskan
Pennsylvanian	Mormon	Hawaiian
South	Interior Southwest	

Hot off the press in 1981 and apparently doing a brisk business in bookstores was Joel Garreau's *The Nine Nations of North America*.[70] This book encompasses the most original and innovative of all schemes of the Old or the New Regionalism. Although perceptive and up-to-date, the regionalizations of Elazar and Gastil are basically revisions of the traditional regional subdivisions of the United States, based on the analysis and interpretation of the Old Regionalism. Not so, however, for Garreau; the book's dust jacket commands: "Forget the traditional map—new realities of power and people are making this continent into *The Nine Nations of North America*"!

Excluding Central America, Garreau divides North America into nine regions (he calls them "nations"); all but two of them cross present national boundaries. This transnational character of Garreau's regionalization is one of its most distinctive characteristics. Of Garreau's nine regions, only one is wholly in the United States and only one is wholly in Canada. Of the other seven, five are mainly in the U.S. The innovative aspect of Garreau's fresh and stimulating book is well exemplified by his region of the Islands. Such factors as the huge Cuban migration into South Florida and the booming cross-Caribbean drug traffic have produced a new regional pattern (the Islands), contends Garreau, that makes Miami's ties to Caracas and Baranquilla stronger than its links to Atlanta or Washington, D.C. Obviously there is exaggeration here, but it is exaggeration to make a significant point; during the 1970s and 1980s (and with earlier background developments) the peoples of North America have been on the move (both within and across national boundaries) in the context of vast economic changes—including the energy boom of western North America and the decline of the industrialized Northeast.

Like much of the New Regionalism, this is grassroots regionalism. Garreau's regionalization was developed on the basis of the journalistic investigations of his colleagues on the *Washington Post,* supplemented by the library work of Garreau and his research assistants. There is no doubt that Garreau's book is close to the pulse beat of our country and our continent. This is regionalism as living history. It is an exciting, provocative book. Yet, there are problems. Is *The Nine Nations of North America* really regionalism or merely journalism with regional datelines? Is it true regionalism or no more than breezy regional reportage? While exceeding the likes of Elazar and Gastil in its timeliness, it lacks their intellectual depth. And in exploding the traditional boundaries of American regionalism in order to make a point, does it not overplay that point by downgrading the persistence of traditional intranational regional divisions and the political power of the traditional national capitals?

But Garreau is probably on target when he says, in effect, that the threat to traditional American regional identities is no longer the homogenizing tendencies of television, jet planes, and interstate highways but, instead, the huge transnational movements of population within North America and the jarring economic forces stemming from the energy boom in western North America, the drug boom of southern North America, and the industrial decline of much of northeastern North America.

Multi-regional approaches. Writers with a multi-regional approach include two writers that are worthy of note. One is the political journalist, Neal R. Peirce. Unlike most meta-regionalists (e.g., Odum, Elazar, Gastil, Garreau) Peirce makes no attempt to provide an original approach to regionalization. Instead, Peirce took as his model for eight contemporary volumes on the traditional regions of America, the 1947 book *Inside U.S.A.* by the late John Gunther.[71] Peirce's eight regions are the Pacific states, the Rocky Mountain states, the Deep South, the Border South, the Mid-Atlantic states, New England, the Great Lakes states, and the

Plains states. Like John Gunther, Peirce crisscrossed the country, visiting all 50 states and conducting numerous interviews as well as drawing upon prodigious library research. Peirce's product is, like Gunther's, fascinating; the treatment is encyclopedic but never boring. The flaw of Peirce's eight-volume series (by far the most comprehensive treatment of American regions by a single author) also resembles that of Gunther's book; the emphasis is, by design, so heavily on the politics and problems of the moment that the regional treatments quickly become dated. Yet, Peirce's regional volumes will long stand as an incomparable treatment of American society and politics in the 1970s.

The second multi-regional authority is the cultural and historical geographer, Donald W. Meinig of Syracuse University, who studies the regions of the western half of America. Although three of Meinig's four regional studies (of Mormonia, the Great Columbia Plain, central Texas, and the Southwest) were published in the middle and late 1960s, his cumulative impact as a regionalist has largely been in the 1970s and 1980s.[72] As superb scholarship, Meinig's studies will likely have greater staying power than the volumes of Peirce. For the regionalist working on any of the areas treated by Meinig, it will be necessary to use his studies as a starting point; this will not always be the case with Peirce's work.

Economic and political approaches. Economic and political sectional rivalries waned during the 1950s and 1960s, but they are on the rise again as, very broadly, the economic growth of the North and the East has slowed or gone into decline and the economic growth of the South and the West has accelerated. This point is, indeed, one of the factors in the rise of the New Regionalism of the 1970s and 1980s. New competition among the regions has also been reflected in responsive pressures within regions. For example, the Pacific Northwest's lumber industry is being strongly challenged by the fast-growing lumber industry of the Southeast, while the economic problems of the Washington Public Power Supply System (WPPSS) are jeopardizing the Pacific Northwest's decades-long advantage of low electric rates.

Although in its scholarly infancy, the new political economy of regionalism is being built up on the basis of a growing shelf of studies by political scientists and economists. Examples include a 1980 study by Kai N. Lee, Donna Lee Klemka, and Marion E. Marts[73] of the perplexing problems of electric power and the economic future of the Pacific Northwest in an era of net-billing by a changing Bonneville Power Administration and nuclear power-plant construction by WPPSS. A comparable study of the Rocky Mountain and Northern Plains states, *Energy, Economic Growth, and Regionalism in the West* by political scientist Lynton R. Hayes and an impassioned popular treatment by Governor Richard D. Lamm and journalist Michael McCarthy of Colorado focus on the difficult challenge of increasing exploitation of that region's energy resources while preserving its quality of life.[74] John Baden, director of the Center for Political Economy and Natural Resources at Montana State University, leads a group of free-market economists who are confronting the problems of large-scale administration of forest, land, and energy resources in the Far West by the U. S. governmental bureaucracy.[75]

Comparative and transnational approaches. Comparative and transnational regionalism is not very well advanced, although Garreau's *Nine Nations* is a clarion call for regionalists to look beyond national boundaries. Robin Winks and others have already done work along this line. Winks' comparison of the American West to comparable regions in Australia and Canada reflects a well-established (although not-well developed) tradition in what has been comparative frontier history. H. C. Allen and W. Turrentine Jackson have also made contributions in this area.[76] Carlos Schwantes' recent study of the radical labor movement in Washington and British Columbia was based on the premise that the proper unit of regional study transcended the national boundary; this, too, reflects a tradition in which earlier scholars (e.g., William J. Trimble on 19th-century mining in the Inland Empire and Paul Sharp on the "Whoop-Up Country" of the Canadian-American West) ignored the border between the U.S. and Canada.[77]

The tradition of transnational regionalism is even more deeply embedded along America's southern boundary as a result of Herbert Bolton's Borderlands concept, which defined regionalism in terms of the impact of Hispanic culture on both sides of the

American-Mexican boundary. Indeed, Joel Garreau's supposedly iconoclastic region of Mexamerica is, in effect, an updated treatment of Bolton's Borderlands region. George M. Fredrickson's widely praised pioneering study of white supremacy in American and South African history is in substance a study in the comparative regionalism of race relations. More recently, a new book of essays edited by Howard Lamar and Leonard Thompson compares the frontier regions of North America and South Africa.[78]

Finally, in his recent presidential address to the American Historical Association, Bernard Bailyn has emphasized regional entities in the form of peripheral areas with these peripheries linked to core localities within vast global systems of centers and margins.[79]

Aspects of the New Regionalism

First, it must be recognized that the New Regionalism has distanced itself in certain crucial respects from the Old Regionalism. The element of reform, which was so important to the Old Regionalism, is largely absent from the New Regionalism. As noted earlier, the Old Regionalism's campaign in favor of the oppressed South and West was largely realized by the major economic changes of the 1940s and 1950s.

There are, however, two recent concepts of regionalism that see the region as a bulwark against oppressive central power in somewhat the same way that some of the Old Regionalists saw things. Ernest Callenbach in his utopian novel, *Ecotopia,* envisioned the revolt of the region of Ecotopia (northern California and the Pacific Northwest) against the frenzied militarism of the national government in the interest of regional and environmental preservation.[80] And in the September 5, 1981 issue of *The Nation,* William Appleman Williams invoked the concept of regional resistance to the national government in pursuit of "backyard autonomy."[81] As in the case of Callenbach's book, Williams has in mind regional centers of power as a counterweight to what he sees as the mindless militarism of Pentagon planners.[82]

Another significant distinction between the Old and the New Regionalism is—except for the National Endowment for the Humanities and certain programs of historic and environmental preservation—the absence of the federal presence. In the 1960s the federal government initiated a strategy of regional uplift for the southern Appalachians, but this effort has apparently been on the wane, and there has been nothing in the 1970s and 1980s equivalent to the vast New Deal action programs of regional renewal in the 1930s. Also in contrast to the Old Regionalism, the West (rather than the South) is the most dynamic seat of the New Regionalism, the role of social science is less than in the 1930s and 1940s, and the role of academia (except in history and the humanities) is narrower than in the 1930s and 1940s.

The great theme of the New Regionalism likewise differs from the primary theme of the Old Regionalism. More than anything else, the passion for reform united the Old Regionalists. For the New Regionalism the surpassing motivation and emotion is the quest for identity—for individual and family identity through identification with the region. The reason for this may be readily seen. As the persistence of regional identities has helped check the nationally homogenizing tendencies of modern technology, the individual has sensed intuitively that the preservation of regional identity is crucial to the preservation of personal identity in the face of those same homogenizing tendencies.

The Future of the New Regionalism

What is the state of the New Regionalism today in comparison to the Old Regionalism? It seems to me that the New Regionalism of 1981 is about where the Old Regionalism was in 1931. In 1931 the best and most vibrant years of the Old Regionalism were in the future. The New Regionalism of the present is less developed than was the Old Regionalism by 1940.

I think that the economic, social, and political trends already under way and in prospect will lead to a continued and increasing emphasis on regionalism. So far nonacademics have been ahead of academics in the regional revival of the 1970s and 1980s. Grassroots regionalism could be a synonym for the New Regionalism. Although I surely could be wrong, I think that academic regionalism will catch up during the 1980s with nonacademic regionalism.

The proximate hesitancy of university scholars to jump aboard the new ship of regionalism stems in part from certain built-in problems and tensions in regard to regionalism. One of these is the pitfall of obsession—the tendency for the regionalist to view the region as the beginning and end of explanation and interpretation. Some of the Old Regionalists did not avoid this pitfall, and, as a result, many scholars have been shy of regionalism ever since. Today the pitfall of regional obsession is, I think, more illusion than reality. There are few regionalists today who do not believe in the complementarity of regional scholarship and general scholarship. For my own part, I would not be happy in a history department which neglected general history in favor of regional history, just as I would not be happy in a history department which emphasized general history to the neglect of regional history.

A second problem for scholarly regionalism is that of regionalization. While the concept of regionalism itself is precise enough, scholars have never been able to agree upon one particular scheme of regionalization for America. This lack of precision is troubling to many scholars. Some simply cannot stand the inherent fluidity of regionalism. In fact, it is the fluidity of regionalism that gives this scholarly strategy the major advantage of flexibility. Thus, every locality is bound to have more than one regional identity. Corvallis and Eugene are, for example, localities in the following regions: the Pacific Northwest, the Pacific Coast, the West, the Willamette Valley, western Oregon, and—to use my own term—the Great Raincoast of North America. Obviously, these regions overlap and interpenetrate each other, but each one encompasses a unique regional reality. It is the flexibility which these various regional identities afford that gives regionalism a valuable multiple precision. Yet, regional identities and their meanings shift, and the task of defining and redefining regional boundaries and realities will always be with us—a persistently interesting challenge but one that can also be frustrating. Those who desire inflexible scholarly certitude will not be comfortable with regionalism. Flux and change seem to be inherent in regionalism, but this is true of the scholarly process as a whole.

Decline of the National Myth

The national myth of America is in decline, while the regional myths live on. Scholars have provided whole libraries of studies that demonstrate the contradiction between the national myth and the national reality. To me the national myth has been at its most basic a compound of abundance and destiny with crucial subthemes of democracy, individualism, equality, classlessness, the frontier, the upward struggle of immigrants, material superiority, pluralism, pragmatism, and a sense of mission in the world. Associated with the national myth was belief in the preordained success of America as a nation and a people.

This myth sustained America through the Civil War, the periodic depressions, and the world wars of the 20th century. Even the most tough-minded and relentless critics of the national reality were sustained in most areas by their ultimate faith in the meaning of America. This confident belief in the national myth was blown to smithereens by the disasters and upheavals of the 1960s and 1970s: the assassinations, the Vietnamese War, the riots in our cities and on our campuses, the soaring crime rate, the shame of Watergate, the setbacks in foreign relations, and the transition from an economy of lavish abundance to one of increasing scarcity.

This is one reason that younger historians of the 1960s and 1970s turned from the study of national themes and issues to research on local communities and topics outside the traditional framework of historiography. These younger historians were no longer buoyed by the sense of the national myth that sustained the likes of Hofstadter, Handlin, Boorstin, Schlesinger (father and son), Potter, and Curti among the older generation of historians. In this sense, the scholarly community of humanists and social scientists as a whole has been intellectually demoralized concurrently with the demythification of our national consciousness that began in the 1960s.

Yet the regional myths live on, and while they do—even though much regional scholarship will be devoted to the contradictions between regional myths and realities—regionalism will flourish. It is just barely possible that, at last in our history and culture, regionalism will not only rival but surpass nationalism in America as a source for good in human life.

The New Regionalism in the West and Northwest

The three predominant themes of West and Pacific Northwest regionalism of the 1970s and 1980s are (1) the individual quest for identity in terms of the region, (2) the symbiosis of art, architecture, litertature, and history with the natural environment, and (3) the tension between the classic and the counter-classic in western history and culture.

Individual Quest for Identity in Terms of the Region

The individual's identification with the region is achieved through emotional and intellectual interaction with its history and culture. In the realm of material culture, individual identification with the region is gained especially in relation to the region's landscape and its architectural heritage. In the sphere of intellectual culture, the individual's identification with the region is largely a response to the media of regional cultural expression.

The individual's quest for regional identification stems mainly from the enormous population growth of the West since World War II. Migration into the West from other regions has been huge and has been magnified by the rippling effect of the post-World War II baby boom. The result is that those raised in pre-World War II western families have sought to rediscover their roots in the West, and contemporary first-generation Westerners have sought to put down roots through identification with the region's cultural and historical heritage. Sometimes the newest Westerner wants a really "quick fix" of regional identification, as in the case of the eager immigrant executives in the booming Lone Star State who enroll in a crash course on "going Texas." But for most Westerners seeking new or renewed regional identification, the more patient processes afforded by the media of regional expression and historic preservation suffice.

In regard to historic preservation, the West is at last beginning to catch up with the Atlantic Coast, a region that long led the nation in preservation activity. As John L. Frisbee III has noted, the

West—exemplified by San Francisco's Ghirardelli Square, Seattle's Pioneer Square, and Denver's Larimer Square—"may well have provided the nation's best examples of commercial preservation." The preserved and restored mining towns of Jacksonville, Oregon, and Virginia City, Montana, are surely Pacific Northwest equivalents of Colonial Williamsburg.[83] Elsewhere in the Pacific Northwest, noteworthy preservation gains range from impressive federal efforts at isolated Ft. Simcoe, Washington, at the Whitman mission near Walla Walla, and at the post of the Hudson's Bay Company near Portland to Wolf Creek Tavern, a gem of private restoration off Interstate 5 in southern Oregon.

All through the Northwest citizens have banded together to preserve the cityscapes of Portland, Seattle, and other communities. State and federal programs are crucial, but, while complacency should never afflict the preservation movement, it seems likely that the indifference, neglect, and cruelty which led to such astrocities as the 1951 destruction of the Portland Hotel are behind us.[84] Losses will occur inevitably, but the preservation successes of the last 15 years give a stability to the region's architectural heritage that will be an ever-increasing source of regional identification.

The print media of regional expression also significantly heighten the Westerner's sense of regional identification. This is nothing new, of course; the promotional magazines *Land of Sunshine* (later *Out West*) in the Southwest and *West Shore* in the Pacific Northwest are early examples of this function.[85] Beginning in the 1960s, however, there has been a burst of new regional publications that have become an important part of the maturing of the New Regionalism in the 1970s and 1980s. California has spawned a host of such publications, including the vibrant *New West* and the historically oriented *American West*. In the state of Washington, Roger Sale has saluted *Seattle Magazine* for its attempt to shake the complacency of native Seattleites,[86] but the effect of that publication in other terms was undoubtedly to heighten the regional identification of newcomers to Seattle (like Sale himself).

Such efforts have been pressed vigorously in Oregon, where three vital Portland publications—the urbane *Oregon Magazine,* the crusading *Willamette Week,* and the acute *Oregon Business*—radiate their influence outward from the metropolitan area.[87]

The print media, however, do not exhaust the individual's opportunity for regional identification. There are, for example, in Oregon the excellent documentary photography of, among others, John Baugness, James Cloutier, and Selina Roberts and the extremely well-done films of Ron Finne.[88] There is also the lively local and regional theater movement, of which I wish to cite two Oregon examples.

One is the documentary drama *Blood and Roses,* by Portland playwright and editor Charles Deemer—a 1980 production that was staged many times in Portland, Salem, Coos Bay, and Springfield among other places. The other example is the long-running 1980 play *Northwest Woman,* that has been performed the length and breadth of Oregon in a production starring Jane Van Boskirk and featuring Edwin R. Bingham as narrator.[89] Both of these plays are typical of the New Regionalism in their blend of contemporary social perspective with the regional past.

In *Blood and Roses,* the episode out of regional history that is dramatized is a Portland longshoremen's strike of 1934, and the contemporary perspective is concern over corporate control of our daily lives. *Northwest Woman* has a similar combination. The current movement for women's rights provides the psychological context for dramatic sketches of four significant Northwest pioneer women. No doubt the vast majority of Pacific Northwesterners had never heard of either the Portland longshoremen's strike or the four pioneer women (except perhaps Narcissa Whitman) before seeing *Blood and Roses* and *Northwest Woman.* But the result, I am confident, for practically all who saw one or both of the productions, was a significant increase in regional consciousness.

The local history, local media, and local historic preservation movements are examples of what might be called "grassroots regionalism." Here the impulse for regionalism is not academic but simply a desire on the part of local people to enrich their lives by deepening their cultural attachments to the heritage of their community. These are, indeed, the efforts that preserve a region's cultural and historical identity at the grassroots, and such efforts give also a heightened personal identity to the individual involved in these endeavors in terms of his or her locality and region.

A remarkable case of grassroots regionalism, in which the emotions and intellects of local residents are tangibly engaged in preserving the Northwest's history and culture, is a beautifully illustrated paperback volume on seven historical landmarks of Lane County, Oregon. Compiled and written by five young men and women between the ages of 14 and 20, *And When They're Gone . . .* uses the method of oral history and historic photographs (supported by archival research) to bond the county's past to its present through histories of seven landmark structures. The sketches of all seven landmarks are highly effective montages of historic photographs and oral reminiscences, but most striking of all is the profile of the Chambers-dahlquist [sic] house, in which the authors have produced a paradigm of the social history of Eugene's last 90 years.

The five young people who wrote *And When They're Gone . . .* said of their project: "We struggled this summer, tracking down names and facts. We struggled and enjoyed. Now, whenever we see an old building, the paint peeling, the roof mossed over, it has a much greater meaning to us—it is no longer merely a house, but a memory of history, people, and stories." In those words and in the following sentence the youthful authors have caught the spirit of grassroots regionalism: "If after reading this book, these and other places arouse your interest, then our efforts are justified." It is not simply a cliche when, these grassroots regionalists declare, "this tour of historic sites affords a wholistic view of our roots and the progression of the past melting into the present; it captures a few moments of a process which, after all, is never at an end."[90]

Symbiosis with the Natural Environment

The West (with a strong assist from the East) has led the environmental movement for the last 15 years. The social base of environmentalism in the West is exemplifed by the phenomenal growth of the Sierra Club, which has undergone transformation from a small society of California hikers and mountain climbers going back to 1892 to an organization whose mass membership in

California forms the core of a potent national association for environmental protection and preservation.

The cultural impact of environmentalism has also been enormous. Gary Snyder of California (who started out in the Pacific Northwest at Reed College) won the Pulitzer Prize in poetry for his volume *Turtle Island* and has become the poet laureate of the American environmental movement.[91] The prolific Southwestern writer Edward Abbey made environmentalism the focus of his fantasy novel, *The Monkey-Wrench Gang*.[92] Nowhere is the fit between cultural creativity and the environment closer than in the contemporary Pacific Northwest. One may plausibly maintain that not until the post-World War II period has the Pacific Northwest produced a regional culture of fiction, poetry, art, and architecture that is truly of the first order. The recent cultural flowering of the Pacific Northwest, however, may well exceed all other regions in its combination of quality and coherence. It is strikingly evident that this achievement rests upon the creative inspiration provided by the Pacific Northwest environment of land, water, and climate.

Historians are at last beginning to relate Pacific Northwest history to the natural environment, a trend foreshadowed by D. W. Meinig's monumental 1968 historical geography of the Great Columbia Plain. Analogous to Meinig's work is the booming field of forest history, which naturally centers more on western Oregon and Washington. The forest history movement encompasses not only publications dealing directly with the forests and the wood-products industry (including monographs by Thomas R. Cox, William Robbins, and Robert Ficken), but also broader social and economic studies such as those by Robert L. Tyler and Carlos A. Schwantes on labor in the logging camps and sawmill towns and Norman H. Clark's study of Everett, Washington and its dependence on the lumber industry.[93]

Related to the broader aspect of forest history, too, is Richard White's recent book on land use, environment, and social change in Island County, Washington. White's book—a landmark volume in the New Regionalism—is notable for its innovative treatment of the "complex relationship between human-induced environmental change and social change" from prehistoric Indian times through the era of white domination into the early 20th century.[94] In a paper of my own, I have elaborated my concept of "the Great Raincoast of North America"—an attempt at a broad interpretation of the regional history of Oregon, Washington, and British Columbia based on the relationship of climate and history.[95]

Yet, what I have called "the creative inspiration provided by the Pacific Northwest environment of land, water, and climate" thus far has had greater impact upon writers of poetry and fiction than upon historians. The rainy weather of western Oregon provided the focal ambience of H. L. Davis' captivating novel of latter-day pioneers, *Honey in the Horn,* and of Don Berry's 1960s fictional trilogy on 19th-century western Oregon Indians and white settlers. Davis' magnificent later novel, *Winds of Morning,* rests both its plot and its symbolism on the distinctive seasonal change and climate in the eastern-Oregon vicinity of The Dalles. The rain and the relentlessly fecund forest are omnipresent in *Sometimes a Great Notion,* Ken Kesey's novel in which a clan of Oregon gyppo loggers is locked in combat not only with their less individualistic neighbors but with the primal force of nature.[96]

More recently, expatriate Virginian Tom Robbins has made the climate and landscape of Puget Sound the backdrop for two unique novels, *Another Roadside Attraction* and *Still Life with Woodpecker.*[97] Barry Holstun Lopez from the Eugene area has provided an original work of naturalism, *Of Wolves and Men,* while the Pacific Northwest environment of terrain, sea, and weather provide the emotive nuclei for Ivan Doig's remarkable 1980 study of James G. Swan, *Winter Brothers* and for his novel, *The Sea Runners.*[99]

The salience of "environment and the human response to it"[100] in Pacific Northwest poetry is by now well established. The orientation to physiography and weather is marked in the poetry of H. L. Davis before 1946, but the flowering of this condition comes later in the poetry of William Stafford, Theodore Roethke, Kenneth O. Hanson, Richard Hugo, Carolyn Kizer, and David Wagoner, to name a few.[101] For the symbiosis of the Northwest's environment and its poetry, the following lines by Theodore Roethke might well be the epigraph:

> . . . this place, where sea and fresh water meet,
> Is important—
> Where the hawks sway out into the wind,
> Without a single wingbeat,
> And eagles sail low over the fir trees,
> And the gulls cry against the crows
> In the curved harbors,
> And the tide rises up against the grass
> Nibbled by sheep and rabbits.[102]

Art and architecture replicate the bond between environment and creativity that we find in poetry and fiction. One must be wary of classifying the immense creative talent of architect Pietro Belluschi's too neatly, but the contributions of Philip Dole and George McMath to the monumental collection *Space, Style, and Architecture*[103] make it clear that the architecture of Belluschi, C. Gilman Davis, and their colleagues in the "Northwest Style" is rooted deep in the Pacific Northwest's past. Such folk styles of building as the environmentally adaptive "Oregon barn," which features a broad sheltering pitched roof and naturally finished native woods, may be seen in innumerable contemporary Pacific Northwest buildings, as well as in A. E. Doyle's early 20th-century seaside structures at Neahkahnie and elsewhere.[104]

The widely heralded school of Northwest painters headed by Mark Tobey, Morris Graves, Kenneth Callahan, Guy Anderson, and C. S. Price is as notable as any of our regional artistic endeavors for its inspiration by the region's weather, water, and land.[105] In his other role as a professional art critic, Tom Robbins has written that the rainfall of the Skagit Valley has "inspired a school of neo-Chinese painters"—Tobey, Graves, and "their gray-on-gray disciples" —who "turned their backs on cubist composition and European color" to use the "shapes and shades" of the "misty" Skagit Valley "as a springboard . . . to paint the visions of the inner eye."[106]

The environmental theme inspired California writer Ernest Callenbach's popular utopian novel *Ecotopia,* which projects the current environmentalist movement of northern California and the Pacific Northwest into a vision of the region as an independent nation.[107] Journalist and regionalist Joel Garreau has followed Callenbach's lead by labeling the Pacific coastal belt from Point

Conception to Cook Inlet as the region of "Ecotopia" in his *Nine Nations of North America.*[108] Aside from the utopian fiction of Callenbach and the regional reportage of Garreau, the key point has been stated by George Venn in regard to the environmental inspiration for Pacific Northwest art and literature: such creativity "moves beyond mere description" as the artist objectifies in fiction, poetry, or art "the experience of human life and death in an immediate locale" with the result that the artist "has internalized environment, taken it as part of himself, and watches and listens and feels for the truth it expresses about the spirit of place, the moment, and the people."[109]

Tension between the Classic and the Counter-Classic

Possibly the deepest fault line in any regional history and culture is that which separates the classic from the counter-classic. By "classic" I mean the region's traditional identity around which its mythology clusters. By "counter-classic" I mean those attributes of regional existence which ordinarily postdate and also differ markedly from the classic regional identity. In the South, the classic phase is represented by what we usually refer to as the Old South, a cultural complex of plantation life and slavery with its "moonlight and magnolias" myth. The counter-classic South is represented by the developments of industrialization, urbanization, and modernization often subsumed under the term "New South." The classic dimension of western history and culture is that ordinarily referred to as the pioneer West or the Old West, with its distinctive mythology focusing on mountain men, cowboys, Indians, prospectors, gunfighters, and outlaws. The counter-classic West is, in terms similar to those of the South, the urbanized, industrialized, and modernized West characterized by recurring technological advance

While there is a rough chronological distinction between the classic and the counter-classic, the classic and the counter-classic have often coexisted (especially in the West) from the 19th century to the present. For example, the California gold rush camps of the 1850s were indeed part of the classic West, but the neighboring San Francisco of the 1850s—one of the newest and most modern cities of America—was decidedly part of the counter-classic West. By the same token, Hollywood and Los Angeles in the 1920s were indubitably part of the counter-classic West, while the Owens Valley (from which Los Angeles was taking its water over the violent protests of the valley's farmers and ranchers) was part of the classic West.

Today the town of Burns and the Steens Mountain area of southeastern Oregon are much more of the classic West than otherwise, while the counter-classic flourishes in Seattle, Portland, Eugene, and Corvallis. The transition between the classic West and the counter-classic West can be abrupt. In an hour or so, one can travel from counter-classic Corvallis to the classic western sawmill town of Valsetz at the end of a long gravel road far up in the Coast Range.[110] Indeed, "transition" is not a wholly satisfactory word, for even in the 1970s and 1980s, the classic and the counter-classic interpenetrate the West just as they did a hundred years ago. This interpenetration is achieved not only by social and cultural comingling but by the looming presence of the monumental western landscape, whose impact is entirely classic. On a very clear day, for example, the classic western profile of Mt. Hood towers grandly over counter-classic Portland.

These are things felt by most of us who live in the West. The contrast and tension between the classic and the counter-classic is central to western regional consciousness. I think, too, that when the tension between the classic and the counter-classic is most acute, we find the greatest regional intellectual and artistic creativity. This was the case with the South in the 1920s-1940s era of the Old Regionalism. The classic South (by no means wholly gone today) endured strongly into the 1920s, 1930s, and 1940s with the Old South attributes of rural life, economic backwardness, and white racism. Advocates of the New South ideology (which went well back into the 19th century) had largely failed in their assault on the rural backwardness that was still pervasive in the 1930s—the economic progressiveness of the New South cities of Atlanta, Birmingham, *et al.* notwithstanding. White racism was institutionalized in the 1930s incarnation of ironclad white supremacy. But counter-classic currents were also swirling from the 1920s to the 1940s, currents that would (with the crucial assistance of federal pressure) sweep away the formal embodiment of white racism in segregation and make the South a synonym for dynamic urban and industrial expansion.

With the notable exception of the Nashville "agrarian" movement centered at Vanderbilt University, the great southern regionalists of the 1920s-1940s mainly represented the counter-classic in southern history and culture. The Chapel Hill regionalists led by sociologist Howard Odum were intent on using academic social science to end the classic southern trap of racial violence and rural poverty.[111] Walter Prescott Webb and J. Frank Dobie of the University of Texas were forging a new consciousness of the classic Southwest in such books as Dobie's *Coronado's Children* and Webb's *Great Plains*.[112] Yet Webb, in his volume *Divided We Stand,* was in the vanguard of those struggling to end the South's (and West's) economic bondage to the financial and industrial citadels of the Northeast.[113]

In Southern literature, a galaxy of remarkably talented writers headed by William Faulkner and Lillian Smith were using regionally focused fiction in an attempt to confront and purge the South of its violent white racism. This endeavor was also of grave concern to W. J. Cash, whose powerful 1941 book *The Mind of the South* presented the tension between the classic and counter-classic South in an excruciating symbiosis of emotion and intellect. In the realm of academic scholarship, V. O. Key and the southern white and black coworkers of Gunnar Myrdal were giving the counter-classic South a new social science through their books on southern politics and race relations.[114] At the same time, C. Vann Woodward was leading a movement of young, liberal, problack white historians, who were rewriting the South's history in terms that would provide a usable past for the counter-classic South that finally became economically, socially, and politically dominant in the 1960s and 1970s.[115]

These were the scholars and artists (mostly white, since blacks were largely excluded from the classic/counter-classic dichotomy) who made the South the most intellectually and artistically creative region in the era of the Old Regionalism. The result has been a new equilibrium in our own time between the classic and the counter-classic in the South, a development whose intellectual history has been brilliantly depicted in three recent books by Richard H. King, Michael O'Brien, and Daniel Joseph Singal.[116] Sociologist John Shelton Reed has shown that the attitudes of the classic South are still widespread below the Mason-Dixon Line,[117] but the ferment and flux of the 1920s-1940s, which eventuated in the rout of segregation and backwardness, relaxed (but did not completely end) the tension between the classic and the counter-classic. Good history, literature, and social science continue to flourish in the South, but with the passing of its regional *raison d'etre* in acute classic/counter-classic tension, the Southern Renaissance of the thirties and forties has run its course with no comparable peak in cultural creativity yet in evidence.

In the New Regionalism of the 1970s and 1980s, the West has supplanted the South as the region of greatest artistic and intellectual vitality, because it is in the West that the tension between the classic and the counter-classic is now most acute. This is reflected in contemporary western history and literature. More and more historians, for example, are writing about the history of the counter-classic West. This trend began as far back as 1965 with publication of Earl Pomeroy's path-breaking *Pacific Slope,* which dwelt heavily on the urban, commercialized, modernized West.[118] Similarly, Gerald D. Nash's *American West in the Twentieth Century* emphasizes the counter-classic, although Nash makes a deep bow to the classic motif of John Wesley Powell and Walter Prescott Webb with his stress on the theme of urban oasis culture in the context of the West's persistent semiarid environment.[119]

At long last, we have a social history of the film industry in Lary May's *Screening Out the Past*[120] whose publication in 1980 aptly coincided with the election of a movie star to the American presidency. Kevin Starr's *Americans and the California Dream* is a unique and brilliant study of the classic western "California Dream" of the good life in the Golden State,[121] while Robert M. Fogelson's *Fragmented Metropolis,* a scathing study of counter-classic Los Angeles, underscores the urban nemesis of the California Dream.[122] The same theme is treated in Starr's novel of contemporary San Francisco life, *Land's End.*

The traditional values of the classic West—courage, loyalty, endurance, individualism—are shown by contemporary writers to be in conflict with the reality of the counter-classic West. This theme is striking in the novels of Larry McMurtry, who is at his best in depicting the failure of classic western values to survive among the hedonism and modern materialism of the burgeoning cities and suburbs of our present West. In *Horseman, Pass By* (filmed and republished as *Hud*), the contradiction between the classic and the counter-classic is posed at its most brutal in the conflict between the cruel materialism of Hud Bannon and Hud's grandfather, who stands for the old ways and old values of ranch life.[124] A similar contrast is found in Ken Kesey's *Sometimes a Great Notion,* which portrays the heroic individualism of the classic western Stamper family at war with the counter-classic bureaucratic mentality of the outside union official, Jonathan B. Draeger.[125] Ivan Doig's moving memoir of his 1940s-1950s boyhood in Montana likewise illustrates the classic western trait of endurance in the persons of his irrepressible grandmother and his father, a staunch, stoic ranch foreman. But Doig also shows the counter-classic western economic trend toward concentrated land ownership, which leaves the Doig family landless amidst Montana's classic western landscape. And Doig himself turns his back on the narrowing opportunities of his classic western Montana life to pursue a writing career in counter-classic Seattle.[126]

Surely the enormous post-World War II surge in urban growth has been a key to the increasing focus on classic vs. counter-classic tension in writing about the West. This, too, is a major element in Larry McMurtry's work. McMurtry (who declared himself "a regionalist" in 1968) followed his fictional trilogy of classic/counter-classic tension in a rural/small-town setting with an urban trilogy published from 1970 to 1975. The three latter novels—*Moving On, All My Friends Are Going to be Strangers,* and *Terms of Endearment*— are a lavishly textured treatment of urban life that boxes the Western compass from Des Moines to Hollywood and from San Francisco to Houston.[127] The three books are so multifarious that they resist simplification, yet McMurtry's rich treatment of urban Texas of the 1960s and 1970s obviously elaborates his conviction that "it is essentially [the] movement from country to subdivision, homeplace to metropolis, that gives life in present-day Texas its passion." McMurtry calls this theme "the Cowboy in the suburb" —that is, the classic western ethos floundering in the counter-classic social reality.[128]

Whereas McMurtry emphasizes the counter-classic West in his urban trilogy, the reverse is true of Wallace Stegner's best novel, *Angle of Repose*. The predominant classic western ambience of Stegner's searing novel is the story of an Easterner whose failure to acculturate to the pioneer West ends in personal tragedy. The story of Stegner's protagonist, Susan Burling Ward, is told against the background of our contemporary West as represented by the novel's narrator (Mr. Ward's grandson), an academic deeply embittered by the counter-classic chaos of Berkeley in the 1960s and by the cold and false sophistication of his own professorial son.[129]

Our own time—the 1960s, 1970s, 1980s—is a great age of reportage,[130] and *The New Yorker* has consistently excelled in this realm. It is significant, therefore, that *The New Yorker* has been a major medium of expression for the New Regionalism of the West and its classic/counter-classic tension. In sketch after sketch during the last 20 years, *New Yorker* writers Calvin Trillin and Philip Hamburger have etched the urban reality of the contemporary counter-classic West.[131] In addition, Jane Kramer's and John McPhee's western books of reportage appeared originally as series in *The New Yorker*.

Kramer's *Last Cowboy*[132] presents the contrast between the classic and counter-classic West at its starkest. Her protagonist Henry Blanton, a West Texas ranch foreman, not only lives the classic western life of a cowboy but identifies passionately with the myth of the classic West portrayed in the television westerns he endlessly watches.[133] Kramer depicts the excruciating tragedy of this "last cowboy" as his dream of finally owning his own land is shattered by the cupidity of his superior in the ranch hierarchy— the manager, Lester Hill. Hill is the antithesis of the classic Westerner, a thorough counter-classic type. He is a suburbanized Texan (with a degree in agriculture from Cornell), who knows nothing about a ranch that really matters. Kramer's nonfiction gem serves as a book-length documentary footnote to the classic/counter-classic conflict in Larry McMurtry's fiction.

The New Yorker's master of reportage is John McPhee, one of America's best writers today. McPhee, an Easterner, has during the 1970s and 1980s turned to the West for the locales of three of his eight books: *Encounters with the Archdruid, Coming into the Country,* and *Basin and Range*—books in which the classic/counter-classic dualism of the West is crucial.[134]

In *Encounters with the Archdruid,* McPhee deals with the environmentalist movement through one of its key chieftains, David Brower, whose dynamic leadership of the Sierra Club helped win several great victories for environmental protection in the West. McPhee presents Brower as an "archdruid" who is tenaciously committed to the preservation of the wilderness and its values, but from McPhee's perspective Brower is also easily seen as an individual blend of the classic and the counter-classic in the West. As a lifelong resident of the *avant garde* university city of Berkeley who commutes to his San Francisco office, Brower lives in the workaday world of the counter-classic Westerner. Yet, Brower can also be viewed as a classic Westerner in his roles as an intrepid mountain climber and wilderness habitue. *Encounters with the Archdruid* also includes a personification of the counter-classic West in Brower's rival, Floyd E. Dominy, who then headed the U. S. Bureau of Reclamation, an organization dedicated to environmentally destructive dam construction in the interest of producing irrigation water for counter-classic agribusiness and kilowatts for counter-classic cities. The relationship between Brower and Dominy is ambiguous; both play for keeps in their high-stakes game over the western environment, yet their personal relations have the almost chivalric quality that characterizes antagonists in the mythical Old West. McPhee's account of their Colorado River raft trip together is a memorable passage in the literature of the New Regionalism of the West.[135] However, despite the personal amiability of Dominy, McPhee clearly casts him in the role of villain to Brower's hero.

McPhee's next book on the West, *Coming into the Country,* deals with Alaska. Here the contradiction between the classic and the counter-classic is even more pointed and arresting than in *Encounters with the Archdruid.* The contrapuntal power of *Coming into the Country* stems from McPhee's acerbic sketch of Anchorage as a remarkably ugly counter-classic metropolis, in contrast to the pristine wilderness of the Brooks Range in the far north[136] and the *soi-disant* classic western life of the contemporary pioneers along the Yukon River. Some of the Yukon settlers appear as slightly mad rightwing fanatics, but all authentically exemplify the classic western values of courage and self-reliance. Some are engaged in a bitter struggle with the Bureau of Land Management, which, in its own way, is carrying out the mandate of the American people to preserve Alaska's classic western landscape.[137]

Coming into the Country is a powerful book and undoubtedly McPhee's best about the West so far, but his recent book, *Basin and Range,* presents implicitly the conflict between the classic and the counter-classic in its most elemental form. The book is about the geologically significant succession of alternating basin valleys and mountain ranges across the breadth of the state of Nevada. *Basin and Range* reads at times too much like a primer on plate tectonics, but its memorable descriptive passages are purely classic western. When it was published there was an inherent drama and poignancy in the book as a result of the environmental threat of the MX missile system. McPhee mentioned the MX missile system in the book only once, but he did not have to mention it more often; it was powerfully evident to the reader that the missile system—the apogee of the anti-human aspect of the counter-classic West—posed a desperate danger to the classic western landscape and ecosystem of McPhee's basin-and-range country.[138]

The political controversy over the MX missile system is a salient reminder that the tension between the classic and the counter-classic in the New Regionalism of the West is not confined to history and literature. The career of Interior Secretary James Watt illustrates this point.[139] It is easy to see Watt as the political point man for the exploiters and developers of the counter-classic West who are doing their utmost, in the name of private profit, to homogenize the West and obliterate its classic heritage. Yet this view of Watt, although a considered one, might be seen by many westerners (including Watt) to be one-sided. Indeed, Watt is an ambiguous figure. Watt's sympathy for the counter-classic ethos of the super-corporation managers makes him an ultra counter-classic Westerner. But it must not be forgotten that the materialistic and exploitative aspect of western individualism is also a significant part of the classic western heritage, as Frederick Jackson Turner emphasized in his essay on "The Significance of the Frontier in American History."[140]

The issues suggested by the career of James Watt have been reflected in some of the writings of Joan Didion, who moves gracefully from fiction to reportage and back again, but in each case from a unitary intellectual heritage of the classic West. A fifth-generation Californian whose western roots go back to an 1846 covered wagon, Didion grew up in Sacramento and went to the University of California at Berkeley.[141] The classic vs. counter-classic western contradiction is strongly imprinted in her two elegant books of reportage dealing with California and the West and in her three piercing novels of California life after 1935.

Didion has not declared any plan to write the social history of post-1935 California, but this is what she has done in her brilliant fictional trilogy of California life: *Run River,* on Central Valley agriculturists; *Play It as It Lays,* on Hollywood, and *A Book of Common Prayer,* on San Francisco.[142] The protagonists in all three novels have a strong sense of the pioneer past, reflecting Didion's statement that "the ethic I was raised in was specifically a Western frontier ethic."[143]

In all three novels the contrast of the counter-classic West with its classic past is almost excruciating, and the theme in each is personal and family dissolution—for the hop growers along the Sacramento River whose society dissolves into the morass of the post-World War II urban boom; for the Nevada-raised starlet who cannot cope with the amoral anomie of contemporary Hollywood; and for the San Francisco sophisticate whose private dreams are shattered by California's radical-shock of the 1970s.

In a sense Didion's fiction does for California what Larry McMurtry's fiction has done for classic-haunted, counter-classic

Texas. Didion has expressed her own version of the classic/counter-classic theme in her declaration that "the tension central to both the Southern and Western experience is . . . [the] inability to distinguish between myth and reality."[144] Indeed, Didion has noted that in her New York period of the 1950s she felt most at home in the company of expatriate Southerners: "They seemed to me to be in New York as I was, on some indefinitely extended leave from wherever they belonged . . ., temporary exiles who always knew when the flights left for New Orleans or Memphis or Richmond or, in my case, California."[145] Didions's western-born affinity for the southern extends into her literary career, for as one reviewer has noted, "like Faulkner, Didion has an overwhelming awareness of human corruption and a sense of unfathomable doom."[146]

Even the sense of "unfathomable doom" so marked in Didion's fiction is moored in her deep appreciation of California's classic western history, for she has written that "it is characteristic of Californians to speak grandly of the past as if it had simultaneously begun, *tablula rasa,* and reached a happy ending on the day the wagons started west . . . . California is a place in which a boom mentality and a sense of Chekhovian loss meet in uneasy suspension; in which the mind is troubled by some buried but ineradicable suspicion that things had better work here, because here, beneath that immense bleached sky, is where we run out of continent."[147]

Not only is Didion strongly regionalist in her fiction, but she has contributed many gleaming gems of regional reportage. Among them are her sketches of Haight-Ashbury hippiedom in San Francisco, the Manson-murders era in Hollywood, California's system of water engineering, and the psychological impact of the Santa Ana wind on the Los Angeles basin, all included in her two books of collected essays, *Slouching toward Bethlehem* and *The White Album.*[148] There is a decidedly more upbeat quality to Didion's nonfiction on the West than her fiction, but this may be simply due to the inherent difference between fiction and nonfiction as modes of expression. Like all of the best regionalists, Didion's regionalism is her own very personal way of pursuing universal truths in thought and feeling; surely there is no resolution in her writing of the classic/counter-classic western dichotomy. This may be because, aside from her incomparable character as a stylist, Didion's strongest quality as a writer—one that transcends her regionalism—is her character as a moralist.[149] The strategy of the moralist is to avoid resolution.

The moralist may well eschew resolution of the tension between ideal and nonideal behavior, but most of us in our daily lives cannot sustain tension without some sort of ultimate resolution. I have been writing about the classic/counter-classic dichotomy in the West as though conflict inevitably characterizes the relationship between the two. Tension will be an almost inevitable characteristic of the classic/counter-classic relationship, but is it not possible for the tension to veer toward resolution and equilibrium? One recent work, I believe, does suggest a resolution of the classic/counter-classic tension. This is a book from the Puget Sound country: *Winter Brothers* by Ivan Doig.

Through his protagonist, the 19th-century pioneer polymath James G. Swan, Doig recaptures the reality and spirit of the classic West along the North Pacific Coast. But there is more than Swan alone in this versatile book, for Doig easily puts himself (and his wife, Carol) into the pages of *Winter Brothers.* Doig presents himself for what he is: a counter-classic urbanite who lives by his skill as a writer, tied to the discipline of the typewriter in the study of his Seattle-area home. Yet, in doing his book on Swan, Doig retraces for himself Swan's life-route along the Northwest coast from Willapa Bay to the Queen Charlotte Islands. For Doig this is not merely a job of conscientious field research for a book in progress. It becomes evident that in visiting and revisiting the scenes and the weathers of Swan's career, Doig is gaining crucial emotional sustenance for his own counter-classic, urbanized, modernized life. Thus, the "winter brothers" are Swan and Doig, bonded in the linkage of the classic and counter-classic West.[150] Doig's winter brothers may well be a metaphor for the resolution of the classic/counter-classic tension. Thus, many of us who live and work in the counter-classic West may find, as Doig has found, renewal from our classic western surroundings and from the brotherhood and sisterhood of classic Westerners of the past.

NOTES

[1] Carey McWilliams, *The New Regionalism in American Literature* (Seattle: University of Washington Book Store, 1930), 1. Howard Odum also used the term "the new regionalism."

[2] Guy Benton Johnson and Guion Griffis Johnson, *Research in Service of Society: The First Fifty Years of the Institute for Research in Social Science at the University of North Carolina* (Chapel Hill: University of North Carolina Press, 1980), chaps. 6-7 and *passim;* Dewey W. Grantham, *The Regional Imagination: The South and Recent American History* (Nashville: Vanderbilt University Press, 1979), chap. 10; Richard H. King, *A Southern Renaissance: The Cultural Awakening of the American South, 1930-1955* (New York: Oxford University Press, 1980), 39-51; Michael O'Brien, *The Idea of the American South, 1920-1941* (Baltimore: Johns Hopkins University Press, 1979), chaps. 2-4; Daniel Joseph Singal, *The War Within: From Victorian to Modernist Thought in the South* (Chapel Hill: University of North Carolina Press, 1982), chaps. 5, 10.

[3] Ronnie Dugger, ed., *Three Men in Texas: Bedichek, Webb, and Dobie— Essays by Their Friends in the Texas Observer* (Austin: University of Texas Press, 1967); William A. Owens, *Three Friends: Roy Bedichek, J. Frank Dobie, Walter Prescott Webb* (Garden City: Doubleday, 1969); Necah S. Furman, *Walter Prescott Webb: His Life and Impact* (Albuquerque: University of New Mexico Press, 1976); Gregory M. Tobin, *The Making of a History: Walter Prescott Webb and The Great Plains* (Austin: University of Texas Press, 1976); Lon Tinkle, *An American Original: The Life of J. Frank Dobie* (Boston: Little, Brown, 1978); Kenneth R. Philip and Elliott West, eds., *Essays on Walter Prescott Webb* (Austin: University of Texas Press, c1976).

[4] O'Brien, *Idea of American South*, chaps. 5-9 and *passim;* Singal, *War Within*, chaps. 7-8, 11.

[5] John F. Bannon, *Herbert Eugene Bolton: The Historian and the Man, 1870-1953* (Tucson: University of Arizona Press, 1978); George R. Stewart, *Storm* (New York: Random House, 1941) and *Fire* (Boston: Houghton Mifflin, 1948), two innovative documentary novels. On Taylor: Richard Steven Street, "The Economist as Humanist: The Career of Paul S. Taylor," *California History,* 58 (Winter 1979/80): 350-61.

[6] Cornelius H. Sullivan, "Regionalism in American Thought: Provincial Ideals from the Gilded Age to the Great Depression" (Ph.D. diss., University of Chicago, 1977). Key works included: Samuel Eliot Morison, *Builders of the Bay Colony* (Boston: Houghton Mifflin, 1930); Kenneth B. Murdock, *Increase Mather: The Foremost American Puritan* (Cambridge: Harvard University Press, 1925); Perry

Miller, *Orthodoxy in Massachusetts, 1630-1650* (Cambridge: Harvard University Press, 1933); F. O. Matthiessen, *American Renaissance: Art and Expression in the Age of Emerson and Whitman* (New York: Oxford University Press, 1941).

[7] Symptomatic of the Wisconsin tradition was its hosting the conference on regionalism at which the papers delivered were published in Merrill Jensen, ed., *Regionalism in America* (Madison: University of Wisconsin Press, 1951). The editor of the book was a historian at Wisconsin, five contributors were Wisconsin faculty members, and two others were former members of the Wisconsin faculty.

[8] Theodore C. Blegen, *Grass Roots History* (Minneapolis: University of Minnesota Press, 1947), a collection of essays and addresses, 1926-1946.

[9] Mari Sandoz, *Old Jules* (Boston: Little, Brown, 1935): Everett Dick, *The Sod-House Frontier, 1854-1890: A Social History of the Northern Plains . . .* (New York: D. Appleton-Century, 1937).

[10] James C. Malin, *Winter Wheat in the Golden Belt of Kansas* (Lawrence: University of Kansas Press, 1944) and *The Grassland of North America* (Lawrence: n. p., 1947).

[11] William D. Rowley, *M. L. Wilson and the Campaign for the Domestic Allotment* (Lincoln: University of Nebraska Press, 1970). On Merriam (the founding editor in 1927 of what "later became the first major Northwestern regional magazine" of literature, *The Frontier*) see: George L. Venn, "Continuity in Northwest Literature," in *Northwest Perspectives: Essays on the Culture of the Pacific Northwest,* ed. Edwin R. Bingham and Glen A. Love (Seattle: University of Washington Press, 1979), 100, 103-4.

[12] Wilbur J. Cash, *The Mind of the South* (New York: Alfred A. Knopf, 1941).

[13] Jerre Mangione, *The Dream and the Deal: The Federal Writers' Project, 1935-1943* (Boston: Little, Brown, 1972). Monty Noam Penkower, *The Federal Writers' Project: A Study in Government Patronage of the Arts* (Urbana: University of Illinois Press, 1977).

[14] Jane De Hart Mathews, *The Federal Theatre, 1935-1939: Plays, Relief, and Politics* (Princeton: Princeton University Press, 1967).

[15] Richard D. McKinzie, *The New Deal for Artists* (Princeton: Princeton University Press, 1973); Charles C. Alexander, *Here the Country Lies: Nationalism and the Arts in Twentieth-Century America* (Bloomington: Indiana University Press, 1980), 182-84.

[16] At least fifty-three books in the "Rivers of America" series were published from 1937 to 1968 by the original publisher, Farrar and Rinehart, and its successors. See, for example, Struthers Burt, *Powder River: Let 'er Buck* (New York: Farrar and Rinehart, 1938).

[17] At least 18 books were published in the "American Folkways" series by Duell, Sloan, and Pearce from 1941 to 1957. Carey McWilliams, *Southern California Country* (New York: Duell, Sloan, and Pearce, 1946); Meridel Le Sueur, *North Star Country* (New York: Duell, Sloan, and Pearce, 1945).

[18] Alexander, *Here the Country Lies,* 179-81; Thomas Hart Benton, *An Artist in America* (New York: R. M. McBride, 1937); Matthew Baigell, *The American Scene: American Painting of the 1930s* (New York: Harry N. Abrams, 1973); James M. Dennis, *Grant Wood: A Study in American Art and Culture* (New York: Viking, 1975). See also, Karal Ann Marling, *Wall-to-Wall America: A Cultural History of Post-Office Murals in the Great Depression* (Minneapolis: University of Minnesota Press, 1982).

[19] Sullivan, "Regionalism in American Thought"; David Shapiro, *Social Realism: Art as a Weapon* (New York: Ungar, 1973).

[20] Joe Klein, *Woody Guthrie: A Life* (New York: Alfred A. Knopf, 1980); Bill C. Malone, *Country Music U. S. A.* (Austin: University of Texas Press, 1968).

[21] Alexander, *Here the Country Lies,* 167-72, 244.

[22] V. O. Key (with the assistance of Alexander Heard), *Southern Politics in State and Nation* (New York: Random House, 1949); Charles McKinley, *Uncle Sam in the Pacific Northwest* (Berkeley: University of California Press, 1952).

[23] O'Brien, *Idea of American South,* 196-97; Donald Davidson, *The Attack on Leviathan: Regionalism and Nationalism in the United States* (Chapel Hill: University of North Carolina Press, 1938); Howard W. Odum and Harry E. Moore, *American Regionalism: A Cultural-Historical Approach to National Integration* (New York: Henry Holt, 1938).

[24] Baker Brownell, *The Human Community: Its Philosophy and Practice for a Time of Crisis* (New York: Harper & Brothers, 1950) and *The College and the Community: A Critical Study of Higher Education* (New York: Harper & Brothers, 1952); Baker Brownell, Joseph Kinsey Howard, and Paul Meadows, *Life in Montana, as Seen in Lonepine, a Small Community* (Missoula: University of Montana, 1945); Richard W. Poston, *Small Town Renaissance: The Story of the Montana Study* (New York: Harper & Brothers, 1950).

[25] Quoted in William Stott, *Documentary Expression and Thirties America* (New York: Oxford University Press, 1973), 241-42.

[26] Wesley Arden Dick, "Visions of Abundance: The Public Power Crusade in the Pacific Northwest in the Era of J. D. Ross and the New Deal" (Ph.D. diss., University of Washington, 1973).

[27] Wilmon H. Droze, *Trees, Prairies, and People: A History of Tree Planting in the Plains States* (Denton: Texas Woman's University, 1977); Donald Holley, *Uncle Sam's Farmers: The New Deal Communities in the Lower Mississippi Valley* (Urbana: University of Illinois Press, 1975); Paul E. Mertz, *New Deal Policy and Southern Rural Poverty* (Baton Rouge: Louisiana State University Press, 1978); Paul K. Conkin, *Tomorrow a New World: The New Deal Community Program* (Ithaca: Cornell University Press, 1959).

[28] McKinley, *Uncle Sam;* Martha Derthick (with the assistance of Gary Bombadier), *Between State and Nation: Regional Organizations of the United States* (Washington, D. C.: Brookings Institution, 1974). On the National Resources Planning Board and its predecessors: Otis L. Graham, *Toward a Planned*

Society: From Roosevelt to Nixon (New York: Oxford University Press, 1976), 52-58; John D. Millett, *The Process and Organization of Government Planning* (New York: Columbia University Press, 1947).

[29] Stott, *Documentary Expression.*

[30] Stott (*Documentary Expression,* 38, 51, 252) emphasizes the importance of Louis Adamic, *My America: 1928-1938* (New York: Harper & Brothers, 1938).

[31] Stott, *Documentary Expression,* 256.

[32] Stott, *Documentary Expression.* Stott's remarkable book was influenced by Warren I. Susman's treatment of documentary media in Susman's essay cited in note 35, below.

[33] Bernard De Voto, *The Year of Decision: 1846* (Boston: Little, Brown, 1943), *Across the Wide Missouri* (Boston: Little, Brown, 1947), and *The Course of Empire* (Boston: Little, Brown, 1952).

[34] Wallace Stegner, *The Uneasy Chair: A Biography of Bernard De Voto* (Garden City: Doubleday, 1974).

[35] Warren I. Susman, "The Thirties," in *The Development of an American Culture,* ed. Stanley Coben and Lorman Ratner (Englewood Cliffs: Prentice-Hall, 1970), 217; Stott, *Documentary Expression,* x, chaps. 14-15.

[36] James Agee and Walker Evans, *Let Us Now Praise Famous Men* (Boston: Little, Brown, 1941). See also, Howell Raines, "Let Us Now Revisit Famous Folk," *New York Times Magazine,* 25 May 1980, 31-46.

[37] Erskine Caldwell and Margaret Bourke-White, *You Have Seen Their Faces* (New York: Viking, 1937).

[38] Merrill Jensen, ed., *Regionalism in America* (Madison: University of Wisconsin Press, 1951). See also, Richard Jensen, "On Modernizing Frederick Jackson Turner: The Historiography of Regionalism," *Western Historical Quarterly,* 11 (July 1980): 307-22.

[39] Johnson and Johnson, *Research in Service,* 66-79 and chaps. 9-10; O'Brien, *Idea of American South,* 90-92.

[40] Lawrance R. Thompson, *Robert Frost,* 3 vols. (New York: Holt, Rinehart, & Winston, 1966-76); John C. Kemp, *Robert Frost and New England: The Poet as Regionalist* (Princeton: Princeton University Press, 1979).

[41] King, *Southern Renaissance,* 256-77.

[42] Kirkpatrick Sale, *Power Shift: The Rise of the Southern Rim and Its Challenge to the Eastern Establishment* (New York: Random House, 1975). See also, Robert A. Caro's study of the alliance of Lyndon B. Johnson and rising Texas industrialists in *The Years of Lyndon Johnson: The Path to Power* (New York: Alfred A. Knopf, 1982).

[43] Walter Prescott Webb, *Divided We Stand: The Crisis of a Frontierless Democracy* (New York: Farrar and Rinehart, 1937).

[44] Howard W. Odum, "The Promise of Regionalism" in Jensen, ed., *Regionalism in America.*

[45] John Shelton Reed, *The Enduring South: Subcultural Persistence in Mass Society* (Lexington: D. C. Heath, 1972).

[46] Raymond D. Gastil, *Cultural Regions of the United States* (Seattle: University of Washington Press, 1975).

[47] Merle Curti et al., *The Making of An American Community: A Case Study of Democracy in a Frontier County* (Stanford: Stanford University Press, 1959); Stephan Thernstrom, *Poverty and Progress: Social Mobility in a Nineteenth Century City* (Cambridge: Harvard University Press, 1964).

[48] The television series, "Roots," was based on Alex Haley, *Roots* (Garden City: Doubleday, 1970); see also, Michael Kammen, ed., *The Past before Us: Contemporary Historical Writing in the United States* (Ithaca: Cornell University Press, 1980), pp. 14, 273. The historical novels of James A. Michener: *Hawaii* (New York: Random House, 1959), *Centennial* (New York: Random House, 1974), and *Chesapeake* (New York: Random House, 1978).

[49] Constance M. Greiff, ed., *Lost America,* 2 vols. (Princeton: Pyne, 1971-72).

[50] Elizabeth D. Mulloy, *The History of the National Trust for Historic Preservation, 1963-73* (Washington, D. C.: Preservation Press, 1976); also, Nathan Weinberg, *Preservation in American Towns and Cities* (Boulder: Westview, 1979).

[51] Roderick Nash, *Wilderness and the American Mind,* revised ed. (New Haven: Yale University Press, 1973).

[52] Ben L. Moon, "City Magazines, Past and Present," *Journalism Quarterly* 47 (Winter 1970): 711-18; Thomas Cekay, "Regionalism Spells Success," *Advertising Age* 52 (June 1, 1981): 810-811.

[53] For information on the regionally oriented programs of the N.E.H., see the annual reports of the N.E.H.

[54] Patricia Cassidy, comp., *The Oregon Committee for the Humanities: The First Ten Years* (Portland: Oregon Committee for the Humanities, 1980), dealing with 1970-1980. Recently published is an intriguing collection of essays in which Oregon humanists confront an issue of compelling public interest: Carolyn M. Buan, ed., *Sweet Reason: Oregon Essays Issue 1: The Ethic of Abundance in an Age of Austerity* (Portland: Oregon Committee for the Humanities, 1982).

[55] James Morton Smith, general ed., *The States and the Nation Series,* 50 vols. (New York: W. W. Norton, 1976-1981).

[56] Gordon B. Dodds, *Oregon: A Bicentennial History* (New York: W. W. Norton, 1977); Norman H. Clark, *Washington: A Bicentennial History* (New York: W. W. Norton, 1976); Richard Jensen, *Illinois: A Bicentennial History* (New York: W. W. Norton, 1978); John A. Williams, *West Virginia: A Bicentennial History* (New York: W. W. Norton, 1976); Virginia V. Hamilton, *Alabama: A Bicentennial History* (New York: W. W. Norton, 1977).

[57] Stott, *Documentary Expression;* McKinzie, *The New Deal for Artists;* Mangione, *The Dream and the Deal;* Penkower, *The Federal Writers' Project;*

Mathews, *The Federal Theatre, 1935-1939;* Lorena Hickok, *One Third of a Nation: Lorena Hickok Reports on the Great Depression,* ed. Richard Lowitt and Maurine Beasley (Urbana: University of Illinois Press, 1981); F. Jack Hurley, *Portrait of a Decade: Roy Stryker and the Development of Documentary Photography in the Thirties* (Baton Rouge: Louisiana State University Press, 1972); Milton Meltzer, *Dorothea Lange: A Photographer's Life* (New York: Farrar, Straus, and Giroux, 1978); *Walker Evans, First and Last* (New York: Harper and Row, 1978). See also, Robert L. Snyder, *Pare Lorentz and the Documentary Film* (Norman: University of Oklahoma Press, 1968).

58 Mertz, *New Deal Policy;* Holley, *Uncle Sam's Farmers;* Donald Worster, *Dust Bowl: The Southern Plains in the 1930s* (New York: Oxford University Press, 1979); Walter J. Stein, *California and the Dust Bowl Migration* (Westport: Greenwood, 1973); Paul Bonnifeld, *The Dust Bowl: Men, Dirt, and Depression* (Albuquerque: University of New Mexico Press, 1979); Droze, *Trees, Prairies, and People.*

59 King, *Southern Renaissance;* O'Brien, *Idea of American South;* Singal, *War Within;* Joseph Blotner, *William Faulkner,* 2 vols. (New York: Random House, 1974); Klein, *Woody Guthrie: A Life;* Stegner, Tobin, *Making of a History;* Furman, *Walter Prescott Webb;* Tinkle, *An American Original;* Bannon, *Herbert Eugene Bolton.*

60 Baigell, *The American Scene;* and *Thomas Hart Benton;* Dennis, *Grant Wood;* Nancy Heller and Julia Williams, *The Regionalists* (New York: Watson-Guptil, 1976); Shapiro, *Social Realism.*

61 Richard Maxwell Brown, "West/Northwest Regionalism and the University of Oregon" (unpub. paper, June 1980).

62 These three centers and other contemporary programs in regionalism are described in the brochure issued in connection with the workshop on "Regionalism in America" held in Oxford, Mississippi, May 14-17, 1980, cosponsored by the University of Mississippi Center for the Study of Southern Culture and the National Endowment for the Humanities.

63 Although far from being definitive (for example, it omits Kevin Starr's key book, *Americans and the California Dream, 1850-1915* (New York: Oxford University Press, 1973), the following work is a valuable listing of authors and titles for the 1970-1979 period: Sue Hart and Elise Winter, comps., *American Regional Culture: A Bibliographic Sampler* (photocopy: Oxford: University of Mississippi Center for the Study of Southern Culture, 1980). See also, the bibliographies in Gastil, *Cultural Regions,* and Joel Garreau, *The Nine Nations of North America* (Boston: Houghton Mifflin, 1981), as well as two comprehensive works that give major emphasis to academic and nonacademic regionalism: Rodman W. Paul and Richard W. Etulain, comps., *The Frontier and the American West* (Arlington Heights: AHM, 1977); Howard R. Lamar, ed., *The Reader's Encyclopedia of the American West* (New York: Thomas Y. Crowell, 1977).

[64] Harry M. Caudill, *Night Comes to the Cumberlands: A Biography of a Depressed Area* (Boston: Little, Brown, 1963) and *My Land is Dying* (New York: E. P. Dutton, 1971). The late K. Ross Toole's role for Montana and the northern Great Plains resembles that of Caudill for Appalachia. Both Caudill and Toole show deep concern for the environmentally and culturally destructive impact of coal mining on their respective regions. See K. Ross Toole, *Twentieth-Century Montana: A State of Extremes* (Norman: University of Oklahoma Press, 1972) and *The Rape of the Great Plains* (Boston: Atlantic-Little, Brown, 1976).

[65] H. Brandt Ayers and Thomas H. Naylor, eds., *You Can't Eat the Magnolias* (New York: McGraw-Hill, 1972); Marshall Frady, *Wallace* (New York: World, 1968), *Billy Graham: A Parable of American Righteousness* (Boston: Little, Brown, 1979), and *Southerners: A Journalist's Odyssey* (New York: New American Library, 1979).

[66] Hugh Davis Graham, *Crisis in Print: Desegregation and the Press in Tennessee* (Nashville: Vanderbilt University Press, 1967); Numan V. Bartley and Hugh Davis Graham, *Southern Elections: County and Precinct Data, 1950-1972* (Baton Rouge: Louisiana State University Press, 1978). An even younger group of historical regionalists working on the South are the editors and contributors of the two books published in 1982 by Greenwood Press, Westport, Connecticut: Orville Vernon Burton and Robert C. McMath, Jr., eds., *Class, Conflict, and Consensus: Antebellum Southern Community Studies* and *Toward a New South?: Studies in Post-Civil War Southern Communities*.

[67] Walker Percy's 1970s-1980s novels, all published in New York by Farrar, Straus, and Giroux, are *Love in the Ruins . . .* (1971), *Lancelot* (1977), and *The Second Coming* (1980).

[68] Daniel J. Elazar, *Cities of the Prairie: the Metropolitan Frontier and American Politics* (New York: Basic Books, 1970), and "Political Culture on the Plains," *Western Historical Quarterly,* 11 (July 1980): 261-83. Also by a political scientist is Ira Sharkansky, *Regionalism in American Politics* (Indianapolis: Bobbs-Merrill, 1970).

[69] Gastil, *Cultural Regions.*

[70] Garreau, *Nine Nations.*

[71] John Gunther, *Inside U. S. A.* (New York: Harper, 1947). All of the following books by Peirce were published by W. W. Norton in New York: Neal R. Peirce, *The Mountain States of America: People, Politics, and Power in the Eight Rocky Mountain States* (1972), *The Pacific States of America: People, Politics, and Power in the Five Pacific Basin States* (1972), *The Great Plains States of America: People, Politics, and Power in the Nine Great Plains States* (1973), *The Deep South States of America: People, Politics, and Power in the Seven Deep South States* (1974), *The Border South States: People, Politics, and Power in the Five Border South States* (1975), and *The New England States: People, Politics, and Power in the Six New England States* (1976); Neal R. Peirce and Michael Barone,

The Mid-Atlantic States of America: People, Politics, and Power in the Five Mid-Atlantic States of America and the Nation's Capital (1977); Neal R. Peirce and John Keefe, The Great Lakes States of America: People, Politics, and Power in the Five Great Lakes States (1980).

72 Donald W. Meinig, "The Mormon Cultural Region: Strategies in the Geography of the American West, 1847-1964," Annals of the Association of American Geographers, 55 (June 1965): 191-220; The Great Columbia Plain: A Historical Geography, 1805-1910 (Seattle: University of Washington Press, 1968); Imperial Texas: An Interpretive Essay in Cultural Geography (Austin: University of Texas Press, 1969); Southwest: Three Peoples in Geographical Change, 1600-1970 (New York: Oxford University Press, 1971); and "The Continuous Shaping of America: A Prospectus for Geographers and Historians," American Historical Review, 83 (December 1978): 1186-1205. Meinig also contributed an important piece in a significant collection of essays by geographers, Donald W. Meinig, " American Wests: Preface to a Geographical Interpretation," in Regions of the United States, ed. John Fraser Hart (New York: Harper & Row, 1972). A provocative new regionalization by a leading geographer is Wilbur Zelinsky, "North America's Vernacular Regions," Annals of the Association of American Geographers, 70 (March 1980): 1-16.

73 Kai N. Lee, Donna Lee Klemka, and Marion E. Marts, Electric Power and the Future of the Pacific Northwest (Seattle: University of Washington Press, 1980).

74 Lynton R. Hayes, Energy, Economic Growth, and Regionalism in the West (Albuquerque: University of New Mexico Press, 1980); Richard D. Lamm and Michael McCarthy, The Angry West: A Vulnerable Land and Its Future (Boston: Houghton Mifflin, 1982).

75 John Baden and Richard L. Stroup, eds., Bureaucracy vs. Environment: The Environmental Costs of Bureaucratic Governance (Ann Arbor: University of Michigan Press, 1981).

76 Robin W. Winks, The Myth of the American Frontier: Its Relevance to America, Canada, and Australia (Leicester: Leicester University Press, 1971); H. C. Allen, Bush and Backwoods: A Comparison of the Frontier in Australia and the United States (East Lansing: Michigan State University Press, 1959); W. Turrentine Jackson, "A Brief Message for the Young and/or Ambitious: Comparative Frontiers as a Field for Investigation," Western Historical Quarterly, 9 (January 1978): 5-18. See also, David H. Miller and Jerome O. Steffen, eds., The Frontier: Comparative Studies (Norman: University of Oklahoma Press, 1977). In his study Winks stresses the invalidity of applying Turner's thesis to Canada and Australia.

77 Carlos A. Schwantes, Radical Heritage: Labor, Socialism, and Reform in Washington and British Columbia, 1885-1917 (Seattle: University of Washington Press, 1979); William J. Trimble, The Mining Advance into the Inland Empire . . . (Madison: University of Wisconsin Press, 1914). Paul F. Sharp, Whoop-Up Country: The Canadian-American West, 1865-1885 (Minneapolis: University of Minnesota Press, 1955).

[78] Herbert E. Bolton, *The Spanish Borderlands: A Chronicle of Old Florida and the Southwest* (New Haven: Yale University Press, 1921); George M. Frederickson, *White Supremacy: A Comparative Study in American and South African History* (New York: Oxford University Press, 1981); Howard Lamar and Leonard Thompson, eds., *The Frontier in History: North America and South Africa Compared* (New Haven: Yale University Press, 1981).

[79] Bernard Bailyn, "The Challenge of Modern Historiography," *American Historical Review,* 87 (February 1982): 13-18, 22.

[80] Ernest Callenbach, *Ecotopia: The Notebooks and Reports of William Weston* (New York: Bantam, 1977).

[81] William Appleman Williams, "Backyard Autonomy," *The Nation* 233 (September 5, 1981): 161, 179-80. See also, Williams, "Radicals and Regionalism," *Democracy* 1 (October 1981): 87-98.

[82] In regard to the regional concepts of Callenbach and Williams, note also Kirkpatrick Sale's concept of "self-sufficient bio-region units" whose basis he lays in his current book, *Human Scale* (New York: Coward, McCann & Geoghegan, 1980).

[83] John L. Frisbee III, "Points West—East—Midwest," *Historic Preservation,* 26 (Oct.-Dec. 1974): 31. On Jacksonville: Nathan Weinberg, *Preservation in American Towns and Cities* (Boulder: Westview, 1979), 150-53; Jack E. Boucher and Marion D. Ross, "Jacksonville in HABS Color," *Historic Preservation* 24 (April-June 1972): 26-30. On Virginia City: John D. Ellingsen, "Ghost Towns in Montana," *Historic Preservation,* 26 (Jan.-Mar. 1974): 24-27. On the continuing struggle for preservation in the West: Tom Huth, "Mining the West: Will Our Heritage Survive?," *Historic Preservation* 33 (May-June 1981): 10-19.

[84] On Seattle: Weinberg, *Preservation,* 196-207; Sally B. Woodbridge, "Industrial Metamorphosis," *Historic Preservation* 30 (April-June 1978): 37-41. On Portland: Joan Guernsey, "An Indomitable Duo Reshapes Portland," *Historic Preservation* 33 (July-Aug. 1981): 40-45; Terence O'Donnell and Thomas Vaughan, *Portland: A Historical Sketch and Guide* (Portland: Oregon Historical Society, 1976).

[85] On *Land of Sunshine* (1894-1935): Edwin R. Bingham, *Charles F. Lummis, Editor of the Southwest* (San Marino: Huntington Library, 1955); Turbese Fiske Lummis and Keith Lummis, *Charles F. Lummis: The Man and His West* (Norman: University of Oklahoma Press, 1975). There is no adequate study of *West Shore,* published in Portland from 1875 to 1891.

[86] Roger Sale, *Seattle: Past to Present* (Seattle: University of Washington Press, 1976), 212-15.

[87] For a pointed survey of city and regional magazines that emphasizes *Pacific Northwest* (Seattle, circulation 55,000), *Oregon Magazine* (circulation 38,000), *Spokane* (circulation nearing 30,000), *Oregon Buiness,* and *Seattle Business Journal,* see, Thomas Cekay, "Regionalism Spells Success," *Advertising Age,* 52

(June 1, 1981): S-10 - S-11. Photographs by Bauguess appear in Steve Siporin, *Cityfold* (Salem: Your Town Press, 1981), dealing with Portland.

88 James Cloutier, *Alpine, Oregon: Photographs of a Small Town in America* (Eugene: Image West, 1977). Selina Roberts is represented in Richard Howorth, ed., *Twelve Oregon Photographers: A Collection of Their Works* (Eugene: Early Worm, 1974). Ron Finne's *Natural Timber Country* (1972) and *Tamanawis Illahee* (1982) are outstanding documentary films about the history of the Pacific Northwest. For a list of many films dealing with the Northwest (by Finne and other independent film makers), contact the Northwest Media Project (P.O. Box 4093, Portland, Oregon 97208), a nonprofit consortium of regional film and video artists.

89 Charles Deemer, *Blood and Roses* (1980); Dorothy Velasco, *The Northwest Woman (1980)*.

90 *And When They're Gone . . . Landmarks of Lane County,* compiled and written by Tim Boldon, Steve Case, Rick Elmer, Judy Jacobson, and Katherine Mithen; supervised by Paula Backus and Kiya Bodding; and edited by Cheryl Pellegrini (Eugene: Lane County Department of Employment and Training, 1980), 2, 6.

91 Gary Snyder, *Turtle Island* (New York: New Directions, 1974). See also, Gary Snyder, *The Back Country* (New York: New Directions, 1968).

92 Edward Abbey, *The Monkey-Wrench Gang* (New York: Avon, 1976).

93 Meinig, *The Great Columbia Plain;* Thomas R. Cox, *Mills and Markets: A History of the Pacific Coast Lumber Industry to 1900* (Seattle: University of Washington Press, 1974); William G. Robbins, *Lumberjacks and Legislators: Political Economy of the U.S. Lumber Industry, 1890-1941* (College Station: Texas A & M University Press, 1982); Robert E. Ficken, *Lumber and Politics: The Career of Mark E. Reed* (Santa Cruz: Forest History Society, 1979); Robert L. Tyler, *Rebels of the Woods: The IWW in the Pacific Northwest* (Eugene: University of Oregon, 1967); Schwantes, *Radical Heritage;* Norman H. Clark, *Mill Town: A Social History of Everett, Washington . . .* (Seattle: University of Washington Press, 1970). The forest history movement has an outstanding medium in the quarterly journal, *Forest History* (1957-).

94 Richard White, *Land Use, Environment, and Social Change: The Shaping of Island County, Washington* (Seattle: University of Washington Press, 1980). Dealing with another region and quite different in character is another outstanding book that deals with the relationships between land use, environment, and society: Donald Worster, *Dust Bowl: The Southern Plains in the 1930s* (New York: Oxford University Press, 1979).

95 Richard Maxwell Brown, "The Great Raincoast of North America" (paper presented at Washington State University, October 30, 1982). George A. Frykman's unpublished paper, "Is There a Pacific Northwest Region? . . ." (1981), is a thoughtful treatment.

[96] H. L. Davis, *Honey in the Horn* (New York: Harper, 1935) and *Winds of Morning* (New York: Morrow, 1952). On Davis, see: Robert A. Bain, *H. L. Davis* (Boise: Boise State University, 1974) and James T. Potts, "H. L. Davis' View: Reclaiming and Recovering the Land," *Oregon Historical Quarterly*, LXXXII (Summer 1981): 117-51. Don Berry, *Trask* (New York: Viking, 1960), *Moontrap* (New York: Viking, 1962), and *To Build a Ship* (New York: Viking, 1963). A sensitive study is Glen A. Love, *Don Berry* (Boise: Boise State University, 1978). Ken Kesey, *Sometimes a Great Notion* (New York: Viking, 1964).

[97] Tom Robbins, *Another Roadside Attraction* (New York: Ballantine, 1972) and *Still Life with Woodpecker* (New York: Bantam, 1980). For Robbins's explicitly stated love of the Northwest rain and its nurturing of his creative impulse, see his essay, "Why I Live Where I Live," *Esquire*, (October 1980), 84.

[98] Barry Holstun Lopez, *Of Wolves and Men* (New York: Charles Scribner's Sons, 1978).

[99] Ivan Doig, *Winter Brothers: A Season at the Edge of America* (New York: Harcourt Brace Jovanovich;, 1980) and *The Sea Runners* (New York: Atheneum, 1982).

[100] George Venn, "Continuity in Northwest Literature," in *Northwest Perspectives: Essays on the Culture of the Pacific Northwest* ed. Edwin R. Bingham and Glen A. Love (Seattle: University of Washington Press, 1979), 99. Venn sees the human response to environment as providing continuity in Northwest literature from 1780 to the present. I see no such continuity; it seems to me that (except for H. L. Davis) the environment does not become important until after *circa* 1940.

[101] Venn, "Continuity," 108-117; Kermit Vanderbilt, "Theodore Roethke as a Northwest Poet," in *Northwest Perspectives*, ed. Bingham and Love, 187-216; Robin Skelton, ed., *Five Poets of the Pacific Northwest* (Seattle: University of Washington Press, 1968), presents the poetry of Hanson, Hugo, Kizer, Stafford, and Wagoner. See also, Allan Seager's biographical study, *The Glass House: The Life of Theodore Roethke* (New York: McGray-Hill, 1968).

[102] Theodore Roethke, "The Rose" (1964), quoted in Venn, "Continuity," 110.

[103] Philip Dole, "Farmhouses and Barns of the Willamette Valley," in *Space, Style, and Structure: Building in Northwest America*, ed. Thomas Vaughn and Virginia Guest Ferriday, 2 vols. (Portland: Oregon Historical Society, 1974), I: 85-93, 219-22; George McMath, "A Regional Style Comes to the City," in *Space, Style, and Structure*, II: 476; George McMath, "The Wood Tradition Expands," in *Space, Style and Structure*, II: 631-32, 644-46.

[104] Jo Stubblebine, Ed., *The Northwest Architecture of Pietro Belluschi* (New York: F. W. Dodge, 1953), 3, cited in Vaughn and Ferriday, *Space, Style, and Structure*, I: 345.

[105] For a convenient collection of reproductions that graphically underscores the linkage of environment to regional painting, see, Puget Sound Group of Northwest Painters, Inc., *The Puget Sound Group of Northwest Painters: First Fifty Years: 1928-1978* (Seattle: Puget Sound Group of Painters, Inc., 1979). See also, Tom Robbins, Bob Peterson, and Don Scott, *Guy Anderson* (Seattle: Gear Works Press, 1965). On C. S. Price: Edwin R. Bingham, "A Contour of Culture in the Pacific Northwest: C. S. Price, Richard Hugo, and Ken Kesey" (unpub. paper, University of Oregon, 1979).

[106] Robbins, *Roadside Attraction,* 57. There seems to be wide agreement with Robbins' perception. For example, in a review of the paintings of Tobey, Callahan, Graves, and Leo Kenney in the August 3, 1981 issue of *Newsweek,* art critic Mark Stevens opined that "the fine gloom" of the Pacific Northwest's "coastal rain forests—the blend of sea, moss, mountain, and fog" were what made the region "so seductive to artists."

[107] Callenbach, *Ecotopia.*

[108] Garreau, *Nine Nations,* 245-86.

[109] Venn, "Continuity," 106. Venn was writing specifically on H. L. Davis's poem, "Rain Crow."

[110] Gary H. Searl and Richard L. Prince, *Valsetz History Project* (Valsetz, Oregon: 1979), an interdisciplinary project in history, geography, and photography cosponsored by the Oregon Committee for the Humanities and the Lane County Geographical Society.

[111] On Odum and the Chapel Hill regionalists: Grantham, *Regional Imagination,* chap. 10; King, *Southern Renaissance,* 39-51; Singal, *War Within,* chaps. 5, 10; Johnson and Johnson, *Research in Service,* chaps. 6-7 and *passim.* A perceptive and sensitive but essentially negative treatment of Odum is O'Brien, *American South,* chaps. 2-4.

[112] J. Frank Dobie, *Coronado's Children* (Dallas: Southwest Press, 1930; reprinted New York: Literary Guild of America, 1931); Walter Prescott Webb, *The Great Plains* (Boston: Ginn, 1931). The biographical and critical literature on Dobie and Webb (as well as their good friend, the self-trained naturalist and philosopher Roy Bedichek of Austin) is growing; salient examples are: Wilbur R. Jacobs, John W. Caughey, and Joe B. Frantz, *Turner, Bolton, and Webb* (Seattle: University of Washington Press, 1965); Dugger, ed., *Three Men in Texas;* Owens, *Three Friends;* Furman, *Walter Prescott Webb;* Tobin, *Making of a History;* Tinkle, *An American Original;* Philp and West, eds., *Essays on Walter Prescott Webb.* A striking attempt by a New Regionalist of our time to distance himself from the Old Regionalists of the 1920s-1940s is Larry McMurtry's critique of Dobie, Webb, and Bedichek: "Southwestern Literature?" in *In a Narrow Grave: Essays on Texas* (Austin: Encino Press, 1968), 31-54.

[113] Walter Prescott Webb, *Divided We Stand: The Crisis of a Frontierless Democracy* (New York: Farrar and Rinehart, 1937).

[114] On Faulkner and Smith: King, *Southern Renaissance,* chaps. 4-8 and *passim;* Cash, *Mind of the South;* Key, *Southern Politics;* Gunnar Myrdal *et al., An American Dilemma: The Negro Problem and Modern Democracy* (New York: Harper and Brothers, 1944).

[115] C. Vann Woodward, *Tom Watson: Agrarian Rebel* (New York: Macmillan, 1938) and *Origins of the New South, 1877-1913* (Baton Rouge: Louisiana State University Press, 1951) were the key works.

[116] King, *Southern Renaissance;* O'Brien, *Idea of American South;* Singal, *War Within.*

[117] Reed, *Enduring South.* See also, Gastil, *Cultural Regions,* 174-204.

[118] Earl Pomeroy, *The Pacific Slope: A History of California, Oregon, Washington, Idaho, Utah, and Nevada* (New York: Alfred A. Knopf, 1965).

[119] Gerald D. Nash, *The American West in the Twentieth Century: A Short History of an Urban Oasis* (1973; reprinted Albuquerque: University of New Mexico Press, 1977).

[120] Lary May, *Screening Out the Past: The Birth of Mass Culture and the Motion Picture Industry* (New York: Oxford University Press, 1980). See also, Robert Sklar, *Movie-Made America* (New York: Random House, 1975).

[121] Starr, *Americans and the California Dream.*

[122] Robert M. Fogelson, *The Fragmented Metropolis: Los Angeles, 1850-1930* (Cambridge: Harvard University Press, 1967).

[123] Kevin Starr, *Land's End* (New York: McGraw Hill, 1979), *a roman a clef* in which pseudonyms for such current figures as Joseph Alioto and Herb Caen form a montage with historical figures like James D. Phelan. A wickedly humorous but apt satire of counter-classic Western suburban phoniness is Cyra McFadden, *The Serial: A Year in the Life of Marin County* (New York: New American Library, 1978).

[124] Larry McMurtry, *Horseman, Pass By* (New York: Harper, 1961), filmed as *Hud* (Paramount, 1963; directed by Martin Ritt and written by Harriet and Irving Ravetch) and republished as *Hud* (New York: Popular Library, n.d.). McMurtry felt that the film was better than his own book, largely because the Ravetchs' screen play strengthened the character of Hud (played by Paul Newman in the movie). McMurtry, "Here's HUD in Your Eye." *Narrow Grave,* 3-19. The critical literature on McMurtry is growing; outstanding is Charles D. Peavy, *Larry McMurtry* (Boston: Twayne, 1977).

[125] Kesey, *Sometimes a Great Notion.* See also, Bruce Carnes, *Ken Kesey* (Boise: Boise State University, 1974), 19-31.

[126] Ivan Doig, *This House of Sky: Landscapes of a Western Mind* (New York: Harcourt Brace Jovanovich, 1978).

[127] McMurtry's rural/small-town trilogy: *Horseman, Pass By* (1961); *Leaving Cheyenne* (New York: Harper, 1963); and *The Last Picture Show* (New York: Dial,

1966). McMurtry's urban trilogy, all published in New York by Simon and Schuster: *Moving On* (1970), *All My Friends Are Going to be Strangers* (1972), and *Terms of Endearment* (1975).

[128] McMurtry, *Narrow Grave*, p. xv. McMurtry's seventh novel, *Somebody's Darling* (New York: Simon and Schuster, 1978), a "Hollywood novel," drops the implicit classic vs. counter-classic tension. On the "Hollywood novel" as a genre in western regional writing, see Walter Wells, *Tycoons and Locusts: A Regional Look at Hollywood Fiction of the 1930s* (Carbondale: Southern Illinois University Press, 1973).

[129] Wallace Stegner, *Angle of Repose* (Garden City: Doubleday, 1971). The protagonist, Susan Burling Ward, is based on Mary Hallock Foote (1847-1938), although Stegner made significant fictional alterations in Mrs. Ward's personal life. See, Rodman W. Paul, ed., *A Victorian Gentlewoman in the West: The Reminiscences of Mary Hallock Foote* (San Marino, Calif.: Huntington Library, 1972).

[130] Aside from the works of Jane Kramer, John McPhee, and Joan Didion, the West has been the subject of some striking examples of reportage: Truman Capote, *In Cold Blood* (New York: Ramdom House, 1965), a sensitive study of rural/small town life on the Great Plains as well as a stunning treatment of the murder of the Clutter family of southwest Kansas; Hunter Thompson's book on the prototypical outlaw motorcycle gang of California, *Hell's Angels* (New York: Ballantine Books, 1967); two works by Tom Wolfe: *The Electric Kool-Aid Acid Test* (New York: Farrar, Straus, and Giroux, 1968) on Ken Kesey and the California counter-culture of the 1960s, and *The Right Stuff* (New York: Farrar, Straus, and Giroux, 1979) with its sketches of the test pilots of Edwards Air Force base and the astronauts of Houston; and Norman Mailer's *The Executioner's Song* (Boston: Little, Brown, 1979), a brilliant fictionalized study of the criminal career of the late Gary Gilmore and a remarkable evocation of the counter-classic *lumpen proletariat* of the West.

[131] For example, see the memorable sketch of booming San Jose by Philip Hamburger in *The New Yorker,* 39 (May 4, 1963): 148-54. In 1962-1966 Hamburger also contributed sketches of the following Western cities in his cross-country "Notes for a Gazetteer" series in *The New Yorker:* Bismarck, Denver, Eugene, Fairbanks, Honolulu, Juneau, Laramie, Sacramento, Salt Lake City, San Antonio, Santa Fe, St. Joseph, and Spokane. From 1970 to 1975 Calvin Trillin contributed sketches of the following Western communities in his "U. S. Journal" series in *The New Yorker:* Crystal City, El Paso, Gallup, Houston, Kansas City, Lander, Los Angeles, Nampa, Pasadena, Provo, Sacramento, Spokane, Tesuque, Truth or Consequences, Valdez, and Watts in Los Angeles.

[132] Jane Kramer, *The Last Cowboy* (New York: Harper and Row, 1977).

[133] Westerns of the counter-classic dimension have been appearing on our television screens—for example, *Dallas, Knott's Landing,* and *Texas. Texas,* especially, emphasizes the conflict between the classic and the counter-classic West, while J. R. Ewing of *Dallas* is an updated, urbanized personification of McMurtry's Hud Bannon.

[134] Published in New York by Farrar, Straus, and Giroux are John McPhee, *Encounters with the Archdruid* (1971), *Coming into the Country* (1977), and *Basin and Range* (1981).

[135] McPhee, *Encounters,* part III; see also, part I for Brower's confrontation with the development-minded geologist, Charles Park, in the Glacier Peak Wilderness of the northern Cascades.

[136] McPhee, *Coming into the Country,* book I: 124-29, and *passim.*

[137] *Ibid.,* book III. Less elegantly written and thinner in treatment than *Coming into the Country* is another striking work of reportage on contemporary Alaska that also presents the classic/counter-classic contrast: Joe McGinniss, *Going to Extremes* (New York: Alfred A. Knopf, 1980).

[138] McPhee, *Basin and Range,* 169-70. Even more explicit is Joel Garreau, who underscores the contrast between the loveliness of the Puget Sound country and the doomsday destructive power of the Trident submarines based there. Garreau, *Nine Nations,* 282-85.

[139] Jerry Adler *et al.,* "James Watt's Land Rush," *Newsweek,* 29 June 1981, 22-32. There are significant resemblances between Floyd Dominy and James Watt, but Watt's attitudes in favor of development far exceed those of Dominy.

[140] Frederick Jackson Turner, *The Frontier in American History* (1920; reprinted, New York: Holt, Rinehart, and Winston, 1962), 18, 37, and *passim.* See also, Ray Allen Billington, *America's Frontier Heritage* (Albuquerque: University of New Mexico Press, 1974), 64-65, 140-50, 163-70, 224-25.

[141] Mark Royden Winchell, *Joan Didion* (Boston: Twayne, 1980), 17-19. Winchell's book is an extremely perceptive study of Didion's writings.

[142] Joan Didion, *Run River* (New York: I. Obolensky, 1963), *Play It as It Lays* (New York: Farrar, Straus, and Giroux, 1970), and *A Book of Common Prayer* (New York: Simon and Schuster, 1977).

[143] Didion (1977) quoted in Winchell, *Joan Didion,* 37.

[144] Didion (1961) quoted in Winchell, 163.

[145] Didion quoted in *ibid.,* 104, 164.

[146] Martha Duffy, *Time,* 10 August 1970, 67-68, quoted in Winchell, *Joan Didion,* 163; see also, Winchell, *Joan Didion,* 93-94, 97-98.

[147] Didion (1965) quoted in Winchell, *Joan Didion,* 174. Didion's perception is similar to Kevin Starr's motif of Americans lured by the "California Dream."

[148] Joan Didion, *Slouching toward Bethlehem* (New York: I. Obolensky, 1968) and *The White Album* (New York: Simon and Schuster, 1979).

[149] Winchell, *Joan Didion,* 32-33.

[150] Doig, *Winter Brothers,* 3-5. This passage keynotes the theme of Doig and Swan as "winter brothers" that is seamlessly woven into the book.

THE NORTHWEST
ENVIRONMENT

The Northwest as a Prehistoric Region

Richard E. Ross and David Brauner

Introduction

Our approach to Pacific Northwest and its boundaries will be to use archaeological data in order to gain a prehistoric perspective. First, however, we must discuss some concepts of regions that are basic to our understanding of the prehistoric information.

Physically, the Northwest comprises two major geographic regions. One is the North Pacific Coast, extending in a narrow strip from southwestern Alaska to California, bounded on the east by the Cascades and Sierras and on the west by the Pacific Ocean. The other is the Intermontane Plateau and Basin region, which extends from British Columbia south through eastern Washington, eastern Oregon, western and southern Idaho into the Great Basin area of Nevada and Utah to the desert area of Arizona, New Mexico, and southeastern California. Obviously, these physiographic regions are not confined exclusively to the northwestern corner of the United States, but they are important to us because of their effect on the culture of the region.

Also of importance is the concept of anthropological culture areas. A "culture area," as used by anthropologists,[1] is a continuous geographical region where the inhabitants share more traits with each other than with people in adjacent areas. Well-defined culture areas have a core which most adequately characterizes the area, as well as marginal areas which exhibit those characteristics to a lesser extent than the core. Frequently it is difficult to precisely place culture-area boundaries, because people of the marginal areas share a number of traits with groups from adjacent regions. Because hunter/gatherers and early agriculturists have a close relationship to their environment, anthropological cultural areas frequently correlate quite closely with geographical and biotic regions.

The concepts of physiographic regions and cultural areas are basic to our understanding of archaeological regions. An archaeological region is roughly defined as the geographical space occupied by a social group larger than a community (maybe in very general terms a tribe), which at a given time should exhibit a high degree of cultural homogenity.[2]

The basic physiographic regions have changed to a greater or lesser extent through the past 15,000 years. This change, of course, has directly affected the prehistoric cultures in the Northwest. Utilizing archaeological and environmental data, we will present a diachronic view and a generalized dynamic model for change and development in the greater Northwest.

Archaeological Evidence

[The earliest direct evidence for human occupation in the Pacific Northwest dates from between 14,000 and 10,000 years ago. This coincides with the end of the last continental glaciation, when ice sheets covered most of Canada and some of Alaska and lobes reached down into what is now the northern tier of the United States. Glacial ice reached south of Spokane, Washington, and across the Idaho Panhandle. Washington, Oregon, and Idaho were greatly affected by the environmental conditions responsible for and fostered by the glaciers. Mean annual temperatures were lower than today and annual rainfall greater. As a consequence of glacial runoff and increased precipitation, much of the Northwest (particularly the Great Basin and southern Plateau) was dominated by lake and marsh systems in basin areas. Open grassland and coniferous forests characterized higher elevations.[3]]

The North Pacific Coast area also would have been considerably different than today. The large glaciers located in the north trapped enough moisture to lower the ocean level several hundred feet. Consequently, the continental shelf was exposed all along the western coast of North America. South of Puget Sound, coastal plains varied in width from a few miles to tens of miles. The grassland environment of those coastal plains could have supported large numbers of grazing animals.

Our knowledge of the first Northwesterners suffers from a lack of data. Available data from a few sites indicate that, as with their contemporaries in the Plains and the Southwest, Northwesterners' economic pursuits seem to have centered on the exploitation of big game animals, including many now-extinct species.[4] Their lithic tool kit, including knives, scrapers, perforators, and large, well-made, leaf-shaped projectile points, displayed affinities with the Plains and Southwest. Apart from the lake areas of the Plateau and Great Basin, the adaptive response of early Northwesterners was not much different than that found throughout western North America and Meso-America.[5]

Between 10,000 and 8,000 years ago, the climate in the Plateau and along the Coasts was still cooler and moister than today, but the continental glaciers were rapidly disappearing and the climate was moderating.[6] With the retreat of the glaciers, precipitation patterns were changing and glacial outwash was significantly reduced. This affected the number and size of lakes in the Plateau and Great Basin. The annual flow of major river systems began to drop, creating suitable habitats along the river canyon floors for human habitation.[7]

Adaptive strategies in the Plateau changed from a combined lake/big game hunting orientation to a river-based orientation involving the exploitation of a variety of land animals ranging from elk and deer to ground squirrels. Fish were exploited, but salmon do not occur in the archaeological record of river sites prior to 8,000 years ago.[8] Culturally, there appears to have been more of a regional orientation and a lessening of influences from the southern Great Basin and the Plains. A lake-centered adaptive strategy persisted in the northern Great Basin,[9] and a big game hunting strategy focused on the vast herds of bison continued on the Plains. Tool styles began to take on more regional distinctions, and experimentation with local raw materials for tool production (as exemplified by artifacts from the Applegate River of southwestern Oregon) reached its peak.[10]

The Coast was changing as well. The retreating glaciers released tremendous quantities of water, and the sea level rose, covering the outer limits of the continental shelf.[11] This phenomenon, which drowned any evidence of previous inhabitants in those areas, would have made the coastal margins an area of rapid physiographic change, with the constantly encroaching ocean causing considerable erosion and creating unstable conditions for biotic communities. Limited information from coastal environments during this time period does not suggest a marine adaptation as yet, although people may well have been living on or near the coast at this time.

Between 8,000 and 4,000 years ago, evidence from several sources, including geology,[12] flora,[13] and fauna,[14] suggests a change to a warmer and drier climate. River-based adaptive strategies continued to be refined, coupled with an increasing emphasis on upland resources in the Plateau. Population expansion may also be inferred from the greater frequency of archeological sites relative to earlier time periods. The beginnings of a winter village complex is indicated by the presence of semi-subterranean houses after 6,000 years ago.[15]

While population expansion may be partially explained by refinements in exploitative strategies, a major protein source also became available in the Columbia River drainage by 8,000 years ago. By this time anadromous fish were present in economically exploitable quantities.[16] Several hypotheses have been put forth to explain the connection between anadromous fish runs, population increase, and new settlement patterns.[17] It seems obvious that anadromous fish eventually played an important role in the subsistence base of the Northwest groups. Exactly when or in what magnitude the runs began is not well known; nor are the dynamics of cultural change in relation to those runs clearly understood. Let it suffice to say that we do have anadromous fish, village sites, and an expanding human population after 8,000 years ago.

Very limited evidence indicates that coastal environments were apparently occupied by peoples who were primarily terrestrially oriented and only infrequently acquired sea mammals.[18] In the northern Great Basin, there appears to have been a strong shift away from the declining lake environment and an increasing emphasis on upland resources.[19] New technologies characterize the lithic tool kit in response to an increasing preference for fine-grained basalts as raw material.[20] The most distinctive artifacts were leaf-shaped or two-pointed projectile points. All evidence points to a stone tool production system that was quite similar from the coast to the interior of the Northwest.

While adaptive strategies were changing, inhabitants of parts of the Northwest also had to contend with catastrophic events. The eruption of Mt. Mazama 7,000 years ago (with accompanying storms, floods, and ash falls) would have had temporary or, in some cases, rather long-term effects on resources. Long-term effects were dictated by distance and direction from the vent. Harold Malde[21] postulated major negative impacts on Northwest cultural systems. This catastrophic view has not been supported archaeologically.[22]

Following the warmer and drier Altithermal period there was a period (from 4,000 to approximately 2,500 years ago) of greater effective precipitation than today, characterized by erosion, downcutting, and considerable siltation in the streams.[23] Erosion and subsequent silting of the streams may have depleted anadromous fish populations until they were no longer economically exploitable.[24] While conditions were detrimental to the spawning success of anadromous fish, the same conditions were beneficial for many upland resources, particularly camas. There was a drastic reduction in the number of archeological sites along interior river systems but an increase in sites located in upland areas. The change evidently occurred with some rapidity, which probably resulted in considerable stress on the cultural system.

While the cause is still problematical, the tool kit from this time period reflects a great deal of change. The rather large leaf-shaped points common prior to 4,000 years ago were rapidly replaced by small crude points, quite possibly reflecting the introduction of the bow/arrow or an increased emphasis on its use. According to some investigators, the manufacturing techniques were continued from an early period, but the morphological aspects of the tools changed drastically.[25] This period also coincides with the appearance of tools and technology necessary to process large quantities of camas for storage and winter consumption. This may reflect a dietary response to expanding camas populations and reduction in the number of salmon available for drying and use as winter food.

Along with the changes evident in the Plateau area, there was more cultural distance evident between the Basin, Plateau, and Coast. By this time coastal environments had stabilized, allowing the establishment of biotic communities which were the source of a dependable food supply. During the latter part of this wet period, we can recognize the establishment of coastal cultures adapted to the multiple resources of riverine, estuarine, and marine habitats, while retaining some upland utilization patterns. Tool kits and settlement patterns reflect these strategies quite strongly, with the presence of harpoon heads, fish hooks, extensive shell middens, houses, and villages.[26]

After 2,500 years ago the erosion and silting tapered off significantly, allowing the reestablishment of anadromous fish populations. This in turn contributed to the establishment of stable coastal communities and a return to a strong river-based orientation in the Plateau. With the climate slowly stabilizing into the modern mode and the return of the fish runs, we begin to see the emergence of the ethnographic pattern that was prevalent until European contact. With large fish runs we see a settlement pattern that again focuses on the rivers. The frequency of archaeological sites along rivers and streams increases dramatically, almost surely reflecting an increase in population density. The anadromous fish runs, coupled with upland resources, certainly increased the carrying capacity of the land and made possible a higher population.

The coastal cultures stabilized their adaptive strategies during this period and became more adept at utilizing those resources. In some northern areas of the Coast, we see more of an orientation towards marine resources (whale hunting)[27] versus a combined riverine, intertidal, estuarine orientation found in the Puget Sound area, on the south coast of Washington, and on the entire coast of Oregon.[28]

Conclusion

Our interpretations of the archaeological data show that physiographic characteristics of the Northwest have changed considerably over the past 15,000 years, and these changes have contributed significantly to the ebb and flow of archaeological regions. There has been a definite trend toward regional differentiation, but cultural characteristics and boundaries have not remained static through time. Many have changed in response to conditions created by special events such as continental glaciation and volcanic activity. At various times in the past, the major physiographic features that help to delineate the geographic regions today were overshadowed by monumental natural events.

The shifting archaeological regions gradually became increasingly specialized to suit different habitats. At the time of European contact, these regions were closely correlated with the present physiographic regions of Coast and Plateau, with a further cultural differentiation between the Plateau and the Basin.

The boundaries of the Northwest ebb and flow according to the criteria used to establish those boundaries. Although the core and marginal areas of the Northwest may have changed in location and intensity, a regional identity has developed through time. That regional identification can be seen in the archaeological evidence of prehistoric adaptation to the resources available in the region. Adaptation to changing environmental conditions through time has helped to shape a Northwest cultural entity (or entities). Two major cultural divisions can be seen between the Coast and the Interior in the later prehistoric period. These areas do not necessarily correlate with present conceptions of the Northwest with its overlay of modern resources. This discrepancy does not invalidate either prehistory or modern concepts, however; it merely reinforces the notion of a changing, dynamic state.

NOTES

[1] A. L. Kroeber, "Cultural and Natural Areas of Native North America," *University of California Publications in American Archaeology and Ethnology* 38 (1939); Clark Wissler, *The American Indian* (New York: D. C. McMurtrie, 1917).

[2] Gordon R. Willey and Phillip Phillips, *Method and Theory in American Archaeology* (Chicago: University of Chicago Press, 1958).

[3] Luther S. Cressman, *Prehistory of the Far West: Homes of Vanished Peoples* (Salt Lake City: University of Utah Press, 1977); Roald Fryxell and Richard Daugherty, *Late Glacial and Post Glacial Geological and Archaeological Chronology of the Columbia Plateau, Washington,* Washington State University Laboratory of Anthropology;, Report of Investigations no. 23 (Pullman, 1963); Henry Hansen, "Postglacial Forest Succession, Climate, and Chronology in the Pacific Northwest," *Transactions of the American Philosophical Society* 37 (1947): 1; Ruth Kirk and Richard Daugherty, *Exploring Washington Archaeology* (Seattle: University of Washington Press, 1978).

[4] Carl E. Gustafson, *The Manis Mastodon Site* (Seattle: Seattle First National Bank, 1978); Ann Irwin and Ula Moody, *The Lind Coulee Site (45GR97),* Washington Archaeological Research Center, Project Report no. 56 (Pullman: Washington State University, 1978).

[5] Stephen F. Bedwell, *Fort Rock Basin: Prehistory and Environment* (Eugene: University of Oregon Books, 1973); Robert B. Butler, *A Guide to Understanding Idaho Archaeology: The Upper Snake and Salmon River Country,* 3rd ed. (Pocatello: Idaho Museum of Natural History, 1978); Ruth Gruhn, *The Archaeology of Wilson Butte Cave, South-Central Idaho,* Occasional Papers of the Idaho State College Museum no. 6 (Pocatello, 1961).

[6] Fryxell and Daugherty, *Glacial Chronology of the Columbia Plateau.*

[7] Alan Marshall, "An Alluvial Chronology of the Lower Palouse River Canyon and its Relation to Local Archaeological Sites" (unpub. M.S. thesis, Washington State University Department of Anthropology, 1971).

[8] David Rice, *The Windust Phase in Lower Snake River Region Prehistory,* Washington State University Laboratory of Anthropology, Report of Investigations no. 50 (Pullman, 1972).

[9] Cressman, *Prehistory of the Far West.*

[10] David Brauner, *The Archaeological Salvage of Sites 35JA52 and 35JA53, Applegate Lake Project, Jackson County, Oregon,* Report prepared for the U.S.

Army Corps of Engineers, Portland District (Corvallis: Oregon State University Department of Anthropology, 1982).

[11] Robert E. Ackerman, "Microblades and Prehistory: Technological and Cultural Considerations for the North Pacific Coast," in *Early Native Americans,* ed. David L. Browman (The Hague: Mouton, 1980); Knut R. Fladmark, "Sea Levels, Shell Middens and Salmon: A Reappraisal of 'A Paleoecological Model for Northwest Coast Prehistory'" (Paper presented at the 44th Annual Meeting of Society for American Archaeology, Vancouver, B.C., 1979).

[12] Roald Fryxell, "Mazama and Glacier Peak Volcanic Ash Layers: Relative Ages," *Science* 147: 1288-90; Fryxell and Daugherty, *Glacial Chronology of the Columbia Plateau;* Hallett Hammatt, "Late Quaternary Geology of the Lower Snake River" (Ph.D. diss., Washington State University Department of Anthropology, 1976); Marshall, "Alluvial Chronology of the Lower Palouse River."

[13] Hansen, "Postglacial Forest Succession in the Pacific Northwest."

[14] Butler, *Guide to Understanding Idaho Archaeology;* Carl E. Gustafson, "Faunal Remains from Marmes Rockshelter and Related Archaeological Sites in the Columbia Basin" (unpub. Ph.D. diss., Washington State University Department of Anthropology, 1972).

[15] Kenneth Ames and James Green, "Lower Clearwater Prehistory: Excavations at Hatwai 1977-1978" (Paper presented at the 23rd Annual Northwest Anthropological Conference, 1980); David Brauner, "Alpowai: the Culture History of the Alpowa Locality" (unpub. Ph.D. diss., Washington State University Department of Anthropology, 1976).

[16] Patrick Thomison, personal communication with author, 1982.

[17] Brauner, "Alpowai"; Luther S. Cressman, "Cultural Sequences at The Dalles, Oregon," *Transactions of the American Philosophical Society* 50 (1960): 10; Randall R. Schalk, "The Structure of an Anadromous Fish Resource," in *For Theory Building in Archaeology,* ed. Lewis R. Binford (San Francisco: Academic Press, 1977).

[18] Ackerman, "Microblades and Prehistory"; Don E. Dumond, "Alaska and the Northwest Coast," in *Ancient Native Americans,* ed. Jesse D. Jennings (San Francisco: W. H. Freeman, 1978).

[19] Cressman, *Prehistory of the Far West.*

[20] Guy Moto, "The Cascade Technique" (unpub. Ph.D. diss., Washington State University Department of Anthropology, 1976).

[21] Harold E. Malde, "The Ecological Significance of Some Unfamiliar Geological Processes," in *The Reconstruction of Past Environments,* eds. James Hester and James Schvenwetter (Taos: Fort Burgwin Research Center, 1964).

[22] Judith Bense, "Cultural Stability on the Lower Snake River during the Altithermal," in *Great Basin Anthropological Conference 1970: Selected Papers,* University of Oregon Anthropological Papers no. 1 (Eugene, 1971); Judith Bense,

"The Cascade Phase: A Study of the Effects of the Altithermal on a Cultural System" (unpub. Ph.D. diss., Washington State University Department of Anthropology, 1972).

[23] Hammatt, "Late Quaternary Geology of the Lower Snake River"; Marshall, "Alluvial Chronology of the Lower Palouse River."

[24] Brauner, "Alpowai."

[25] Brauner, "Alpowai."

[26] Donald H. Mitchell, "Archaeology of the Gulf of Georgia area, A Natural Region and its Cultural Types," *Syesis* 4 (1971): 1; Richard E. Ross, Sandra Lee Snyder, and Barbara Atkinson, "The Umpqua/ Eden Site: Marine/Riverine Exploitation on the Central Oregon Coast," in forthcoming volume on coastal prehistory, ed. David Yesner (Society for American Archaeology).

[27] Marian Fisken, "Whale Bone Studies," in *Ozette Archaeological Project Interim Final Report, Phase XIII,* ed. Richard Daugherty, Washington Archaeological Research Center (Pullman: Washington State University, 1980).

[28] Knut Fladmark, "A Paleoecological Model for Northwest Coast Prehistory" (unpub. Ph.D. diss., University of Calgary Department of Anthropology, 1974); Tom E. Roll, "The Archaeology of Minard: A Case Study of a Late Prehistoric Northwest Coast Procurement System" (unpub. Ph.D. diss., Washington State University Department of Anthropology, 1974); Ross, Snyder and Atkinson, "The Umpqua/Eden Site."

The Altered Landscape:
Social Change and the Land in
the Pacific Northwest

Richard White

Any region of the United States, no matter how one defines regional criteria and boundaries, is a physical place with its own geography and climate, its own flora and fauna. Once this rather obvious statement was the heart of regionalism. During the early 20th century, geographical determinists argued that environment translated readily into culture, social structure, personality, and politics. In their crudest formulations, determinists argued, for instance, that rugged land regularly produced rugged individualists.

Even in the current intellectual climate, where the only things still being recycled are simplistic social theories, this kind of geographical determinism has so far failed to make a comeback.[1] Still, reports of its demise may be premature. Geographical determinism, after all, seems no more unlikely than the currently fashionable assertions that laissez-faire economics and appeals to greed will create universal prosperity and social justice, and that militarism will prevent war. Nevertheless, geographical determinism remains momentarily dead, although its unfortunate legacy has been to turn attention away from regional studies of the realtionship between the environment and the human societies which inhabit the land.

In a real sense, the determinists had gotten it all backwards. As George Perkins Marsh noticed more than a century ago, the land shaped societies decidedly less often than societies shaped the land.[2] The implication of Marsh's insight is that a region is less likely to get men to match its mountains, than mountains to match its men (and women). This neat reversal is, however, too simple. Nature is not infinitely malleable. In the end the relationship between landscape and society, between environment and culture, is reciprocal. Human beings create landscapes, and these landscapes in turn have consequences for the society which created them.

The Northwest is, at least superficially, an apt place to examine the reciprocal influences of land and society. To Easterners, Northwesterners seem particularly tender in their concern for the land. This is an opinion maintained despite years of Hanford's nuclear wastes leaking into the Columbia River and eventually Dixie Lee Ray leaking into the political system. It is an apt region, too, because, by defining the Pacific Northwest narrowly as everything between the Cascades and the Pacific and between British Columbia and California, it is possible to create a crudely homogeneous environmental region to study. Here vast changes have taken place in the land; a society has arisen, which claims (for vague and ill-defined reasons) to be regionally distinctive; and a vocal concern for the land has become a legitimate political issue.

In the Pacific Northwest, as in any region of the United States, there are diverse feelings and opinions about the land. Personal feelings and opinions, however, are not really at issue here; my concern is with how they develop, what power they exert, and with what results. These are basically historical questions even though they are often defined in excessively presentist and functional terms.

History matters a great deal in understanding the regional relationship to environment, but history cannot be confused with myth. What the American West spawns (for the good, I think) are the great myths of American culture which revolve around the clash of civilization and savagery and nature. These are, however, cultural divisions and must be understood as such; they are not useful historical divisions of the past. Untamed nature plays only a minor role in the history of the Northwest (or any part of the West). The high country of the Cascades and Olympics was (and still is) wilderness, but calling the land American settlers found "wilderness" only obscures the relationship between people and the land.

The first American settlers who penetrated into western Oregon and Washington entered a relatively stable and productive environment. For centuries Indian peoples had been burning for-ests and prairies, encouraging some species and discouraging others; more recently, they had adopted exotic plants and animals such as the potato and the horse. The species composition of both the forests and prairies were to a significant degree the result of Indian practices.[3] The Northwest that American settlers found was an Indian-managed Northwest. This point is an important one. Any environment inhabited by human beings is, to varying degrees, a human-dominated ecosystem. The question is not domination per se, nor civilization versus wilderness, but rather how an environ-ment is dominated and with what results. In the 1840s the environ-ment west of the Cascades remained not only stable and productive, but also botanically distinctive. Indians manipulated native species, and few exotics were introduced; the managed ecosystem main-tained itself without costly imports or serious deterioration.

White settlement destroyed the Indian Northwest. Indeed most whites failed to recognize that it even existed. Farmers simply mistook Indian handiwork for virgin nature. They sought out the prairies and openings to farm in preference to the massive fir forests, without realizing that Indian burning often created and maintained these prairies and shaped the species composition of both prairie and forest.[4] Treating those Indians who survived the ravages of smallpox and influenza, murder and war, and displace-ment to reservations as so many primitive pyromaniacs, settlers banished the fires and in so doing began to change the forest composition and the balance between prairie and forest in ways they did not suspect.[5] Settlers might think that they were putting the mark of human use on the land as they displaced the Indians and plowed and fenced and planted, but they were only reordering the land and imposing a different vision, one developed far from the place they settled.

Early settlers in the Pacific Northwest almost automatically sought familiar landscapes. They were newcomers in what remains a region of newcomers, and the familiar was not the native. Settlers, therefore, sought not so much to create as to recreate. A frontier in this sense was not the cutting edge of change, but rather the most conservative region of the country. As historians are increasingly

emphasizing, settlement was not a process of individualists breaking ties and heading west, but instead the relocation of existing
kinship groups and community groups. The connections between
settlers in the Willamette Valley or the Puget Sound region created a
web of kin and old neighbors.[6] Settlers husbanded the familiar, and
the new land became merely a foundation upon which to reestab-
lish existing ways.

Settlers brought with them to the new land an idea of an
ordered landscape—a cultural model, rather than a specific ecology.
What was meaningful for the frontier farmer was the traditional
sense of landscape reflected in the census categorization of land as
either improved or unimproved. Improved land was essentially
that from which native plants and animals had been eradicated;
unimproved land was where they remained. In the traditional
mixed farming of the Midwest and Border South (from which most
migrants came), these categories implied different perceptions and
uses of the land.[7] Farmers invested great labor in improved land,
fenced it, and limited its production to familiar useful species. They
controlled it by means that went back centuries to other continents.

Unimproved land was not untouched, but it was largely
unexamined. Early diary accounts of western Washington, for
example, often praised the land's beauty, but few diarists either
knew, noticed, or named specific plants. Someone like James
Swan, who took a detailed interest and delight in the peoples,
plants, and animals of the native Northwest, was unique and
eccentric.[8] Most settlers contented themselves with hunting the
land's game, destroying its predators, and releasing their cattle and
hogs to fatten on (and destroy) camas and other native plants of the
region. However, unimproved land, no matter how altered, still
retained marks of older systems and different orders.

Of course, not all improved land was the same. In western
Oregon different farming systems emerged within a decade of
settlement, but nonetheless, the agricultural landscape still lacked
the variety and distinctiveness of the unimproved land it replaced.
A prairie wheat field in Oregon differed little from a prairie wheat
field in Illinois, while a native prairie in Oregon differed a great deal
ecologically from a native prairie in Illinois.[9]

Anglo-American influence on the Pacific Northwest, then, began simply as a result of attempts to impose old ways on a new place. As long as settlers remained subsistence farmers, domestic considerations shaped production decisions. These considerations seem to have been clearly utilitarian: farmers managed the land to feed and clothe their families. But arguments of simple utility are deceptive and deserve closer examination. To say something is useful explains little. It is not that people want only the useful, but rather that people define as useful and necessary whatever it is that they want. For instance, people have to eat, but why do they eat what they do? Northwestern Indians relied on salmon for animal protein; the whites largely preferred pork. Both pigs and salmon are useful sources of protein and, on the Northwestern frontier, salmon were arguably more useful since they were rarely known to get into the fields and destroy growing crops. Yet frontier whites preferred the pig, even though in some areas hogs became ecological frankensteins that ate up both Indian and white food sources.[10]

Utility clearly lies in the eye of the beholder (or rather the beholder's culture), and the Northwest settler's eye had a narrow range of vision indeed. Faced with the majestic forests of the region, T. J. Cram, a member of one of the government's expeditions of the 1850s, could only dismiss the trees as "timber of inferior quality for everything but spars, yards, and piles."[11] Cram's crabbed view of the forest is a fair sample of unreflective utilitarianism, which even on its own terms is limited and shortsighted. Its arguments are necessarily geared to a present and culturally limited utility. To the immigrant, the usefulness of something new may not be immediately apparent, or its possible uses may be considered culturally unacceptable. The useful always exists within constricted cultural and temporal boundaries.

The logic of unreflective utility quickly established itself in the Northwest. The native landscape was neither sacred nor sentimental; it was merely an opportunity. And opportunity quickly became the opportunity to make not just a living but a profit. This change was part of the larger transition to commercial farming in the United States. Its consequences appeared in the attitudes of northwestern farmers and through them in the landscape. As Walter Crockett, an early settler in Washington Territory, phrased it, his main object in settlement was:

> to get the land subdued and wilde nature out of it. When that is accomplished we can increase our crops to a very large amount and the high prices of everything that is raised here will make the cultivation of the soil a very profitable business.(sic)[12]

Crockett's ambitions and those of the settlers in the Willamette Valley for large profits in the commercial market were doomed to frustration for much of the 19th century. Farmers producing staple crops increasingly operated in a world market over which they could exert little influence. A farmer could accurately plan what his family would need, but he could not predict what the price of wheat would be or what specialty crop would sell. In relatively isolated, commercially marginal areas like the Pacific Northwest, what was profitable could change yearly. Some farms became a kaleidoscope of different crops and animals, while other farmers engaged in steady staple crop production could not compete and actually abandoned land. In both cases care of the land suffered, exotic weeds invaded the fields, and fertility declined. In the Willamette Valley there was actually an absolute decline in improved land between 1880 and 1900.[13]

By the end of the 19th century, agricultural settlement had significantly contributed to a less distinctive northwestern landscape, one that was increasingly shaped by markets hundreds or even thousands of miles away. By introducing exotic species into the region and by trying to make it over in the image of other places, settlers had sparked an ecological invasion one botanist characterized as the most cataclysmic event in the natural history of the area since the Ice Age. In 1919 an examination of a seemingly native prairie landscape in the Willamette Valley revealed that one-half the species of grasses present were not indigenous.[14]

In time, such introductions combined with surviving native species might have formed a new stable landscape. But the domination of the agricultural economy by large and impersonal markets insured that the only criteria of success in farming would be profit, and profit came only to those who quickly adjusted their fields to market demands. Thus commercial farming usually insured ecological instability. As the 20th century wore on, weeds and insects were only held at bay by increasingly costly applications of energy and poison to the land. There was little unique or regionally distinctive about successful farming in the Pacific Northwest.

The impact of the market reached well beyond the farmer's fields into the forests which surrounded them. Initially, the 19th century market demanded only fir, and available technology limited logging to areas only a mile or two from tidewater.[15] The resulting logging for piles, masts, and spars produced operations of prodigious wastefulness, but surprisingly little ecological damage resulted. Loggers left cedar and hemlock standing as well as those Douglas fir either too large or too diseased to be cut. These trees provided the seeds necessary for the rapid repropogation of the forest. In Island County, Washington an untrained eye could mistake land cut 30 years before for a virgin forest.[16] That the forest could maintain itself was, however, an accident. Loggers did not plan for sustained yield. It simply was not yet profitable to engage in the sort of lumbering that would destroy the forest. Again, the real forces at work were market forces. Concern with the land or the communities upon it was subordinate to making money. Advocates of the free market claimed then, as now, that private profits eventually translate into healthy communities and stable environments. The history of the Pacific Northwest belies this.

With the depletion of the forests of Michigan, Minnesota, and Wisconsin, accompanied by improvements in logging technology, changes in transportation and markets, and an influx of logging capital, the real assault on northwestern forests accelerated after the turn of the century.[17] The donkey engine (a steampowered winch that could drag logs to a central place for shipment) and logging railroads allowed the logging of areas far removed from tidewater. The markets gradually expanded to include cedar and hemlock. Loggers took out immense amounts of timber cheaply and efficiently, but they left huge amounts of waste. Stumps, tops, branches, and trees shattered in the felling amounted to an average of 24,000 cubic feet of waste per acre. When this slash ignited, it burned at temperatures as high as 1,814 degrees and consumed not only the slash but 89 percent of the duff layer on the forest floor.

The seedlings that sprang up from fallen seeds in the wake of logging were often destroyed in these fires, which left unpromising conditions for any new trees that might follow them. By destroying the humus, fire lessened the moisture retention of the soil which was essential for the germination and survival of Douglas fir seedlings. It changed the nutrient balance of the soil and altered its ph. The sudden abundance of potassium, nitrogen, and calcium released from debris by burning encouraged those seedlings that survived to develop shallow root structures and large crowns and thus made them vulnerable to even short droughts. The black ash and charred debris also exacerbated drought by increasing heat retention in the soil on hot summer days by 25 degrees or more.[18] Even to get a second crop of seedlings on the land following fires was difficult, since loggers no longer left an abundance of cull trees, and the logging of small tracts which could be reseeded by neighboring forests gave way to operations that covered huge areas.

Lumbermen cared little about all this. They realized the utility of protecting standing forests, but they ignored the fires that devastated cutover lands. Lumbermen claimed taxes prevented them from reforesting the lands they cut, but the evidence indicates such claims were specious. The real problem was that market prices did not justify restocking the forest.[19] The logging companies cut and ran, and as a 1927 Forest Service report concluded, "whatever reproduction takes place, does so, for the most part, in spite of present methods, not as a result of them." Foresters estimated that 40 percent of privately held land in the Douglas fir region was not reforesting at all and that reforestation on most of the remainder was inadequate.[20] In a good part of the reforestation that did take place, the returning trees were not Douglas fir, but rather alder.[21]

By the early 20th century the new lumber industry, unlike farming, promised to provide a unique Northwestern landscape. It consisted of miles of huge shattered stumps surrounded by debris which, when accidentally ignited, burst into fires that burned for much of the summer. These devastated forests produced little but fire and bracken and filled the bays and rivers with eroded soil and logging debris, wiping out the spawning beds of the salmon. The ruin of the forest brought a generation of Northwesterners abruptly to the realization that ecology and society were connected; it became apparent that it is impossible to maintain human institutions, build roads, support schools, and meet public needs on a wasteland.[22]

It is, however, naive to believe that the mere recognition of a problem insures its solution. The response to the logged-off lands took shape within the same cultural boundaries that produced the problem. The result was a back-to-the-land movement which was a complex brew of commercialism, class interest, and sincerely held agrarian beliefs.[23]

The movement to settle the logged-off lands of the Pacific Northwest, like similar back-to-the-land movements in Michigan, Minnesota, Wisconsin, and the arid West, justified itself largely in regional terms. The northwestern back-to-the-land movement originated in the cities. City people promoted it, and ultimately the movement served urban interests. The West, and the Pacific Northwest in particular, have always been largely urban regions, but Westerners often manage to reconcile an urban reality with antiurban rhetoric. Proponents of the settlement of logged-off lands proceeded from the assumption that the cities were overpopulated while the rural districts were correspondingly underpopulated. From this fundamental imbalance flowed the myriad of social problems—unemployment, poverty, disease, moral decline—which they feared could destroy the Northwest and eventually the nation. This rhetoric was antiurban, but it paradoxically served urban interests. Blaming urban ills on too many poor people in the city not only avoided any serious analysis of the economic and social system, it proposed a simple solution to a pressing environmental problem. Urban poverty could be eliminated by shipping the poor to the logged-off lands, which they would then redeem with their labor. Ideally, the socially expendable poor of the cities would cultivate the surrounding land and alleviate the need to import millions of dollars worth of dairy products, pork, poultry, and vegetables from outside the Northwest. Not only would these new settlers retain needed capital in the area, they would also consume the products of urban industries and thus stimulate urban prosperity.[24]

This vision was partly a response to the wasteland left behind by the loggers, but it was also a rejection of the forest itself. It represented an inability to come to terms with the realities of the ecology of the Northwest. Boosters of the movement denounced the Forest Service for its fledgling attempts to replant the forest on federal lands. When one enthusiast condemned the Forest Service for "trying to grow trees on land that should grow men," he was only underlining the logic of the whole movement.[25]

Having denounced the city to serve the city's ends and having rejected the forest, the boosters of settlement offered all the venerable agrarian homilies. They argued that the attraction of people to the soil was instinctive, that urban life was unnatural, and that moral and civic virtue sprang directly from agriculture. They put these evocative and emotional appeals, however, firmly within a commercial context. Organizations from local chambers of commerce to the state government of Washington assured settlers that farming logged-off lands would surely make them comfortable and might very well make them rich.[26]

To read the propaganda of these years is to witness the creation of a cultural landscape, but one which had only the most tenuous relation to the environmental realities of the land. The primitive soil science of the era before 1930 was of little help in guiding settlement. All soil seemed capable of producing something marketable, if only by supporting cows and chickens. When boosters claimed that the "land which grew the sturdy evergreen will grow anything else," few challenged them. As late as 1931, the state director of agriculture for Washington advised prospective settlers to choose land with plenty of big stumps because such land was certain to be fertile. In the promotional literature, the region's biggest drawbacks became assets. The logging debris which made land clearing so tedious and expensive became "fuel for all time . . . at the doors of the home." The heavy rains which leached the limited fertility of thin soils were "just enough to make everything grow to perfection."[27]

How many people were convinced by this propaganda is impossible to determine, but people did settle these lands. Western Washington alone gained 17,000 farms between 1900 and 1920, and 15,000 of them were under 50 acres, the farm size typical of the cutover region. By 1940 there were 36,370 such farms in western Washington.[28] The ethnicity and social origins of these settlers shifted over time. Predominantly Scandinavian between 1900 and 1920, by the 1930s the flood of settlement was made up of drought-stricken migrants from the northern plains and urban workers who often sought little more than a small plot to grow food while they searched for work.

Settled on infertile lands and provided with little capital, these farmers were anachronisms in the commercial economy.[29] Rural virtue didn't feed their families. Even boosters, while arguing that federal aid for settlement could fix matters, conceded that "isolation from markets, lack of roads, lack of neighbors, and lack of school facilities" often made farming logged-off lands a "life of dreary existence . . . without any practical rewards."[30] State and federal surveys only verified such subjective impressions. The movement weakened in the 1920s, but quickened again in the 1930s as the cities disgorged their desperate poor, and environmental and eco-nomic disaster on the plains pushed people west. The cutover lands were hardly a haven. A survey in 1939 found that one-third of the farmers had been on relief sometime in the past two years, and among those who had settled in the 1930s, the figure was over 50 percent.[31]

The damage the movement inflicted was not confined to the settlers. Their hilly infertile farms suffered with them. Depending on farming techniques and terrain, they eventually turned their fields into dense patches of bracken, watched them erode down hillsides, or abandoned them to the alder which thrived on the degraded land and replaced the original forests of Douglas fir.[32] Even those rare areas (such as the floodplains of the Willamette) where logged-off farms eventually became productive benefitted the original settlers little. This was a post-World War II develop-ment that demanded both flood control and a capital investment the original settlers could not muster.[33]

The collapse of the back-to-the-land movement at the end of the Great Depression, while a blessing to both land and people, did nothing to check the commercial forces shaping the Northwest.

Concern with the regional landscape now resided largely within the organized conservation movement, which had probably always been more powerful than the back-to-the-land movements. Conservation, like the market, provided a national context in which regional groups operated.

Conservation represented a reaction to the environmental disasters and waste brought by unrestrained entrepreneurial capitalism. The movement itself, however, was neither anticapitalist nor antidevelopment. As Samuel Hays has persuasively demonstrated, conservationists of the late 19th and early 20th centuries shared with corporate executives a strong belief in efficiency and planning as opposed to unrestrained competition. Their major goal was efficient production, with an emphasis on the renewal of resources whenever possible. In practice, conservation bureaucrats and corporate bureaucrats have always worked well together.[34]

National conservationists such as Gifford Pinchot worked through the federal bureaucracy, but from necessity they had to deal not only with national groups (such as large corporations) but also with various regional groups (such as local conservationists interested in specific issues, municipalities, and local economic interests). All of these people put claims upon the public lands; in practice conservation in the Northwest was the result of shifting, complicated alliances between various interest groups and federal (and later state) bureaucrats. For example, irrigators, cattlemen, and members of the Oregon Alpine Club supported early forest reserves in the Cascades; sheep owners and miners opposed them. Federal management did not completely remove market influences from the land; it did, however, narrow the range in which these influences operated.[35]

On federal and state lands the landscape evolved within the framework of national development policy, instead of within the older arena of unrestrained use. At any given time this planned use pleased some groups and antagonized others, depending largely on whom the planning benefited. Quite often demands for states' rights or regional rights in such issues represented no more than the protests of those special interests who had lost out in the bureaucratic planning process, while pious support for conservation measures came from those groups who benefited from the same process. Economic interests remained decisive in shaping the public lands, but now an advantage went to those groups who could at least claim that the resources they used were renewable and that their activities were compatible with other uses. In practice, this meant that "guild organizations of lumbermen and stockmen" came to shape federal policy in much of the Northwest.[36]

This description of early conservation policy in the Northwest seemingly neglects an important segment of the movement—the preservationists like John Muir, who sought to preserve land for scenery and recreation. Most of these people, however, also fit into the larger framework of planned land use for economic development. For a surprisingly long time, preservationists in Oregon concerned themselves largely with maintaining strips of scenic virgin timber along the highways for the tourists they zealously tried to attract. Scenery was but another engine for development. By such early 20th century standards, a recent governor of California who advocated sparing only enough redwoods to flank the highways might rank as a preservationist.[37]

By the mid-20th century, planned development with an emphasis on renewable resources and a devotion to preserving scenery were all ensconced in northwestern land use. These basic tenets of conservation, however, were not always synonomous with a healthy environment. Nor were the conservationists who promoted them primarily concerned with the regional ecology. Conservation, too, reflected the needs of powerful enonomic groups within society. In the woods, conservation and economic rationalization produced managed forests, which grew ecologically simpler and simpler. At the extreme they have become genetically selected, chemically fertilized, aerially sprayed tree farms.

Like any radically simplified form of monoculture, these forests can become costly to maintain, and the poisoning of their predators and competitors can quickly shade over into the poisoning of human residents. The recent controversy over dioxins is a single example of this. The benefits of this policy largely accrue to the large timber companies. These forests are efficient, but efficiency is measured largely in terms of corporate profits and government revenues. The recent controversy over log exports shows that not everyone feels such measures reflect the larger economic wellbeing of the region, let alone the environmental health of the forest.[38]

Similarly, local attempts to preserve scenery and wild resources often approached the land as a sort of environmental supermarket, in which one could choose to preserve certain natural populations while destroying others. As hunting and fishing became important to local and regional economies, both sportsmen and those who served their needs recognized that the wild populations they depended on were dangerously near elimination. The result was a flood of concern and regulation: hunting seasons enforced by local and state officials, laws to preserve shellfish beds, laws to ban fish traps and fish wheels, and the stocking of streams and lakes with hatchery-bred fish. Eventually such concerns encompassed attempts to preserve water quality, to protect the spawning beds of salmon, and to perpetuate endangered species. Most of this originally occurred, however, because a dollar value could be put on certain wild game populations.

Sportsmen became an economic interest group who secured members of a state bureaucracy (the fish and game agents) to serve their interests. The victories of sportsmen were victories over competing economic groups such as the canning companies who ran fish traps, the mill companies who polluted the rivers, or the Indian fishermen who competed for the catch. In many instances sportsmen's victories benefited the environment; in others, such as the Indian fishing controversy, conservation was a cynical mask. In virtually all cases, however, the aims of sportsmen remained quite selective. They could at once protect game animals and sponsor "predator days" to eliminate those species who competed with them for game. Until recently, the measures they sought had little sense of ecological balance and often rendered the regional ecology, if anything, less stable. Fish hatcheries, game farms, elaborate regulations, and a new bureaucracy are necessary to maintain the desired wild populations. These animals have often become mere commodities, valued not according to their place in the regional ecology, but rather according to their marketability. Like many state and local parks, they are maintained to attract visitors and further economic development.[39]

Over the last decade many of the historical trends described here have been challenged and sometimes blunted. Ecology and ecosystem have entered common speech; environmentalists in the Northwest and elsewhere have searched for a language and a convincing rationale for creating a stable and ecologically distinctive environment. The results have been mixed. Wilderness areas have been preserved, the tendency to equate economic growth with wasteful consumption and environmental damage has been challenged, and the tendency of capitalism to reduce everything on the planet to a commodity has been questioned. Yet it would be premature to argue that the forces that have shaped the American landscape since settlement are no longer pertinent to its future.

In fact, environmentalism is currently receiving a vigorous counter-challenge. It can be forcefully attacked, in part, because it has too often been content with mystical or semireligious rationales for its efforts or else has taken the stance of a continuing protest against recurrent environmental catastrophes. The land ethic Aldo Leopold spoke of—a coherent vision of the human place in the ecosystem—has yet to be forcefully articulated. The real and vital connections between human societies and the natural world need to be stressed and understood. It is a dimension of human history too often oversimplified or neglected. The Northwest will certainly remain a center of environmental conflict, and it is a conflict to which the historical issues sketched here are pertinent.

Nearly a century and a half of American settlement has produced a regional landscape which has grown increasingly less distinctive and progressively less stable. That Northwesterners have not allowed natural systems to function without interference is neither surprising nor objectionable; all human societies shape their environment. What is more noteworthy is that alterations of the Northwest landscape have often proceeded with reckless disregard for the environmental limits of the area, as if ecosystems operated on a profit motive. Northwesterners have frequently acted as if the natural world exists largely as something to buy and sell and as if the regional ecology were infinitely malleable. The history of the region already shows that environmental destruction has social costs, but as long as these costs are borne by the powerless, this is an easy lesson to ignore.

The results of environmental destabilization and regional homogeneity may not be immediately catastrophic, but the costs are there, and they are incremental. The northwestern landscape, still a recent one, already grows increasingly costly to maintain and increasingly vulnerable to disruption. The costs of maintaining it are largely public; the profits of destroying it remain private. In an era which appears bent on repudiating public cost, this does not bode well for the land. Nor does it bode well for a distinctive regionalism in a section of the country which has repeatedly resorted to its mountains, woods, rivers, and oceans as symbols and sources of its distinctiveness. Northwesterners may still claim to be unique, but they will do so amid a landscape that reflects commercial homogeneity and ecological precariousness—a place where regional concerns and influence over the land have been thoroughly subordinated to national capitalist development. The mountains may then stand like skeletons, dead remains of an older and far more distinctive place.

NOTES

[1] The kind of geographical determinism I have in mind here is seen in Ellen Semple, *American History and Its Geographic Conditions* (Boston: Houghton Mifflin, 1903) and even in Walter Prescott Webb, *The Great Plains* (Boston: Ginn and Company, 1931). For what still remains a thoughtful attempt to come to terms with regionalism see Vernon Carstensen, "The Development and Application of Regional-Sectional Concepts, 1900-1950," *Regionalism in America,* ed. Merrill Jensen (Madison: University of Wisconsin Press, 1965), 99-118.

[2] George Perkins Marsh, *Man and Nature* (Cambridge, Mass.: Harvard University Press, 1965).

[3] Richard White, *Land Use, Environment, and Social Change: The Shaping of Island County, Washington* (Seattle: University of Washington Press, 1980), 1-33; Jerry Charles Towle, "Woodland in the Willamette Valley: A Historical Geography" (Ph.D. Diss., University of Oregon, 1975), 36-37.

[4] Towle, "Woodland in the Willamette," 36-37; William Bowen, *The Willamette Valley: Migration and Settlement on the Oregon Frontier* (Seattle: University of Washington Press, 1978), 60-61; White, *Land Use, Environment and Social Change,* 35-53.

[5] Towle, "Woodland in the Willamette," 80.

[6] Bowen, *Willamette Valley,* 52; John Mack Faragher, *Women and Men on the Oregon Trail* (New Haven: Yale University Press, 1979), 34.

[7] A good account of this traditional agrarian world is found in Faragher, *Women and Men,* 40-65.

[8] James Swan, "Scenes in Washington Territory," newspaper articles in Swan Papers, University of Washington Library. For an inspired and insightful treatment of Swan's relationship with the Pacific Northwest see Ivan Doig, *Winter Brothers: A Season at the Edge of America* (New York: Harcourt, Brace, and Jovanovich, 1980).

[9] Towle, "Woodland in the Willamette," 34-35; Bowen, *Willamette Valley,* 94.

[10] For a cultural critique of utility see Marshall Sahlins, *Culture and Practical Reason* (Chicago: University of Chicago Press, 1976), 129-139, 166-179. For the example of the pig, see White, *Land Use, Environment, and Social Change,* 48-49.

[11] "Topographical Memoir of Captain T. J. Cram," *House Executive Document 114* (serial 1014), 35th Cong., 2nd sess., 66.

[12] Walter Crockett to Dr. Black, 15 October, 1853, Manuscript Collection, University of Washington Library.

[13] Towle, "Woodland in the Willamette," 77; White, *Land Use, Environment and Social Change,* 69.

[14] Towle, "Woodland in the Willamette," 34; White, *Land Use, Environment and Social Change,* 68-70.

[15] The most complete account of the 19th century lumber industry is in Thomas Cox, *Mills and Markets: A History of the Pacific Coast Lumber Industry to 1900* (Seattle: University of Washington Press, 1974).

[16] White, *Land Use, Environment and Social Change,* 91.

[17] Cox, *Mills and Markets,* 284-96.

[18] White, *Land Use, Environment and Social Change,* 106-109.

[19] White, *Land Use, Environment and Social Change,* 96-196.

[20] Thornton Munger, *Timber Growing Practices in the Douglas Fir Region,* U.S. Department of Agriculture, Department Bulletin no. 1493 (June 1927), 14.

[21] U.S. Department of Agriculture, *Forest Statistics for San Juan, Island, and Kitsap Counties,* Pacific Northwest Forest and Range Experiment Station, Forest Service Report 142: 5, 20.

[22] White, *Land Use, Environment and Social Change,* 106-14.

[23] I have treated this far more fully in Richard White, "Poor Men on Poor Lands: The Back to the Land Movement of the Early Twentieth Century—A Case Study," *Pacific Historical Review* 49 (Feb. 1980): 105-31.

[24] White, "Back to the Land Movement," 105-31.

[25] Washington Logged-off Land Association, *Proceedings of the Washington Logged-off Land Association* (Seattle, 1909), 28-29.

[26] A. R. Hathaway, "Call of the Land," *Little Logged-off Lands* 1 (May 1914): 14; Joel Shoemaker, "Let the State Clear the Logged-off Lands," *Little Logged-off Lands* 1 (June 1912): 33-34; *Island County, Washington, A World Beater* (n.p., n.d.).

[27] Joel Shoemaker, "Wonderful Opportunities in Logged-off Lands," *Pacific Northwest Commerce,* 5: 16; C. W. Scharff, "Redeeming the Wooded Wilderness of Washington," *Little Logged-off Lands* 1: 19-20; "Logged-off Paradise," *Little Logged-off Lands,* 1: 22; Shoemaker, "Independence on Little Logged-off Farms, *Little Logged-off Lands.* 1: 16; C. J. Zintheo, "This Man Says Stumps Are a Blessing Not a Curse," *Little Logged-off Lands,* 1: 23; C. J. Zintheo, "The Logged-off Land Problem and Its Solution," *Pacific Lumber Trade Journal* 16 (January 1911): 55-58; H. K. Benson, "Utilization of Waste Wood," *Little Logged-off Lands,* 1: 12; Washington Logged-off Lands Association, *Proceedings,* 11, 28-29; *Seattle Post Intelligencer,* 3 September 1931, p. 1.

[28] U.S. Department of Commerce, Bureau of the Census: *Twelfth Census, Agriculture, 1900,* Vol. 5, pt. 1: 135-39; *Thirteenth Census, Agriculture, 1910,*

Vol. 7: 840-43; *Fourteenth Census, Agriculture, 1920,* Vol. 6, pt. 3: 292-95; *Fifteenth Census, Agriculture, 1930,* Vol. 2, pt. 3: 430-33, 436-39; *Sixteenth Census, Agriculture, 1940,* Vol. 1, pt. 6: 548-51, 556-59.

29 E. R. Johnson and E. D. Strait, *Farming the Logged-off Uplands in Western Washington,* U.S. Department of Agriculture, Department Bulletin 1236 (July 1924), 19-20; Glenn Hoover, "Rural Settlement in Western Washington" (M.A. thesis, University of Washington, 1922), 44.

30 "Washington's Logged-off Land Problems Discussed," *Pacific Lumber Trade Journal* 17 (June 1911): 41-43.

31 Richard Wakefield and Paul Landis, *The Drought Farmer Adjusts to the West,* Washington Agricultural Experiment Station Bulletin 378 (Pullman: Washington State University, 1939), 22; Carl P. Helsig, *Settlement Experience and Opportunities on the Cutover Lands of Western Washington,* Washington Agricultural Experiment Station Bulletin 399 (Pullman: Washington State University, 1941), 5, 30, 33.

32 For a fuller discussion of this see, White, "Poor Men on Poor Lands," 126-128.

33 Towle, "Woodland in the Willamette," 121-23.

34 Samual Hays, *Conservation and the Gospel of Efficiency,* (Cambridge: Harvard University Press, 1959).

35 Lawrence Rakestraw, "Sheep Grazing in the Cascade Range: John Minto versus John Muir," *Pacific Historical Review* 27 (November 1958): 371-82; Rakestraw, "Uncle Sam's Forest Reserves," *Pacific Northwest Quarterly* 44 (October 1953): 145-49; Rakestraw, "Before McNary: The Northwest Conservationist, 1889-1913," *Pacific Northwest Quarterly* 51 (April 1960): 49-56.

36 Lawrence Rakestraw, "The West, States Rights, and Conservation: A Study of Six Public Land Conferences," *Pacific Northwest Quarterly* 48 (July 1957): 89, 97-98. For the quote see, Rakestraw, "Sheep Grazing in the Cascade Range," 382.

37 Thomas Cox, "The Crusade to Save Oregon's Scenery," *Pacific Historical Review* 37 (May 1968): 181, 188-89, 193-94; Thomas Cox, "Conservation by Subterfuge: Robert W. Sawyer and the Birth of the Oregon State Parks," *Pacific Northwest Quarterly* 64 (January 1973): 21-29.

38 Steve Woodruff, "Exporting Timber: Jobs Across the Sea," *Willamette Week,* 2 June 1980.

39 White, *Land Use, Environment, and Social Change,* 148-153.

Desert, Sagebrush, and the Pacific Northwest

Judith Austin

There are obvious and real differences between the Pacific Northwest that lies west of the Cascade divide and the Pacific Northwest east of it. Primarily because of the Columbia River, the area to the east is historically and economically part of the Pacific Northwest;[1] yet a sense of distinction between the two areas has always been perceived by people on both sides of the Cascades, even if it has been little articulated by historians.[2] The differences between the two major parts of the region have persisted and will persist despite political changes and technological improvements, and any valid characterization of the Pacific Northwest cannot ignore these distinctions.

What follows is an effort to outline some of the factors that make the land on the other side of the Cascades different, in the hope that future consideration of the Pacific Northwest as a whole may include "my side" more than has been the case thus far. Toward that end, it may be useful to note where I come from geographically and, if you will, spiritually. I am that rare creature, a third-generation native of southern California. Child of a couple of desert rats who grew up in the little towns behind Los Angeles in the first quarter of this century, I was introduced to the desert even before gas rationing was lifted after World War II; thus I was raised with the true Westerner's sense of the irrelevancy of distance. When I was nine I was carried off to the wilds of Manhattan Island for 17½ years of absolute urban, mid-Atlantic living. Because we kept a car (a fact that marked us as rather odd people in New York City), I learned there what it is like to live in a heavily wooded country where there is frequent precipitation.

We went west often, usually by car, occasionally by train. My parents held that we reached the eastern fringes of the West when we got something more than bread and meat in a hamburger. But I realized early that the transition begins (perhaps at the same geographical point) in a different way; the West begins where the landforms become more visible and more significant than what covers the land. By that, I do not mean the point at which farmers can no longer plant and harvest crops economically with or without irrigation. I mean the point at which it is possible to *see* the landforms—to look across country and see not just trees and undergrowth, but the permanent texture of the land. I suspect that the western sense and acceptance of distance stems from the visibility of landforms. Many of those who crossed the continent on the overland trails noted their surprise at how far away things were that they could see; over the decades we have adapted our sense of what distance we can cover without giving much thought to that reality.

When I returned to the West in 1967, I came to a part of the country that had the sense of distance and space that I knew from my birthplace. I arrived in Boise by train, in the middle of the night, for a job interview the next morning. When I woke up and looked out my hotel window at the Boise Ridge which reaches above town, I was hooked. I had never been west of the Cascades. While I had some vague mental image of Oregon as green and wet, my first view of it some months later was Malheur County, which is about as deserty a landscape as you will find anywhere in the country. It was some time before I got to the Willamette Valley or any other part of western Oregon or western Washington. The landscape on the west side of the Cascades certainly seemed familiar, after all those years in the East. But it is not what I was raised to see as western.

As I have observed the differences in topography and climate in the years since my return west, I have also become more aware of the historical and cultural differences among the various parts of the region, and of the various senses of loyalty and identity that exist here. Anyone familiar with Idaho's history and present cultural complexity will understand why the southeastern part of the state, almost totally a part of the Pacific Northwest geographically, is oriented culturally and economically toward the Great Basin kingdom whose capital is Salt Lake City. Less pervasive differences also exist in that part of Idaho north of the Salmon or Clearwater rivers, where Spokane is by far the nearest big-city presence. On a smaller scale, residents of far southeastern Oregon turn to Boise, rather than Portland or Salem, for just about everything. But those in the far northeastern corner of Oregon, in Wallowa County, may look to the small town of Enterprise (the county seat) more than to the more substantial communities of Clarkston, Washington, and Lewiston, Idaho, which are no farther away but out of state.[3]

These differences, however—aside from the Mormon presence, which is unique in many ways—could exist anywhere. The significant differences between the areas east and west of the Cascades are those created by the environment's effect on the history of the interior, made more complex by the common history of the region. For reasons of both history and geography (thus of politics and economics), we are tied together; realignment of borders, whether in accord with various 19th-century plans or a future "Nine Nations of North America" pattern would not change that. We who live on the eastern side of the mountains recognize the shared heritage, manmade and natural. But we have always been at least a little uneasy about it, because it has sometimes tended to obscure us and our significant differences from the west side.

Some of those who listen as we grumble that the interior Northwest is often overlooked or ignored would argue that our situation is in no way unique; all states and regions have such divisions and resentments, most often between the big city or capital and the hinterlands. Maybe. But if the parallel were exact, the Willamette Valley would hold the same view of Portland as does eastern Oregon, and Bellingham and Walla Walla would look at Olympia and Seattle in the same way. To some extent, of course, they do. But I think there are some valid reasons why our situation is different.

Chiefly, settlement patterns are different. In New York or Pennsylvania or Illinois, the timespan of permanent broad-based settlement throughout the state was shorter, and the spread of population was more regular. The white men and women who came into this region east of the Cascades in the first decades did not come to settle. The first were fur trappers and traders, and their forts in the interior were expected to remain only as long as the extractive business of gathering beaver pelts lasted. Missionaries were by definition not settlers (their purpose too was in a sense extractive); their ties to the home board or equivalent were very clear, no matter how long they lived in the West. And those who came to mine in the 1860s were after all engaged in a transitory, extractive business.

Mostly, the interior Northwest was an area to be hurried across or to be milked of its riches—human, animal, mineral, and eventually vegetable. That is what its identity rested on. There is some evidence that for many people, the east-of-the-Cascades Northwest does not now have a much more positive identity. A friend reported to me his daughter's experience as a freshman in one of the Willamette Valley's small liberal arts colleges. When asked by a fellow student where she was from, she said with some pride that, while she had grown up in California, she was born in Oregon—in Redmond. "Oh," said her questioner (a Salem resident), "that doesn't count—that's not really Oregon." It may not be, by Willamette Valley standards. But the junipers and sagebrush around Redmond are typical of more of the state than are the unirrigated farmlands and Douglas fir forests near Salem, and central Oregon boasts sawmills and agriculture as surely as the Willamette Valley.

Differences have been blurred by the fact that the people of the interior Northwest are not so very different from the people west of the Cascades. In the early years of white settlement, many of those who came to the interior came up the Columbia River from the Willamette Valley.[4] Enterprising businessmen from Portland set up shop in the towns that served mining camps.[5] The Oregon Steam Navigation Company, which provided the first real commercial transportation into the interior, was a Portland company. Many of the early farmers and ranchers in the interior were from the Willamette Valley, although some of the larger ranchers came from California and hired the sons of Portland businessmen to spend summers working on them.[6] If anything, the population of the interior was and is more homogeneous than that west of the Cascades.

None of these moves eastward took place rapidly. The interior population was composed largely of people who had been settled for some time west of the mountains. Economically, the focus continued to be on the coast and Willamette Valley (and especially, until the railroads finally crossed the Cascades to Puget Sound in the 1880s, on Portland). Dorothy Johansen's speculations on early migrants shaping the nature of later populations perhaps hold as well on the east side as on the west side of the Cascades.[7]

The two sides of the Cascades share more history than just the people who settled the country. The three modern states were a political whole until Washington Territory was spun off in 1853. Ten years later, to quote Earl Pomeroy's summary, "the Territory of Idaho brought under one ungainly jurisdiction a miscellany of geographical leftovers that socially and economically still look about as much to Washington, Oregon, and Utah as to each other."[8] By the turn of the century, all three states contained populations strongly representative of the north central states; Idaho's population was drawn more from the Middle Border area, while Washington's was more form the Old Northwest and Oregon's fell in between.[9] This distribution has considerably influenced politics (in Idaho Territory and eastern Oregon in particular) and shows up most particularly in tensions between appointive and elective officials in the early years of the former.[10] Politically each state has a history of being maverick, especially in its electoral structures.[11]

The three states have shared problems of transportation, communication, and marketing as well throughout their collective history. Pomeroy has summarized the long-term effects: "Basically the Northwest's limitations [in the mid-20th century] were still what they had been: it depended on selling its resources in other markets, and its marketable resources were few."[12]

Nonetheless, life east of the mountains *is* different. As I suggested earlier, it can be argued that the interior Northwest is more "west" than the western part of the region. One relatively standard distinction is that the West is that area in which water, or the lack thereof, has had special significance.[13] Technically, that excludes the region west of the Cascades; although, as long as political and logistical decisions about the Columbia Basin are made on the west side of the mountains, I would not detach the two sections on those grounds. A more detailed and thoughtful delineation was laid down by the distinguished historian John Caughey in his essay "Toward an Understanding of the West":

> To begin with, it had better be stressed that this is a land where the environment has to be taken into account. It may be lavish in resources, but unlike a South Sea Island with its coconuts and bread-fruit [or the Pacific Northwest coast with its dependable precipitation], it does not automatically nourish. The mark of the land is strong on its history, and the facts of geography are these:
>
> First, it is a big country, a land of distances, of remoteness. The problem of transportation has always been uppermost for those who wanted to use or develop the West.
>
> Second, it is a rugged land, a land of sharp uplifts, canyons, and gorges, a region complex in topography and with a great deal of exposed geology. The multiplicity of landforms—the alternation of plains, mountains, basins, mesas, valleys—complicates the transportation problem.
>
> It also sets up a broad diversity of climates. The isothermal lines climb the mountains more rapidly than they do the degrees of latitude. Zones of climate ranging from subtropical to arctic may be only a few miles apart, and the precipitation on one side of a mountain range often is much greater than on the other side.[14]

Look, one writer says, "for the dry, blowing soil, check for magpies, try to catch the smell of sage."[15] Those are western, desert sights and smells. They are not the look and smell of money, the way a pulp mill or new-sawn lumber is to the timber industry. But they represent richness to residents of the Palouse of northern Idaho and eastern Washington, the wheat country of north-central Oregon along the Columbia, and the dry farmlands of south-central Idaho. Sage and dust smell like money to those who know that, with more water, the desert land just beyond the edges of their irrigated acres would be more rich farmland.

But where there is no topsoil left to blow, where the sage is too stunted and dry to give off much aroma, where magpies are not found, the land will be sterile and poor. There are vast stretches of eastern Oregon and Washington and south-central Idaho that are the latter sort of country. And some other areas, while not yet so barren, have lost fertility in a region that cannot afford such losses.[16]

To the uninitiated, this interior Northwest seems empty—not only of people but of native fauna (except in the forested areas that lie chiefly on its edges and on the slopes of the Blue Mountains) and of native flora that require much water. Donald Meinig, in his extraordinary study of the Columbia Plain, might often be speaking of the whole region: "This is not a bountiful land for people who could only glean directly from nature. [It] had no good animal staple, few usable plants, and little material for fire and shelter." And—excepting only the wheat country—it seems a country that did not regenerate the wealth extracted from it until massive amounts of money for irrigation projects were poured in. A perceptive student of settlement on the "pioneer fringes" of the world has said, "If one were to contour the difficulties of settlement, central and southeastern Oregon would be a Himalaya on the human map of the United States."[17]

Michael Harrington, in his study of poverty in this country, *The Other Americans,* speaks of "property-owning poverty." He identifies a handful of regions in which "farmers [are] dependent on their farms as the main source of income but [are] unable to make an adequate living from farming."[18] One of his regions is the Pacific Northwest. Harrington's book was published in 1962, but some of those farms are still there, barely hanging on with wives (and husbands) working part time in nearby towns to bridge the economic gaps. Nor is the problem a recent one; failure or near failure has been an all-too-common experience. Early in the days of the Boise Project—one of the first United States Reclamation Service undertakings early in this century—Frederick Newell, chief of the Service, commented: "It is hardhearted, perhaps, to turn out the first man, but the second man is just as deserving of aid from the Government as the first one."[19] Newell might have noted that the second was as likely to fail as the first, unless he had rare understanding of the problems of irrigated farming. In a more ironic tone, Oregon's fine writer H. L. Davis spoke of homesteaders and packrats as parallel species:

> They [packrats] had the fun of planning big; maybe that was all they wanted or expected. If that is so, their living in [deserted] homestead houses was the most appropriate of all earthly coincidences, for they,

more perfectly than any other created thing, exemplified the people
whom they supplanted. If there is ever a monument to busted
homesteaders, the pack-rat deserves to be on it. He is nature's one
victim of the homesteaders' never-failing curse—a fury for beginning
things and leaving them one-fourth done. It may have been from them
that he learned his habits.[20]

Some of the impression of poverty is misleading. The appearance of many farms and ranches in the interior clashes with the
"family farm" image of neat, green fields, with equally neat red or
white houses and outbuildings. In the interior country, colors
often seem almost bleached out of the land and the structures on it.
This is a sign not necessarily of poverty but of the desert reality that
wind and weather and dryness will take their toll no matter what.[21]

And there is now another, statistical response to Harrington's
concern. Idahoans have gotten a good deal of kidding from friends
elsewhere about a 1980 government report indicating that we have
a higher number of millionaires per capita than any other state. We
were surprised, until we looked at what has happened recently to
land values and reminded ourselves of the size of the average ranch
and the cost of the equipment necessary to work a viable farm.
Such establishments may carry with them their own noneconomic
problems. In "The Size of Things: A Memoir," William Kittredge
poignantly describes both the beauty and difficulties of his childhood ranch home in the Warner Valley of south-central Oregon.
The factors of size and "mechanical precision" that made it viable
also made it "emotionally uninhabitable," he says. It was " . . . too
huge to be walked and understood as a place for living, scaled
beyond human dimension, for the convenience of machinery."[22]

The larger parallel to "property-owning poverty" is the
nonmining, agricultural or resource-dependent ghost town. The
interior Northwest is dotted with them, especially in those areas
where attempted irrigation projects failed.[23] Shaniko, Oregon, was
once a major wool-marketing town in southern Sherman County, a
gateway to the entire central Oregon district. Now it is a collection
of alternately lovely and shabby buildings—most deserted—clumped
as if for protection from the wind and isolation up there on the
plateau. Silcott, Washington, now at best an extension of Clarkston,

was once a town all its own with some pride, serving the local farming and sheep-ranching community, warehousing grain, and servicing a large orchard area. But farming on that fringe could only be subsistence farming, and Silcott became a victim of modern highways and the agricultural depression of the 1920s.[24]

A somewhat different and much more recent ghost town is Kinzua, Oregon, at the far western fringe of the Blue Mountains. As the crow flies, it is about 40 miles east of Shaniko, but it is in a different world altogether. It was a company lumber town on the classic model, with railroad and store and bar and carwash and everything else owned by Kinzua Pine Mills. In 1978, the company moved all its operations to Heppner, some 50 miles northeast. Company employees could buy their houses, but not the land they were on; the company decided to let the forest take over—to return the whole area to trees. Had the town not died in 1978, it surely would have in 1981, given what happened to the timber industry in the Northwest. Its downfall, like many such towns in the interior Northwest, was attributable to two factors: changing technology and changing transportation patterns. Heppner has better access to outside areas and more room to build a fine new mill to replace the outmoded one that had long been crowded into Kinzua's narrow valley.

Many smaller communities of the interior were begun in anticipation of communications networks, as they were elsewhere. With a sparse population, more than our share of them have faded or at least shrunk when passed by. Few communities have been as ingenious as Prineville, Oregon, or Waterville, Washington, which built their own railroad spur lines to connect with main lines. Only Prineville's has survived (and generally prospered) thanks to an ample resource base (primarily timber) that furnishes it with goods to carry.[25]

The local rail lines, like the ghost towns and the homesteaders (and the packrats), represent a kind of stubbornness at work in this region that is not always the most useful quality. Aldo Leopold wrote of an area where "[t]here is, as yet, no sense of pride in the husbandry of wild plants and animals, no sense of shame in the proprietorship of a sick landscape."[26] Leopold was speaking of what has happened to the original rangeland of Oregon and Utah: the bunchgrass destroyed by overgrazing and replaced by cheatgrass that is edible by deer, cattle, or sheep only in its very young stages. Moreover, cheatgrass burns all too readily in the dry fall of the Northwest, holds soil poorly, and is a physical irritant to man and animal alike once its sharp awns have matured and dried in the summer sun. Donald Meinig goes further. There is, he says (albeit in referring to an earlier time), a stubbornness to be found here about "new ways," about "scientific farming" that holds firm until the farmer can more or less discover the truth for himself.[27]

This is not universal, of course; there are ranchers who work closely with Bureau of Land Management staff to improve range, rotate grazing, and guard against overgrazing. But we in the interior are awfully close to the basics in a lot of places. It is not easy to go along with nature when you are farming in desert or running range cattle and sheep in near desert. Man's manipulations tend not to be farsighted enough, while nature's ability to change matters rapidly is great. Drought is an obvious example, but consider what will happen in 1982. A wet spring in 1981 produced heavy range cover; the usual dry summer produced a record quantity of range fires fueled by that cover. In order to reseed adequately (if money can be found in the Bureau of Land Management's budget to reseed, which is questionable in an era of Reaganomics) many herds of cattle and bands of sheep will have to be cut back rather drastically. The surviving range simply will not—by BLM standards—hold more, and reseeded areas must, for the best range land, be left for a season or two without grazing. The ranchers caught in the middle of the problem cannot, in many cases, abide being told by federal employees what they know to be true: that for their long-range survival they may have to accommodate short-term near disaster.[28]

Outside control of the land and thus the economy of the interior Northwest has been a force in the region since first settlement. It has always been heavily dependent on outside capital, whether private or public. The inland Northwest "frontier"—poked at by fur trappers and missionaries and miners—was breached on a permanent basis about the time the Turnerian frontier was closing down. Oregon had transcontinental rail connections by 1883, southern Idaho by 1884. The Northern Pacific finally crossed the Cascades of Washington in 1887, offering the Puget Sound area alternatives to a roundabout rail route up the Columbia Gorge and to a difficult water route on the river itself. The Great Northern reached Seattle five years later. Money built the railroads (eastern money, by and large) and they in turn provided better markets for a part of the country that had few before that time. The railroads (and thus eastern money) profoundly influenced settlement and development patterns.[29]

Money and railroads brought people, especially to the Yakima country. Above all else (in this century especially), money has made possible irrigated farming. While small systems existed about as early as settlement (e.g., Henry Harmon Spalding's in the 1830s, Mormon irrigation in southeastern Idaho by 1860, and plenty of small private ditches in the Boise area and the Columbia Basin by the 1870s), only with substantial commitments of private development funds could substantial networks of dams and canals even be contemplated. And only the resources of the federal government could finance the enormous systems that have made possible the growth of southern Idaho and much of the farmland of central and eastern Oregon and the Columbia Basin. Furthermore, the necessary technology did not exist in any useful sense until this century, as the long list of projects that failed amply demonstrates.[30]

This is, therefore, new country by and large, even by Northwest standards. That newness is, I believe, part of the explanation for the lack of much written history, and perhaps also for a renewed sense of the need to preserve history, which I see on a day-to-day basis in my own work. Especially in the irrigated areas, settlement has come well within the lifetimes of people still alive and active. We are seeing a lot of 75th anniversaries in our part of the world, and a very few centennials. Many such celebrations produce special editions of the local newspapers, often reflecting what a town thinks it is more than what in fact it is. One 50th-anniversary paper from central Oregon, published in 1955, emphasizes the enormous growth that was the history of those still there and, in a rare burst of honesty, describes the town as "just emerging from the juvenile stage of merely learning to be a town."[31] Both reminiscences and historical sketches in that same special edition are colored by a sense of the vast distance crossed to come to the community—and to go anywhere from it. The viewpoint is typical of the region, as much so now as ever.

However, despite some perceptions to the contrary, the isolation reflected is one of places rather than of people. And we who live on the east side of the mountains often feel ourselves misperceived because of a provinciality to the west. Two examples of such misperception appeared in the 1960s in the admirable alumni magazine of the University of Oregon; I will summarize them for you.

In 1920 Dr. Bernard Daly left a fund to the community of Lakeview, Oregon, to help send its high school graduates to college. Dr. Daly reportedly confided shortly before his death that "this remote country was in desperate need of the kind of refinement that only educated men and women could bring to it."[32] In 1963, an article entitled "Can Education 'Save' Lakeview?" appeared in *Old Oregon.* The essay examined the town and the impact of the Daly Fund on it. As Ken Metzler, editor of *Old Oregon,* said, Lakeview "is unmistakeably [sic] western; its economy is built of lumber and cattle and sheep and the great outdoors."[33] Metzler sketched the community as being essentially nonintellectual—even suggesting that it is anti-intellectual—and a "man's town." More significantly, the chairman of the board overseeing the fund said to him: "We have to face the fact that this community is producing more educated men and women than it is capable of absorbing into its own economy. In many areas of specialization, the community simply has no need for these people. And there's no doubt that the Daly Fund is taking away some of our best people."[34]

At one point, the community seriously considered abandoning all federal funding for vocational agriculture, changing its mind only when it learned that students could not participate in Future Farmers of America if there was no federal funding involved. Metzler described the community's support of the initial plan to abandon federal vo-ag as a "typical brand of eastern Oregon conservatism." Some of it may also have been the sense that those on the front lines know as much as the feds. The community was, after all, maverick enough to strongly support Wayne Morse.[35]

While noting that "capital and labor applied to natural resources . . . makes taxable wealth," in Lakeview at least, Metzler goes on to say: "If the impression of Lakeview is one of simple conservatism and anti-intellectualism, it should be noted that an occasional bright corner appears . . . ." The example given is the late University of Oregon history professor Paul Dull, who got 120 people out for a two-hour presentation sponsored by the American Association of University Women. The presence of an AAUW chapter in an isolated town of less than 3,000 people says something about "simple conservatism and anti-intellectualism." But Lakeview, Metzler believed, "needs . . . outside stimulation that will penetrate the sagebrush curtain of geographic isolation that separates Lakeview from the outside world."

Responses to Metzler's article were sharp;[36] the pithiest was a comment that "[t]he people are not isolated—only the land is." Other letters—notably one from a former Lakeview high school principal—suggested that Metzler saw what he assumed would be there, not what really *was* there.

In 1981 Lakeview is dying around the edges; with problems in the cattle industry and far more in the lumber industry, there are many houses and ranches for sale. But the town clearly has not lost faith in itself. The bright young people in the BLM district office there care about the community, and the high school graduates of 1981 sport t-shirts crowded with all their classmates' names.

Six years after the Lakeview article, Metzler tackled Madras, another east-of-the-Cascades town. He had learned a lot. The title of the article—a quotation from one of the town's citizens—was "College Has Ruined Many a Fine Sheepherder." The most interesting aspect of the article (especially in light of the earlier piece) was Metzler's explanation of why Madras was selected for examination in the first place. The alumni office wanted to learn what the town's view of college and of the University of Oregon was. To their surprise, the *Old Oregon* staff discovered that the most immediate impression was created by the university's Pine Mountain Observatory (some 50 miles southeast of Madras), which was seen as a positive presence in the area.

But back on campus the staff had found, on coffee breaks spent in the Union, a split into two factions. There was an elitist view that Madras was not capable of understanding universities and their role; furthermore, since Jefferson County (of which Madras is the county seat) had fewer residents than the University of Oregon had students, it did not matter what they thought. The egalitarian view was that "this elitist attitude is exactly the kind of aloof, snobbish nonsense that gets the citizens of Oregon angry about higher education. People in Madras are citizens of the state . . . . Ignoring the people of Madras because of their alleged isolation and provinciality is a foolish act, a little like cutting off your foot because it is so isolated from your center of intellectual thought."[37]

Metzler's view when he studied Lakeview and that of some university people toward Madras may help explain the prickliness of many who live to the east. Ours may not be the Northwest of plush mountainsides carpeted with Douglas fir—when you are on the east side of the Cascades, even the Douglas fir are less luxuriant, their wood more brittle—but it *is* the Pacific Northwest in its essential orientation.[38] Most of all (far more than the lovely country west of the mountains) it is visibly, texturally, and economically the West. Some residents have had sharp comments about the folk to the west; one miner in the Pueblo Mountains of far southeastern Oregon said of his fellow Oregonians west of the Cascades, "Well, they're funny people in the Valley—not enough distance; can't see out."[39] One hopes he said it with sympathy and humor, but probably it was merely with exasperation. Similarly, a historian from the interior Northwest, commenting on the dearth of research and writing on the region, suggests: "Most scholars are on the other side [of the mountains] and they do not seem much interested in this very different environment; perhaps the rains and fogs have covered their glasses and windshields and they don't see much distance."[40]

There are at least three exceptions to that generalization. Among senior Northwest scholars, several reside east of the mountains: Merle Wells, whose interest has been primarily in the region's 19th-century political history; George Frykman, who has recently been looking at regionalism per se; and the late Herman Deutsch.[41] Deutsch's comments on the Inland Empire might be applied to the region as a whole:

> East-west communications have tended to flatten the Cascades, and settlement of the Columbia Basin has encouraged travel across what in the recent past has been regarded as an arid no man's land. The former isolation between the various portions of Washington may soon become a matter of history. Whether the conquest of physical divisions will redound to greater homogeneity for the entire Pacific Northwest or whether state particularism will assume greater prominence because of diminished intra-state sectionalism will be a matter for the next generation of Inland Empire historians to reveal.[42]

I am extremely wary of environmental determinism, but cultural and historic differences are in this setting based on the environment. Such differences will persist; east-west communications may have flattened the Cascades for those who drive cars, but not for the rainclouds. The reticence of those clouds east of the mountains has shaped the land there, and it has shaped what people can do with the land. Most of the "next generation" of Northwest historians have dealt thus far only with very particular, narrow aspects of the region's history. We need to study the Pacific Northwest as a whole, and to consider its differences as carefully as its continuities.

NOTES

[1] For a provocative discussion of the Columbia-Snake river system's role in linking the Northwest, see Edward L. Ullman, "Rivers as Regional Bonds: The Columbia-Snake Example," *Geographical Review* 41 (April, 1951): 210-25.

[2] It is my impression that Oregonians have done more writing about their east-of-the-Cascades country than have Idahoans or Washingtonians. The work of Phil Brogan, Ralph Friedman, Miles Potter, Raymond Hatten, Keith Clark, and Samuel Dicken, among others, does not seem to have an equivalent for the other two states. *High & Mighty: Random Sketches of the Deschutes Country,* edited by Thomas Vaughan (Portland: Oregon Historical Society, 1981), while flawed in its definition of the region it is about, is nonetheless an admirable example of Oregonian self-study.

[3] Jim Riggs, "Story of a Home (Well, not Exactly . . .) Birth," Portland *Oregonian,* 7 June 1981, *Northwest Magazine* section, 6.

[4] D. W. Meinig, *The Great Columbia Plain: A Historical Geography* (Seattle: University of Washington Press, 1968), 504-507.

[5] Mining towns are an example of a distinctive interior settlement pattern. Mining towns began simultaneously with almost any mining activity, while most agricultural communities tended to develop after there was a farm or ranch settlement.

[6] Peter Kooi Simpson, "A Social History of the Cattle Industry in Southeastern Oregon, 1869-1912" (unpub. Ph.D. diss., University of Oregon, 1973), 327. Simpson also states that leadership in Harney County has continued to come from those whose roots are in the Willamette Valley (*Ibid.,* 179). A fragmented, impressionistic, and thoroughly delightful account of the cattle industry in Harney and Malheur counties is contained in Anne Shannon Monroe, *Feelin' Fine! Bill Hanley's Book* (Garden City, N.Y.: Doubleday, Doran & Co., 1931), a collection of the bits and pieces that pioneer cattleman Bill Hanley left about.

[7] Dorothy O. Johansen, "A Working Hypothesis for the Study of Migrations," *Pacific Historical Review* 36 (February 1967): 1-12. Johansen's Oregon in this article is west of the Cascades.

[8] Earl Pomeroy, *The Pacific Slope: A History of California, Oregon, Washington, Idaho, Utah and Nevada,* 2nd ed. (Seattle: University of Washington Press, 1973), 64. Pomeroy's emphasis on regional historical continuities does not imply a lack of understanding of the discontinuities, although it does tend to obscure them.

9 Census data from 1900 indicate that almost one-third of the population in Idaho and Oregon and well over one-third in Washington came from the North Central states. *Twelfth Census of the United States: Population, Part I* (Washington, D.C.: Government Printing Office, 1901), cxlv, cxlvi.

10 Pomeroy, *Pacific Slope,* 78. For a description of some of Idaho's problems with Middle Border Southern sympathizers after the Civil War, see Merle W. Wells, "S. R. Howlett's War with the Idaho Legislature, 1866-1867," *Idaho Yesterdays* 20/1 (Spring 1976): 20-27; and Owen Wister, "The Second Missouri Compromise," reprinted in the same issue. The whole region is treated in more detail in Merle W. Wells, "Idaho and the Civil War," *Rendezvous* 11/2 (Fall 1976): 9-26.

11 See the chapters on Idaho, Oregon, and Washington in Frank Jonas, ed., *Politics in the American West* (Salt Lake City: University of Utah Press, 1969), 180-200, 296-325, 382-415.

12 Pomeroy, *Pacific Slope,* 308.

13 Jonas, *Politics in the West,* 3.

14 John W. Caughey, "Toward an Understanding of the West," *Utah Historical Quarterly* 27 (January 1959): 11.

15 Daniel Jack Chasan, "Prosperity in the Palouse," *Pacific Northwest* 15 (September 1981): 30.

16 Simpson, "Social History," 13.

17 Meinig, *Great Columbia Plain,* 20; Isaiah Bowman, *The Pioneer Fringe* (New York: American Geographical Society, 1931; reprinted, New York: Books for Libraries [Arno Press], 1971), 110.

18 Michael Harrington, *The Other America: Poverty in the United States* (New York: Macmillan, 1962), 44.

19 Quoted in Charles Coate, "Federal-Local Relationships on the Boise and Minidoka Projects, 1904-1926," *Idaho Yesterdays* 25/2 (Summer 1981): 4.

20 H. L. Davis, "Back to the Land—Oregon, 1907," *American Mercury* 16 (March 1929): 117-151.

21 In some cases, while houses are unoccupied, the land is not by any means abandoned; ranchers have become wealthy enough to move to town. Bowman, *Pioneer Fringe,* 108.

22 William Kittredge, "The Size of Things: A Memoir," *Pacific Northwest* 15 (June 1981): 31.

23 E. R. Jackman and R. A. Long list 25 homesteading ghost towns that were born and died between 1910 and 1920. E. R. Jackman and R. A. Long, *The Oregon Desert* (Caldwell, Idaho: Caxton Printers, Ltd., 1965), 397-98.

24 Jacqueline Day-Ames, "Changing Social Networks in a Rural American Community" (undated manuscript, copy courtesy of the author), *passim.* Interestingly enough, Silcott has been intensively studied by archaeologists,

anthropologists, and ethnographers as something of a model nonsurviving community of the late 19th and early 20th centuries, and a great deal of documentation, oral and written, exists. See William H. Adams, *Archaeological Excavations at Silcott, Washington: The Data Inventory,* Washington State University Laboratory of Anthropology (Pullman, 1975), and William H. Adams, *Silcott, Washington: Ethnoarchaeology of a Rural American Community,* Washington State University Laboratory of Anthropology (Pullman, 1977).

[25] Meinig, *Great Columbia Plain,* 434; John F. Due and Frances Juris, *Rails to the Ochoco Country: The City of Prineville Railway* (San Marino, California: Golden West Books, 1968).

[26] Aldo Leopold, "Cheat Takes Over," *A Sand County Almanac with Other Essays on Conservation from Round River* (New York: Oxford University Press, 1966), 158.

[27] Meinig, *Great Columbia Plain, passim* (especially Chapter 19).

[28] For a concise discussion of the problems of grazing in the desert country of eastern Oregon, see Jackman and Long, *The Oregon Desert,* 304-318.

[29] For the impact of the railroads on regional economic growth in the 1880s and 1980s, see the June 1966 issue of *Oregon Historical Quarterly,* especially: Peter A. Shroyer, "Oregon Sheep, Wool and Woolens Industries," *Oregon Historical Quarterly* (June 1966), 125-138; and George E. Carter, "The Cattle Industry of Eastern Oregon, 1880-90," *Oregon Historical Quarterly* (June 1966), 139-159. Idaho had had rail access via the Kelton (Utah) stage route since 1869. It was a long and dusty link between Boise and the Central Pacific, but it made possible ready business with the East that had not been feasible when everything had to go to or come from the westward.

[30] See, for example, Hugh Lovin, "Footnote to History: The Reservoir . . . Would not Hold Water," *Idaho Yesterdays* 24/1 (Spring 1980): 12-19, and Mikel H. Williams, *The History and Development of the Carey Act in Idaho* (Boise: Idaho Department of Reclamation, 1970).

[31] *Redmond* (Oregon) *Spokesman,* 22 August 1955, sec. 2, p. 2.

[32] Ken Metzler, "Can Education 'Save' Lakeview?" *Old Oregon* 43 (August-September 1963): 10.

[33] *Ibid.,* 8.

[34] Ted Conn, quoted in *ibid.,* 11.

[35] *Ibid.,* 11. However illogical the federal policy may be, it does help one to see why there is a certain antifederal attitude abroad in the land—and why communities are susceptible to compromise.

[36] *Ibid.,* 13. Letters in response appeared in *Old Oregon* 43 (October-November 1963): 30-31.

[37] Ken Metzler, "College Has Ruined Many a Fine Sheepherder," *Old Oregon* (September-October 1969): 15.

[38] Thomas R. Cox, "International and Domestic Trade and their Impact on the Utilization of North America's Pacific Coast Forests to 1914" (paper presented at World Forest Depletion Conference, Oakland University, Rochester, Michigan, 13 May 1981), 2-7. Cox discusses the impact of climate and topography on commercial forests in the region.

[39] Warren DuPre Smith, *The Scenic Treasure House of Oregon* (Portland: Binfords & Mort, 1941), 122-123.

[40] G. Thomas Edwards, Walla Walla, personal communication, 6 July 1981.

[41] George W. Fuller certainly deals with the interior Pacific Northwest—arguably overbalancing to the east and especially to the Spokane/Inland Empire area. However, Fuller barely edged into the 20th century, and his work is strictly narrative history. George W. Fuller, *History of the Pacific Northwest* (New York: Alfred A. Knopf, 1931).

[42] Herman Deutsch, "The Evolution of Territorial and State Boundaries in the Inland Empire of the Pacific Northwest," *Pacific Northwest Quarterly* 51 (July 1960): 131.

REGIONAL IDENTITY IN THE NORTHWEST

Pacific Northwest Writing: Reaching for Regional Identity

Edwin R. Bingham

What constitutes regional writing? Can each region or subregion claim a body of work that could only have come out of its particular milieu? Are creative people nourished and influenced by a sense of place? And what about the dimension of time and circumstance as well as location?

On one level and for some areas the answers seem obvious. If the sea can be viewed as a region, Herman Melville or Joseph Conrad or John Masefield come readily to mind. The American Southwest is beautifully evoked in the work of Willa Cather or Paul Horgan. Who has dealt with the south more powerfully and more sensitively than William Faulkner or Wilbur Cash or William Styron?

The most effective interpreters of a place write out of intimate knowledge and experience. Take the case of Mark Twain and his biography of the Mississippi River. *Life on the Mississippi* began as a series of articles in the *Atlantic Monthly*. These vignettes are distillations from Twain's boyhood and youth which had lain undisturbed in his memory until he chose to call them forth. However, when he decided to publish the early pieces in book form, he returned to the river to freshen his recollections and to bring the river up to date. Thus, the second part of the book is skillful reportage, sharp with the detail of recent observation. Yet, by comparison with the earlier portion, the writing is flat, one-dimensional, and neither as aesthetically impressive nor as convincing as the *Atlantic* essays.[1]

Substitute the Pacific Northwest for the Mississippi River and the Twain example suggests a similar division in northwestern

151

writing. On the one hand is much of the worshipful and sentimental writing that focuses directly, sometimes relentlessly, on the Pacific Northwest. On the other hand is the work of writers who express their regional commitment through criticism as well as celebration, and who use the Northwest as the specific setting for their efforts to develop universal themes or dilemmas. From the early days of white settlement, the Pacific Northwest can show writing that not only effectively reflects the region but also displays a measure of literary merit and at times genuine literary distinction. To support this thesis, I will examine and assess the work of one writer from each of four successive literary generations in the Pacific Northwest: William L. Adams, Charles Erskine Scott Wood, H. L. Davis, and Richard Hugo.

William L. Adams

The Oregon Country had its literary frontier, one that could claim the first novelist (Margaret Jewett Bailey) and the first newspaper (the Oregon *Spectator*) on the Pacific Slope. Even before Bailey's novel *The Grains, or Passages in the Life of Ruth Rover* (1854), William L. Adams, an eccentric and talented midwestern Whig, published a play that poked fun at leading Democrats of territorial Oregon. Adams named his satire *Treason, Strategems, and Spoils, a Play in Five Acts by Breakspear.* The play was first published in five installments in the Portland *Oregonian* in February and March of 1852. In early April it appeared in pamphlet form.

In its day *Treason, Stratagems and Spoils* was a best seller in Oregon Territory, but its popularity was fleeting. The pamphlet was soon out of print, and an attempt at reprinting around 1899 seems to have been abortive. No wonder, for the play is comprehensible only to persons intimately acquainted with Oregon politics in the early 1850s. Not until 1968 did Yale University publish a scholarly edition painstakingly edited by George N. Belknap.[2] Adam's play is local literature with a vengeance. As a piece of skillful and polished writing, the satire does not deserve the obscurity it has suffered.

William Lysander Adams was born February 5, 1821 in a northeastern Ohio town on the shores of Lake Erie, the son of a

Whig land speculator and Great Lakes ship captain who was probably an early follower of Alexander Campbell and his Disciples of Christ. Adams was educated first at Knox College in Galesburg, Illinois and then at Bethany College in Virginia (where Alexander Campbell was founder-president). At Bethany, Adams acquired a deep anti-Mormon bias that shows up conspicuously in *Treason, Strategems, and Spoils.*

After teaching school for a year or so in Illinois, Adams, at the age of 27, set off overland for Oregon in 1848. With him went a small but select personal library including Shakespeare, a large volume of British poets (including Chaucer, Spenser, Burns, Byron, Coleridge, and Scott), *Gulliver's Travels,* Fox's *Book of Martyrs,* Dryden's poems, Pope's translation of the *Iliad,* Thomson's *Seasons,* Von Rotteck's *History of the World,* and Virgil (in Latin). George Belknap believes that Adams was the best-read Oregonian of his day.[3]

On the Oregon frontier William Adams was quick to make his presence felt. He delivered the oration at the Yamhill County Independence Day celebration and began to contribute political essays and verse to the Whig *Oregonian.* His major target was the coterie of Democrats who made up a backwoods political machine known as the Salem Clique. The Willamette Valley was overwhelmingly Democratic, and Adams did his utmost to pillory the party leaders in his play.

The key political issue in 1851 was the location of the territorial capital. A strongly Democratic Legislative Assembly in 1850 passed an act locating the capital in Salem, the penitentiary in Portland, and the university in Corvallis. John P. Gaines, territorial governor appointed by Whig president Zachary Taylor, claimed the act was null and void, because the basic legislation creating the territory limited each territorial statute to a single object and the Location Act embraced three objects. The opening of the third regular session of the territorial assembly found 18 of 22 members of the House and 8 of the 9 members of the Council meeting in Salem. However, Whig Governor Gaines remained in Oregon City with four Whig House members, one Whig Council member, and two of the three justices of the territorial Supreme Court (both

Whigs). The third member of the court, Judge O. C. Pratt, joined his fellow Democrats in Salem. The Location Act drew the lines clearly between Democrats and Whigs, and Adams exploited the cleavage in his play.

The plot of *Treason, Stratagems, and Spoils* revolves around the Democrats' subversive plans to detach the territory from the United States and form a Pacific empire under the rule of Brigham Young, with Mormon Apostle Parley P. Pratt as governor of California and Orville C. Pratt (thinly disguised in the play behind the pseudonym Judge) as governor of Oregon. Judge is ostensibly the central conspirator, aided and abetted by Chicopee (really Asahel Bush, editor of the *Oregon Statesman*), Uncle Ned, (really Matthew Deady, member of the Legislative Council), Grub (William H. Wilson, proprietor of the Salem townsite in trust for the Methodist Oregon Institute), Park (Samuel Parker, president of the Council), and a number of lesser characters. All pseudonyms were readily recognized by the satire's readers. It was generally understood that Adams was perpetrating a joke when he made Orville C. Pratt the main instigator of the revolt. Most readers knew that Bush, or Chicopee, was the real power among the Democrats.

Adams, a strong prohibitionist at this time, portrayed the Democrats as drunkards as well as spoilsmen and traitors. Further, the link with the Mormons and polygamy was designed to cast additional opprobrium on the party of the people. Throughout the satire, the Democratic leaders demonstrate contempt for their constituents, cupidity for land and bribes, enthusiasm for plurality of wives, lust for liquor, and hatred of Governor Gaines and his fellow Whigs. The play closes rather inconclusively in the lumber room of Grub's grocery (a euphemism for saloon) with most of the Democratic chiefs strewn over the premises in drunken slumber. Judge exits limping from his fall into an empty barrel.

The play is structured along the lines of classic satire. A quotation from Bryon on the title page sets the mood and manner: "Prepare for rhyme—I'll publish right or wrong, Fools are my theme—let satire be my song." Lines are rendered either in free verse or rhymed couplets. The quality and sophistication of the writing is impressive. The following selection of representative passages should make the point. Judge and Chickopee are in a Salem inn. Judge explains what it is that recommends Chicopee to him as a partner in conspiracy and spokesman through his newspaper:

> Your talents rare, for double tongued deceit,
> And foul disguise, for feigning truest love,
> And harboring rankest, deadliest hate;
> Your conscience, of an Indian-rubber kind,
> And your political, chameleon skin;
> Your Cossack onslaught, bluffing impudence;
> Your swaggering, bullying, lying tone;
> Your restless, chaffing, scorning, envying,
> Broil-loving temper, have recommended
> You to me, as one to whom I safely
> Might commit the arguing of my cause
> Before the people, whom I wish to gull.[4]

Chicopee's response suggests the aggressive, vehement editorial attacks that characterized antebellum journalism and became generally known as the "Oregon Style":

> Your speech becomes you now, most honored judge,
> Full well, and shows that you my talents rare
> Appreciate.
>   . . . . Have I not branded Gaines with infamy,
> And spattered him all o'er with leprous blots,
>   . . . . Have I not held him up to public scorn,
> As an old, pampered, shallow minded swine,
> Feeding and grunting round the public crib,
> Eating the corn, and casting back the husks
> To the poor, lank, cadaverous people.[5]

In form, and for the most part in language, the play has little hint of the far western frontier. It reads like something out of Boston or, more accurately, early 18th century England. But its characters of course are exclusively local, and Adams spices the dialogue with American slang and a smattering of the Chinook jargon. In fact, one of the most interesting figures is Park, a pure product of the American fur trade frontier. Nominally, his real-life counterpart is Samuel Parker, president of the Council, but actually Park is almost pure invention. It suited Adam's satiric purposes to present the head of the Council as an ignorant former mountain man and a master of the malapropism. George Belknap points out that Park's speech may have been modeled after the American fur trapper patois so skillfully employed by English traveler George Frederick Ruxton in his *Life in the Far West*. On the other hand, as Belknap acknowledges, Adams would have come into contact with the real thing through association with former mountain men who had settled in the Willamette Valley (Joe Meek, for example, or Robert Newell or Osborne Russell).[6] At any rate, Park can be very funny.

When Judge, in Act III, Scene 2, asks Park how goes the business in the Council chamber, the latter replies:

>   Swimminly, sir,
> The way we expatch business thar's a sight.
> Our corn-cracker, judge, has ground all the gristes
> Your honor has sent to the mill—tharfore,
> Having no business directly on hand—
> I, being the *cheerman* of the consarn,
> Tuck the liberty to exmiss the boys
> Till you had Chick tote in another griste—
> Or ruther, we tuck a *siny-diny*
> Adjournment to the old favorite stand,
> Where Grub keeps the o-be-joyful on hand.
> We waited a right smart while for business,
> But none coming, the boys begun to swar
> They was all dry—so I just let 'em rip.[7]

Later on, in an inspired moment, Adams has Judge translate a Latin legal term into Chinook jargon so that Park can comprehend its meaning.[8] Finally, toward the end of the play, Park mounts a pile of bacon to unload this diatribe against the United States Constitution:

> Attention tillicums! whilst I, standing
> On a more firmer foundation, proceed
> To drap a few appertinent remarks,
> Without any diabolical flourish,
> Or logical circumlocution. I wish
> To make a few delusions to the negative
> Quality of that intimous "directory" institution
> Of these United States. That institution, gentlemen
> Was writ, as I've heard, by that villainous
> Tory, and red-coat Britisher, J. Q. Adams,

*   *   *   *   *   *

Don't you see, gentlemen, how it composes
Hereditary secession on the *Presidents*?
The second article of that institution
Says the President "*shall*" hold his office
For four accessary years. Now, hosses,
Jist notice, it don't say he "shant hold it
No longer." So it's simply "*directory*,"
And he mout sit in his cheer forever,
According to a proper instruction
Of that document.[9]

Treason, Strategems, and *Spoils* was not only the first product of Oregon's literary frontier, but it is decisively the best piece of writing from the pioneer period. It is the work of a perceptive and learned man with a keen sense of humor and a sharp ear for speech patterns. Instead of sentimentalizing the frontiersmen, Adams held up the movers and shakers of early Oregon to ridicule, suggesting that satire can cleave closer to the truth than romance.

Is the play truly regional literature? No and Yes. It was written by a recent arrival in studied literary style that is laden with classical allusions. On the other hand, Adams knew the politics of Oregon at first hand, and the plot he unfolds and the characters he creates could have occurred nowhere but in the Willamette Valley. Further, through the persona of Park, Adams adroitly exploits the speech and attitudes found on the American far western frontier.

In his later years Adams turned away from religion to become a free thinker. He continued to write, producing a promotional tract called *Oregon As It Is* (1873) and *History of Medicine and Surgery from the Earliest Times* (1888), but his best work by far is *Treason, Strategems, and Spoils.* Along with James Swan's *The Northwest Coast, or, Three Years' Residence in Washington Territory* (1857), Adams's play gives the early Pacific Northwest a literary foundation of which it need not be ashamed.

Charles Erskine Scott Wood

A generation after William L. Adams, a kindred spirit appeared in the Pacific Northwest. Charles Erskine Scott Wood, like Adams, was born on the shores of Lake Erie. Both men found opportunity and satisfaction in the Pacific Northwest. Like Adams too, Wood was a poet and a satirist, though Wood's satire had a national rather than a local focus. Both were men of the world as well as writers. Adams was a doctor and gentleman farmer; Wood was a soldier, attorney, and land agent. Both men had diverse talents and moved from conservative backgrounds and opinions into unconventionality.

Charles Erskine Scott Wood, the second son of a naval surgeon, was born in Erie, Pennsylvania in 1852. When his father retired in 1866 as Surgeon General, the family moved to Rosewood Glen, a small farm on the outskirts of Baltimore. Erskine (the name Wood preferred) received an appointment-at-large to the United States Military Academy from President Grant. Cadet Wood resented the West Point regimen, and when he should have been reading military technical manuals, he was checking out of the Academy library some of the same classical works that went west with Adams a quarter of a century earlier.

Wood was graduated as second lieutenant in the infantry in 1874 and, according to common practice in the case of cadets with undistinguished academy records, was assigned to duty on the western frontier. From his first station at Fort Bidwell, California, Wood's company was sent to Vancouver Barracks in Washington Territory. The long march passed through southeastern Oregon, and that high desert country made a deep and lasting impression on the young lieutenant. He was fascinated by what he later called in his poetry the "signs of the desert." During 30 years of living in Oregon Wood was to return many times to the Harney desert, and that region furnished the setting for most of his poetry.

Wood spent ten active years in the Army, but not always on the frontier. In the late fall of 1878 he returned to the East to marry Nannie Moale Smith, a Baltimore belle. As adjutant of the Military Academy in the early 1880s, he met and entertained Mark Twain, who liked to visit the cadets and their officers. As a favor to Twain, Adjutant Wood surreptitiously commandeered the Academy press to print about a dozen copies of *1601*, Twain's scatological fabrication of fireside conversation in Queen Elizabeth's chambers. Shortly before he resigned his commission, Lieutenant Wood wangled detached service in New York to take a law degree at Columbia.

Armed with his LL.B., Wood left the Army in 1884 and opened a law office in Portland, where he practiced for more than 30 years. Nannie and Wood reared five children and established a distinctive Portland household in an exclusive residential area in the west hills known as "The Heights." Wood's neighbors and associates were proper and affluent Oregonians—the Corbetts, the Ayres, the Dolphs, the Lewises. Wood was given the title of Colonel in the Oregon militia, and he joined the elitist Arlington Club. His practice (initially mostly maritime law) brought him a substantial income, and he served Lazard Freres, a New York international banking firm, as overseer of the sprawling Willamette Valley and Cascade Mountain Wagon Road grant stretching from Albany to the Idaho border. Wood was handsome, articulate, and witty, with enough irreverence and romanticism to save him from complacency.

Beneath his gilt-edged credentials, C.E.S. Wood was also an artist, a writer, and a rebel. From early youth he had literary ambitions. More than once he considered forsaking West Point for a writing career. During and after his Army years, he wrote articles on his Alaskan and Indian campaign adventures for magazines like *Century* and *North American Review*. In the 1890s he moved toward what he called philosophical anarchism. His, of course, was an anarchism of the word rather than of the deed. He was a heavy contributor of verse, short stories, and editorial impressions to *Pacific Monthly,* a Portland literary and promotional magazine. In 1901 Wood published *A Book of Tales,* a graceful rendering of Indian legends he had picked up in Alaska, northern California, and eastern Oregon.[10]

More important than any of this work was a long poem that Wood originally called *Civilization* but later renamed *Poet in the Desert.* The setting was Harney Valley, which stretched from the western edge of Steens Mountain and was watered by the Blitzen River. The poem deals with the Poet who enters the desert seeking a panacea for the ills of society. It is radical and freighted with criticism of capitalism. The work consists of a series of Psalm-like segments (55 in all) of varying length, with freedom as the theme.

Poet in the Desert is as expressive of the poet's love for southeastern Oregon as of its author's anarchistic creed. Max Eastman said the poem contained too much propaganda and not enough poetry; Emma Goldman insisted that it was the other way around. Anthologists have invariably selected the stanzas describing and celebrating the desert rather than those bearing the anarchistic message. Wood's understanding of and affection for what he called the "lean and stricken land" comes through clearly in passages such as the following:

> Behold the signs of the Desert:
> A buzzard afloat on airy seas,
> Alone between two infinities,
> As I am alone between two infinities;
> A juniper tree on a rocky hillside,
> Dark signal calling from afar off,
> That the weary may rest in shade;
>
>   *   *   *   *   *
>
> A basaltic cliff, embroidered with lichens,
> Illumined by the sun, orange and yellow,
> The work of a great painter,
> Careless in the splash of his brush.
>
>   *   *   *   *   *
>
> Behold the signs of the Desert:
> The stagnant water-hole, trampled with hoofs;
> About it shine the white bones of those
> Who came too late.
> A whirling dust-pillar, waltz of Wind and Earth;
> Glistening black walls of obsidian
> Where the wild tribes fashioned their arrowheads.
> The ground with fragments is strewn,
> Just as they dropped them,
> The strokes of the makers undimmed
> Through the dumb and desperate years;
> But the hunters have gone forever.
>
>   *   *   *   *   *
>
> The prowler of the night,
> The lean coyote,
> Slips to his rocky fastnesses,
> And noiselessly, through the gray sage,
> Jack-rabbits shuttle.

Now, from the castellated cliffs,
Rock-ravens launch their proud black sails.
Orioles begin to twitter.
A red-bird, dipped in sunrise,
Cracks from a poplar top
His exultant whip above a silver world.[11]

In *Poet in the Desert,* Wood's performance is uneven. There are melodramatic vignettes of sweatshop and mine. There are passages of calm beauty cleanly wrought. There is an ostentations hymn to bastardy. There are tributes to nature rich in imagery and restrained in statement. One reviewer described the work as a series of alternate "rhapsodies and recriminations."[12] *Poet in the Desert* appeared first in 1915. Three more editions followed. In the poem's various versions, the continuous struggle within Wood between poet and propagandist is evident. However, there is consensus that Wood is most effective when dealing with the desert landscape that he loved.

Aside from *Poet in the Desert* Wood wrote dozens of independent verses, most of them on western themes. The best of these is "First Snow":

The cows are bawling in the mountains.
The snowflakes fall.
They are leaving the pools and pebbled fountains.
Troubled, they bawl.
They are winding down the mountain's shoulders
Through the open pines,
The wild-rose thickets, and the granite boulders
In broken lines.
Each calf trots close beside its mother
And so they go,
Bawling and calling to one another
About the snow.[13]

"First Snow" was the lead poem in a slender volume called *Poems from the Ranges* (1927). One other piece from that collection— "The Cattle Camp—Night—" is worth quoting here:

Bring sagebrush—bitter smelling sagebrush,
Bitter and spicy sweet:
Desert weed to desert fire,

Flame tongues twisting high and higher,
While softly the horses' feet
Pound and crush the desert dust.
Down from the upper dark a nightjar's cry
Drops like a plummet; the wall of lava rock
Towers like a fortress frowning on the sky.
One by one the cattle fold their knees.
A wakeful cow grumbles deep and low,
Age-old jungle sound of age-old woe.
Night lets fall her veil of mysteries.
Tinkle of spurs—the night guard.
Arcturus, great bear warden, torchlike, sweeps
Upon his watch; the lake is myriad-starred.
The cow camp sleeps.
A cuckoo-owl sobs sadly and is still.
Beyond the outer ramparts of the dark,
Unhappy, pained, and shrill,
Coyotes bark.[14]

Although he was a transplant from the East and South and despite the fact that he deserted Oregon for California in his early 60s, the thirty-some years he spent in Oregon constitute C.E.S. Wood's most creative period. At the same time he was writing poetry, Wood tried his hand at satire. He contributed a number of dialogues to *The Masses,* a radical but refreshingly nondoctrinaire New York magazine edited by Max Eastman and John Reed. The conversations are set in heaven and they involve God (Wood's alter ego), St. Peter, Rabelais, the Devil, Teddy Roosevelt, Margaret Sanger, and other historical and contemporary characters. The dialogues revolve around issues such as censorship, militarism, pacifism, birth control, and companionate marriage. Wood pokes fun at prudes, superpatriots, and bigots. The pieces were collected, added to, and published in 1927 by Vanguard Press under the title *Heavenly Discourse.*

Heavenly Discourse was by far Wood's most popular work, yet throughout his long career he thought of himself as first of all a poet. And it is as poet that Wood emerges as a regional writer of some skill and significance. Through *Poet in the Desert* and his western verse, C.E.S. Wood brings a remote southeastern corner of the Pacific Northwest into clear and compelling focus.

H. L. Davis

The first native Northwesterner to achieve genuine literary stature was H. L. Davis. Although ultimately he left the Northwest for the Southwest, Davis had the look and feel of the land and people of his youth fixed fast in his mind and heart and he drew on this knowledge over the years with consummate skill to produce a number of novels, short stories, poems, and essays.

Harold Lenoir Davis was born in Yoncalla, Oregon in 1896. Beyond rather casual training in the public schools of rural Oregon, he was self-educated. He went to work when he was nine, setting type on a country newspaper. That was followed by hit-and-miss work in a variety of jobs—cowboy, sheep herder, hop picker, surveyor, editor, and deputy sheriff.

Davis grew up fast through his association with this backwash of second-generation Oregon homesteaders and herders. His rural rambling kept him in intimate contact with the contours, the climate, and the plants and wildlife of the land, not to mention the variety of human beings he met along the way. He soaked up his varied experiences and impressions and began setting them down on paper, first in poetry and then in short stories and sketches. He found outlets for his early work in Harriett Monroe's *Poetry,* Harold G. Merriam's *Frontier,* and H. L. Mencken's *American Mercury.* Unlike Adams or Wood, Davis turned writing into a career. He wrote almost exclusively about the Pacific Northwest, interpreting the region both as he knew it firsthand and historically, as it developed through the impact of successive overland migrations.[15]

It is appropriate to begin with Davis's poetry, for although his verse is little known today, Davis, like Wood, thought of himself first of all as a poet. In one way the two are alike. Each has a sharp eye for the environment and can describe a scene or setting in rich and telling detail. But Wood worked from setting to ideology and argument, while Davis fused description with human experience, as in his poem "The Threshing-Floor":

> See, in a dead vine,
> How many blackbirds are swinging—the lives there
> In vines and in dead leaves that need no help of you.

Rein your horse into the salal, young man, follow down
The clearest ground, this frosty day, to the threshing-floor.
Red is women close together in the broken weeds,
Watching the horses: red dresses and blue,
Thin cloth of early-day dresses spread among the burrs.

Yellow is where the threshing-floor is, and horses' hoofs
Beat the grain-heads into chaff; and cold wind
Strews chaff over the bushes and to the eyes.

Women call to the horse-driver, and laugh out
At the man behind the horses who catches the horse-droppings
With his hands to keep the grain clean.
                                    And, crippled old man,
You shake in this cold wind, yet have come out-of-doors
To see your grain threshed again: under the sky, clearer
Than a beach, you standing skaking, and face the chaff with
        red eyes.

I fork a horse on the hill above the threshing-floor.
Driver and bundle-handlers, the ones in red dresses,
I must lose none of this; because men I have known
Are less simple, or are secret as birds in vines.[16]

Closer in content to Wood's western verse is Davis's "Proud Riders"
which gives the title to a collection of Davis's poems. But again,
Davis goes beyond description to provide a human dimension that
Wood's poetry seldom achieves:

We rode hard, and brought the cattle from brushy springs,
From heavy dying thickets, leaves wet as snow;
From high places, white-grasses and dry in the wind;
Draws where the quaken-asps were yellow and white,
And the leaves spun and spun like money spinning.
We poured them on to the trail, and rode for town.

Men in the fields leaned forward in the wind,
Stood in the stubble and watched the cattle passing.
The wind bowed all, the stubble shook like a shirt.
We threw the reins by the yellow and black fields, and rode,
And came, riding together, into the town
Which is by the gray bridge, where the alders are.
The white-barked alder trees dropping big leaves
Yellow and black, into the cold black water.
Children, little cold boys, watched after us—

The freezing wind flapped their clothes like windmill paddles.
Down the flat frosty road we crowded the herd:
High stepped the horses for us, proud riders in autumn.[17]

These two poems and others such as "The Rain Crow" and "A Hill Come Out of the Sea," suggest a rebellion brewing in Davis, not so much against C.E.S. Wood but against the sentimental, pretty, contrived writing that was all too typical of the Pacific Northwest in the late 19th and early 20th century. In fact, in 1927 H. L. Davis and James Stevens issued a malicious manifesto entitled *Status Rerum* that deplored the low and artificial standards set by Northwest writers of their day. Davis and Stevens complained that most writers in the region (and the pamphlet named names) did not understand their native grounds either environmentally or historically. The result, they asserted, was alien, rootless, imitative work that neither realized the region in its own terms nor connected it with the human condition.[18]

H. L. Davis spent the rest of his life producing work, most of it in prose, that is legitimately and unmistakably Northwestern in setting and tone but that deserves consideration within the mainstream of serious American literature. In 1929 in a sketch called "Back to the Land—Oregon, 1907," Davis rehearses one of the lines he pursues later in *Honey in the Horn.* The sketch deals with the dismal course of the 1907 homestead rush into eastern Oregon. A passage at the close of the story exemplifies what Mark Twain once called "the curse of the land":

> But the feeling that I had the oftenest, and the most clearly, when we rode in to make a night-camp in one of the old houses, among the ruins of work wasted, was one of abashment and shame. It was as if we were prying upon somebody's hurried, childish extravagances which were none of our business, and ought, out of decency to be left secret. The people who built them had no need to be reminded of their mistakes, being either dead or too old to profit by them. And the newcomers had mistakes enough of their own, including the one they had made in coming there at all.[19]

H. L. Davis is best known for his picaresque novel *Honey in the Horn,* which claimed both the Harper and the Pulitzer prizes. In this, his first novel, Davis reacts against the lethal hallelujahs raised up to the Oregon pioneers, producing a ranging, sardonic commentary on some of their sons and daughters who drifted across the Oregon Country in a turbid backwash that parodies the westward crossing in the middle of the 19th century. The corrective Davis applies is overly rigorous, but on the whole it is healthy. Critics divide on the novel's merit. Indeed, there are those who deny it is a novel at all. Clay and Luce, the teenage nonhero and nonheroine, are not fully realized and their relationship seems artistically unfinished. The figures they meet on their travels are often one-dimensional types rather than human beings. Hyperbole and the tall tale permeate the novel and press hard at times on the reader's credulity. The humor is raucous, indelicate, and drawn-out, quite in contrast to the brevity, subtlety, and general propriety of the wit that Randall Mills insists appealed most to the proper Oregonians. However, Davis was dealing with the back-country settlers and the itinerant workers who passed among them—the hop harvesters, horse traders, and wagon tramps—early in the 20th century. Outside the cities, in southern Oregon valleys, coastal hamlets, or isolated little communities east of the Cascades, the tone of the Pacific Northwest was likely to be border or southern rural, with speech patterns and broad tastes in humor that reflected their close-to-the-soil origins.

Honey in the Horn follows the essentially aimless wanderings of Clay, a young fugitive from the law, and Luce, daughter of a traveling horse trader. The two join a group of cattle raisers in the Coast Range who decide to flee the rain and migrate with stock and wagons to eastern Oregon, where pastures are dryer if not greener. This permits Davis to treat ironically an eastward trek of nondescript settlers. He comments savagely on the rapacity and mendacity of small-time promoters hoping to fatten when the railroads come to the physically and culturally barren land of the Columbia plateau. About the only concession to the typical "western" in *Honey in the Horn* is a lynching episode, which results in the hanging of an innocent man, or more accurately, a man innocent of the crime charged against him. There is little in the novel to encourage a 20th century "Great Migration" to the Pacific Northwest.

Davis is a sure craftsman deeply concerned with precision, with the exact phrase to trace the path of wind through the tall grass or the adroit summation of character in a sentence like: "She knew how to look a man up and down as if she were taking stock of all his capabilities and concealing her admiration for them."[20]

In *Honey in the Horn,* Davis introduces a broad national audience to the Oregon Country—its coast, its valleys, and its high desert. He rudely shatters the pattern of the traditional western, substituting a rambling plot, unconventional and sometimes grotesque characters, and an appropriately ambiguous ending. Davis stretches his readers' frame of reference to take them past the particularities of western materials to an understanding of universal meanings.

After *Honey in the Horn,* Davis wrote four more novels and published two collections of short stories, but this is not the place to examine the complete Davis canon. The essential point is that in H. L. Davis the Pacific Northwest found a shrewd, skillful, sensitive interpreter. He wrote pungently and convincingly (and on the whole, honestly) of a region that kindled and sustained his creativity through a long and distinguished career.

Richard Hugo

Despite the work of C.E.S. Wood and, to a greater extent, H. L. Davis, most Pacific Northwest poets before World War II neither understood nor credibly reflected their natural surroundings. Indians rode "sable-maned coursers," and "limpid" rivers with "roseate ripples" hurried "to be buried in the bitter moon-mad sea."[21] The artificial, consciously classical, effete style that pained and infuriated Davis and James Stevens long marred Northwest poetry, especially when the Native American served as subject. For example, in "The Last Taschastas," Joaquin Miller, an Oregon poet before he left the Cascades for the Sierras, shapes his Indian hero in the image of Longfellow's Hiawatha:

> In belt of wampum, in battle fashion
> An Indian watches with wild desire.
> He is red with paint, he is black with passion;
> And grand as a god in his savage ire,
> He leans and listens till stars are a-fire.[22]

Richard Hugo's poetry is probably closer to the region than that of any other Pacific Northwest poet. His poem "Tahola" will suggest how far the present generation of Pacific Northwest poets have come in the treatment of regional themes:

Where sea breaks inland, claiming the Quinalt
In a half saltwater lake, canoes turn gray
Waiting for the runs. The store makes money
But the two cafes, not open, rot in spray.
Baskets you can buy are rumored Cherokee.
When kings run wild, girls use salmon oil
To stain a doll's face real. The best house
Was never envied for its tile. Cars
And philosophic eyes are coated by the sea.

Whites pay well to motor up the river,
Harvest blackmouth, humpbacks, silvers,
Jacks and sea run cuts. Where rain assaults
The virgin timber and the fishpools boil,
The whites pry stories from the guide
With bourbon. Sunset, and they putt downriver
Singing. But the wind, the sea
Make all music language, dead as a wet drum.

When whites drive off and the money's gone
A hundred mongrels bark. Indians
Should mend the tribal nets in moonlight,
Not drink more and hum a white man's tune
They heard upstream. What about the words?
Something about war, translated by the sea
And wind into a song a doll sang
Long ago, riding a crude wave in.[23]

Like Davis, Richard Hugo is a native Northwesterner. He was born in Seattle in 1923 and never left the state of Washington until he was 19. Hugo grew up in a permissive but starkly reticent household. Left with grandparents when he was two and they were past 50, he wandered at will through the long days of childhood. His grandparents demanded no chores, and meals were often eaten in unbroken silence. From the age of nine he began to write. With woods and water on every hand, he soaked in the juices and textures of his environment. He fished for shiners or bullheads in the Duwamish slough. Directions took on special meanings. From the roof of his house, Hugo looked west to the hills of affluent Seattleites and beyond to the massive sweep of the Olympics. The dusky green foothills of the Cascades rose to the east, and beyond them, in his mind's eye lay the Atlantic seaboard. East meant knowledge, wisdom, culture. But north was the direction that fascinated and compelled the poet. Time and again it crops up in his work:

> . . . .   The river
> when the backed-up tide lets go
> flows the only north the birds believe.
> North is easy. North is never love.[24]

Despite the natural beauty around him and the freedom to savor it, much of Hugo's boyhood was marked by loneliness, rejection, and violence. Living near the river in the flatlands, Hugo felt awkward and inferior in the shadow of the well-dressed, confident boys and girls of West Hill. West Seattle he remembers:

> . . . was not a district it was an ideal. It towered
> over the sources of felt debasement; the filthy, loud
> belching steel mill, the only slow river, the immigrants
> hanging on to their odd ways, Indians drunk in the
> unswept taverns, the commercial fishermen, tugboat
> workers and mill workers with their coarse manners.[25]

Twice Hugo lived briefly with friendly West Hill families, but he failed to fit in and came back to his grandparents, who received him without a word. Escape of a sort came with the onset of World War II. In November of 1942, Richard Hugo, at 19, volunteered for the Army Air Forces. He won his wings as a bombardier and was sent to Italy. He flew 35 combat missions, one of which counted 30 percent casualties. He was lucky to come home alive. The war experience taught him to live with others, but it seared his psyche so that if he went to bed sober, he suffered from wrenching anxiety dreams. Moreover, one vital corner of innocence remained. He returned, in his words, "A man in all ways except the important one."[26]

After the war Hugo moved back with his grandparents, but he enrolled in the University of Washington on the G. I. Bill, majoring in creative writing. In the academic year 1947-1948, Hugo studied with Theodore Roethke, recently arrived from the Midwest. On the way to the university on a street car while thinking about Roethke, Hugo had a conversion experience. It came to him with quiet certitude that he would be writing poems all his life. He became a Roethke disciple.

Writing was a struggle, but one poem, "Duwamish," came easily and pointed to the river's power to trigger the poet's imagination:

> This river colors day. On bright days
> here, the sun is always setting or obscured
> by one cloud. Or the shade extended
> to the far bank just before you came.
> And what should flare, the Chinese red
> of a searun's fin, the futile roses,
> unkept cherry trees in spring, is muted.
> For the river, there is late November
> only, and the color of a slow winter.[27]

A book and several poems later, in "Duwamish Head," Hugo pays explicit homage to the river as creative source:

> My vision started at this river mouth,
> on a slack tide, trying to catch bullheads
> in a hopeless mud. The pier was caving
> from the weight of gulls. Wail of tug
> and trawl, a town not growing up
> across the bay, rotten pay for kings—
> these went by me like the secret dawns
> the sea brought in. I saw the seaperch
> turn and briefly flare around a pile
> and disappear. I heard bent men
> beg a sole to look less like a stone.[28]

Richard Hugo's first two collections of poems, *Run of Jacks* (1961) and *The Death of the Kapowsin Tavern* (1965), attest to his reliance on the Pacific Northwest as the wellspring of his work. He continually evokes images of sea and salmon, gull and crane, decaying tavern and defeated Indian. Hugo's is not the essentially benign and nostalgic vision of Wood. He is closer to Davis, but Hugo's writing is more personal, more painful, more anxiety-ridden. He distills poetry out of pollution, alienation, and torment:

This river helped me play an easy role—
To be alone, to drink, to fail.[29]

*   *   *

Jacks don't run. Mills go on polluting
and the river hot with sewage steams.[30]

*   *   *

When the world hurts, I come back alone
along the river, certain the salt
of vague eyes makes me ready for the sea.
And the river says: you're not unique—
learn now there is one direction only—
north, and, though terror to believe,
quickly found by river and never love.[31]

Despite Hugo's rising national visibility, he remains, to a substantial degree, a poet of place—whether it be Seattle, Italy, or western Montana. But Hugo uses locale or environment to release anxieties and emotions that lie deep within, and, through poetry, he gives them meanings that go far beyond the frightened and lonely self.

Paint it grand with mountains, but the scrub
some gypo left, the one-o-one in ruts
from constant rain, shabby meadows
elks create, fog that fakes the ocean's
outer rim will smear your canvas, turn
your art as savage as the Indian
who bums you for a muscatel in Forks.

What is harsh is the bone-infecting,
sound-deranging, forest-brooding damp;
moss that hangs on maples like disease.[32]

*   *   *

The solitude I felt in my youth later became
license to write a poem . . . .
I suppose our landscapes choose us and writing
a poem is a momentary burst of self-acceptance in
alien country. If mine chose me, they don't let
go easily.
Re-reading those early poems, and remembering
how I once was, I can see that along the river
my defeats and fears turned into raw ore, my
loneliness became a dramatic toy, the desolation

I felt make me a citizen of that ignored and
unique world. Even one with the fish in the
brackish water backed up on the in-tide from a
bay to the north that, on our clear bright days,
glittered blue and clean.[34]

Conclusion

It is neither prudent nor possible to argue that the Pacific
Northwest *determined* the work of Adams, Wood, Davis, and
Hugo; nor is there any really persuasive evidence that the region
has generated a "school" of writers. It does seem that these four
were aware, each in his distinctive way, of their surroundings as
something more than backdrop. In practicing their craft, Adams,
Wood, Davis, and Hugo took advantage of their environment.
They drew nourishment and perhaps inspiration from their surroundings. Out of the ways each experienced and understood the
world around him, each was able to draw substance for creative
work. And Davis and Hugo were able to sound universal themes
within a milieu that is limited and particular.

This is not to suggest that every writer in the Pacific Northwest
either strives for or attains identity with the region. When all is said,
place is a realm of the mind and heart, and the immediate locale
may or may not be relevant to the writer's purpose. For William L.
Adams, C.E.S. Wood, H. L. Davis, and Richard Hugo, it was.

NOTES

[1] For the *Atlantic Monthly* and "Life on the Mississippi" episode see Henry Nash Smith, *Mark Twain: the Development of a Writer* (Cambridge: Harvard University Press, 1962), 72.

[2] William L. Adams, *A Melodrame Entitled "Treason, Stratagems, and Spoils,"* ed. George N. Belknap (Hamden: Archon Books, 1968). Biographical information on Adams is drawn from Belknap's introduction.

[3] *Ibid.,* 1.

[4] *Ibid.,* 59.

[5] *Ibid.*

[6] *Ibid.,* 102.

[7] *Ibid.,* 95-96.

[8] *Ibid.,* 15.

[9] *Ibid.,* 146.

[10] Biographical details on C.E.S. Wood may be found in Edwin R. Bingham, "Charles Erskine Scott Wood: An Era and a Realm," *Northwest Review,* I (Summer, 1958)

[11] Charles Erskine Scott Wood, *The Poet in the Desert* (Portland: F. W. Baltes, 1918), 4-5, 30-31.

[12] Gustave Davidson, review, *Saturday Review of Literature,* XXXII (4 June 1949): 18.

[13] Sara Bard Field, ed., *Collected Works of Charles Erskine Scott Wood* (New York: Vanguard, 1949), 3.

[14] *Ibid.,* 8.

[15] Biographical data on H. L. Davis rest largely on an essay by George Armstrong in Edwin R. Bingham and Glen A. Love, *Northwest Perspectives: Essays on Literature and Culture* (Eugene: University of Oregon, and Seattle: University of Washington Press, 1979), 168-85.

[16] H. L. Davis, *Proud Riders and Other Poems* (New York: Harper & Brothers, 1942), 21.

[17] *Ibid.,* 63.

[18] H. L. Davis and James Stevens, *Status Rerum: A Manifesto upon the Present Condition of Northwestern Literature Containing Several Near-Libelous Utterances upon Persons in the Public Eye* (The Dalles, Oregon: privately printed, 1927)

[19] H. L. Davis, *Team Bells Woke Me and Other Stories* (New York: William Morrow, 1953), 171-72.

[20] H. L. Davis, *Honey in the Horn* (New York: Harper & Brothers, 1935), 116.

[21] Sam Simpson, "Beautiful Willamette," in W. T. Burney, ed., *The Gold-Gated West: Songs and Poems by Samuel L. Simpson* (Philadelphia: Lippincott, 1911), 19.

[22] Joaquin Miller, "The Last Taschastas," in *Songs of the Sierras,* Joaquin Miller's Poems, vol. II (San Francisco: Whitaker & Ray, 1909), 109.

[23] Richard Hugo, "Tahola," in *Five Poets of the Pacific Northwest,* ed. Robin Skelton (Seattle: University of Washington Press, 1964), 30; Richard Hugo, "The Real West Marginal Way," in *American Poets in 1976,* ed. William Heyen (Indianapolis: Bobbs-Merill, 1976), 107.

[24] Richard Hugo, "Duwamish No. 2," in *The Slackwater Review* (Special Issue, 1978): 97.

[25] Richard Hugo, "The Real West Marginal Way," 114.

[26] *Ibid.,* 120.

[27] Hugo, in *The Slackwater Review,* 85.

[28] *Ibid.,* 102.

[29] *Ibid.,* 104.

[30] *Ibid.,* 103.

[31] *Ibid.,* 97.

[32] *Ibid.,* 74.

[33] Hugo, "Real West Marginal Way," 125-26.

"New Era": Growing Up East of the Cascades 1937-1950

Jarold Ramsey

East of the Cascades and many long years ago (at the rate the world is changing now), before we had enough water for shade trees and electricity for yard-lights, I could look out of our upstairs bedroom windows at night and count on two hands the other dry-land families who lived on Agency Plains with us. Friendly yellow lights, Aladdins and Colemans like ours, beaconing through the living-room windows of the Evicks, the Greens, the Linkses, the Luellings, Joe Burns, the other Ramseys; and if I looked out after 10 o'clock, no house lights were visible under the starry sky. I sometimes wondered, leaning out of bed to peer into that darkness, when did the Indians go to bed, when they lived around here?

In the daylight, I was always impressed by the fact that Agency Plains is a kind of mesa, maybe 12 miles long and wide, a flat little world ringed with basalt cliffs and cut off from the general lay of the land on all sides: by the deep canyon of the Deschutes River on the west and north sides, by the dry valley of Paxton and Gateway to the east, and by Willow Creek and the town of Madras on the south. "Agency," because the western rims overlook the Warm Springs Indian Agency across the river, where bands of Wascos, Wishrams, Teninos, and Paiutes were settled by the Indian Treaty of 1855.

When my grandparents and their kinfolks arrived from Missouri in 1900 to take up their homestead claims on those rims, a Wasco leader named Jim Jackson crossed the river and climbed up to see what kind of people they were, these newcomers. He returned and reported to his sons, including Charlie (who told me the story as an old man a few years ago), that they seemed to be decent folks, but didn't know much of anything about the country and would probably need a lot of help. So Jim Jackson became a regular visitor and field hand, and his son Charlie and my Uncle Stub grew up as agemates and pals, and one of Charlie's sons, Zane, and my cousin Leslie were buddies in school, and another of Charlie's boys, Vern, and I were friendly in college together. When Vern graduated (the first of his people to do so), he returned to Warm Springs and began to make news as a farsighted, development-minded Tribal Secretary.

In the local newspaper, *The Madras Pioneer,* our community was celebrated weekly in a column titled "Agency Plains-Mud Springs Items," as reported by a refined old lady who was paid for her newsgathering by the inch. Her coverage was wonderfully thorough, right down to the births of puppies and the deaths of old dogs, letters from distant relatives and former neighbors, and weekly trips to town ("So-and-so motored to town on business last Friday"). Every week the reporter would call my mother to ask for news, and if there wasn't anything to report from our household, she would invariably ask about the "doings" of other families on the Plains. My mother would always decline this invitation to serve as "an unnamed but reputable source"—her restraint disappointed not only the columnist but my older brother and me.

As a matter of fact, gossip ran in a much swifter and freer channel than the newspaper, anyway. All the families on the Plains subscribed to a party-line telephone service, with hand-cranked battery-powered telephones, and wire that ran, variously, on poles, fence-posts, rooftops, abandoned farm machinery, and, inevitably, the ground. Each family had its own signal, generated by short and long turns of the crank. Ours was a *long* and a *short.* When someone called a number, *everybody's* phone rang, and we assumed that any conversation would begin with at least two or three silent listeners. This deplorable but universal practice was known as "rubbering." Some families seemed to be the subject of rubbering more than others; that was the price they had to pay, we reckoned, for living more colorful and conspicuous lives. The current drain in

really extreme cases of eavesdropping could render the conversation virtually inaudible for all parties, a clear case of sin betraying
itself.

A dedicated rubberer could even determine the identity of the
caller by the distinctive way he or she rang numbers. And of course
any call that went through "Central" in Madras was *ipso facto*
worth checking out, because it might be an emergency, or even
Long Distance. There was a special General Emergency number—
five *longs,* I believe—which everybody was supposed to answer
(like the bell in a New England village or our nuclear-age "hot
lines"), but I don't recall that this extreme measure was ever used,
not even the day the Second World War ended. We were a
restrained community, and anyway, rubbering made it unnecessary.

When my brother grew old enough to call up girls, and be
called by them, the inherent tensions of such communications
were magnified by the likelihood that love's shy intimacies would
be shared by an invisible but appreciative audience. So he devised
the following deterrent. He rang a girl's number one night after
supper, and after all the intruding receivers had clicked on in his
ear, he suavely announced like Don Ameche, "Good evening, and
welcome to the Agency Plains Listening Club! We have an exciting
conversation for you tonight . . . ." Then he named in welcome
four or five of our most notorious rubberers. The effect, he later
reported, was like startled frogs jumping back into the pond—click
after embarrassed click until the line between him and his girl
friend was free and private.

Our house sat by its lonesome at the head of a dry canyon
leading west into the chasm of the Deschutes River; nowadays
Highway 26 from Portland bends due south in front of the place.
By local legend it was the site of an Indian camp; Indian friends of
my father's like Wesley Smith and Charlie Jackson said so. Whenever we plowed up the garden or the hayfields east and north of the
house, jasper and obsidian arrowheads or basalt grinding stones,
wonderfully smooth to the touch, would emerge. To this day I am
unable to walk across a plowed field or even a vacant lot without
looking for arrowheads—one of life's great innocent mindless
pleasures, as Thoreau knew. The best arrowpoint finder amongst

us was our one-eyed cousin Billy, who could virtually find points at will by a sixth sense he had. We all had boxes of artifacts, to be hauled out and shown to visitors from the city, and then put back. The real pleasure, as with so many things, was in the finding.

Our house was built in the first homestead years, around 1910 I believe. We were the third family (all intermarried) to move into it, in 1938, the year after I was born. Like most of the other houses on the Plains, it was tall, gaunt, and paintless. Seen from a distance by an outsider, it must have cried aloud for trees, and paint, and side-rooms to break up its stark lines, but such refinements were years to come. There were various outbuildings close by: a little wash-house, a garage, and a tin-roofed shop, which concealed a two-hole privy on its back side. My parents added a large chicken house, and we celebrated its fragrant newness in a world of weathered buildings by hosting a memorable dance in it. The next day we laid down straw and installed the chickens; there were no more dances after that.

North of the house, right on the edge of the canyon for drainage, were the barn, granaries, and a rickety corral. Generally we kept two cows, one to milk and one to freshen; in winter, when it was my turn, I milked by lantern light morning and night sitting on a T-shaped stool, feeling heroically abused. What a medley of smells—pure essence of cow, odors of fresh and sour milk, stink of bag balm, and redeeming it all, the mild summery scent of the hay in the mow, where no one had ever yet broken a neck jumping from the rafters.

It was much the same on every other farm thereabouts. Like most western farm communities, ours was almost tribally homogeneous; there was a Way, and we all lived it. For one thing, these families, now in their third generations, had arrived here at the same time, around 1901 (my father's next oldest sister, Leda, was the first white child born on the Plains, a major article of Ramsey pride). And many of them came from English/German farm communities in northern Missouri. But why in the world did they come?

A few years ago I visited that rich hill-and-river country around Moberly, Missouri, and went away more puzzled than ever about the motives of Grandpa Billy Ramsey and his fellow emigres.

There, the soil is black and apparently bottomless; here, it is gray, mineral, parched, and so thin over the rimrocks you'd have to anchor cornstalks with guy-wires—but we never tried to raise field-corn. Back there, the growing season is both long and intense, almost violent; out here, it is short and uncertain, with frost possible every month, withering winds likely every afternoon, and 15 inches of moisture in a good wet year. Grandpa Billy cut his first crop of seed wheat with a handscythe, and Grandma gathered it with a garden rake. What did they think about their great move, as they worked through that pitiful first harvest? Grandpa Billy was 51 years old; Grandma, his second wife, was in her thirties. Well, this was no paradise they'd come out to, and taking dominion over all that sagebrush, juniper, and rock under that immutable sky would be the work of generations. "So be it," I imagine my grandparents and their yeoman neighbors saying, Missouri-style. "If a man can't do a job in 10 years, why then let him take 30, and raise some sons and daughters to help."

Why did they come out to the Oregon desert? For people who seemed so dour and pragmatic to me as a child 40 years later, the probable answer is surprisingly romantic. Those Missouri farmers had been hearing for a decade that the great American frontier was closed—no more virgin land—and no doubt they shrugged the news off with apparent indifference, being already landed if not gentry. When word came back in 1900 that the frontier was reopening a crack, with lands in the central plateaus of Oregon open to quarter-section homestead claims, the unexpected chance to wester and pioneer must have been irrestible. They sold out and went, and learned a new life.

No doubt the late reports from the Promised Land were extravagant, after their kind. If this was one of the last regions in western America to be homesteaded, they found out *why* it was soon enough, in terms of soil and climate. But they had to come, I think. If I can only speculate as to why they came, I know in my heart why they stayed, through drought and homesickness and crop failures and the Great Depression. They stayed because the land—so bleak and austere that even the Indians had only lived there seasonally—claimed them body and soul.

The autumn before my father died, I took him and my mother and my own family on a little trip through Vermont and New Hampshire, as far as the White Mountains. Above the lovely old town of Plymouth, surveying the hills in their gold and scarlet and enduring green, and smelling the smoke of autumn in the air, he said, "Well, if I *couldn't* live in Central Oregon, I guess this wouldn't be bad." He was being polite, in his gruff way, to our New Hampshire host; but what he meant, having watched the setting sun back-tracking each night along the south slopes of Mt. Jefferson every October of his life, was that he knew something better for himself.

If I were a serious ethnographer, attempting a systematic description and analysis of our little culture, I would have to pause here and offer an account of the games, recreations, and social, fraternal, and religious organizations of Agency Plains. It would be a brief account. Churches we had none—the Methodists, Baptists, Free Methodists, Christians, and Episcopalians amongst us all met in Madras; if there were any Catholics, they kept a low profile amidst such a staunchly Protestant bunch. Lodges, also located in Madras, were important, dividing our families between the Masons and the Eastern Star on the one hand, and the Odd Fellows and the Rebekahs on the other. A few families figured in both fraternal sets, which shared a dusty second-story lodge hall in downtown Madras, catty-corner from the hotel.

Lodge initiations and dances were their preeminent social events of the year. I can still smell the dust raised on those interminable evenings, first by the new officers sashaying around the floor in close-order ceremonial drill (what my father liked to call "threading the needle"), and then by the whole assembly, even children, dancing the night away (even until midnight), perhaps to a hotlicks Indian combo from Warm Springs.

The one truly native Agency Plains social organization in my childhood was known as "The Neighborly Club." In theory it included every woman on the Plains; it met at a rotation of houses on the third Thursday of every month. In our bleak and isolated circumstances, its civilizing influence was considerable. It brought rank newcomers and young brides into the bosom of the female community; it fostered the higher forms of gossiping and the exchange of recipes. And it exposed us country kids to the theory and practice of birthday parties, festive programs, and genteel entertainments—as in the elaborate Halloween and Christmas programs the Club used to put on, to which even the menfolk were invited.

Once my mother and another lady presented a Halloween skit for the children, in which my mother was to be accosted by the lady, disguised as a witch. Just as the witch laid hands on her victim, my older brother, then about five, violently sprang to her rescue with hands, feet, and teeth, all the while yelling vile curses. Finally, he was subdued and carried, still howling, to a bedroom. The poor ruffled witch asked if anybody could tell her where such a nice little boy could have learned such bad language in our neighborhood. Meanwhile, banished to the bedroom, my brother was no doubt pondering the perils and paradoxes of aesthetic detachment.

By city or even small-town standards, our recreations and pastimes were few and far between. Here again, I suppose, we paid the cultural price of being a belated frontier community, cut off by one or more generations from the folkways of the "old country" in Missouri or even the Willamette Valley. We had no fiddlers, folk singers, designated storytellers, brass bands or social choirs; square dancing came on the scene much later, brought in by Idahoans. Our sports were noncompetitive and unsocial—fishing, hunting, looking for artifacts, sledding; I remember watching the Indians playing their intense and gregarious bone games at Warm Springs celebrations with real envy. For the women, flower gardening was *de rigeur;* men simply didn't have hobbies, apart from tinkering incessantly with their machines. Neither were we adventuresome readers, although most families subscribed to *Colliers, The Saturday Evening Post, The Readers Digest, The National Geographic,* and *The Oregon Farmer.* The most carefully read books were the Bible and the "Sears and Sawbuck" and "Monkey Wards" catalogs. On our battery radios, we favored gloomy old Gabriel Heatter for news, "The Jack Benny Show," and "Lum and Abner."

In place of formal pastimes and leisure pursuits, it seems to me, we preoccupied ourselves imaginatively with *character.* Character in the old sense of distinctive personality was our TV, our stage, our cinema and music hall, our literature. Out of the necessity of getting along with a fixed field of neighbors and relatives, rural communities like ours made a virtue, indeed a kind of art, of celebrating individual personality. I remember no conversations as animated and delicious as those in which some dour farmer's latest sayings and doings were reported and then interpreted in the light of earlier episodes. "Well, old Fritz has done it again," someone would offer. "What now?" "Well, he and the missus had the minister out for Sunday dinner, and when the minister said grace and asked for a special blessing on President Roosevelt, old Fritz, he pounds the table and says, 'By God, not in this house!' "

Rarely did such accounts aim at censure or take the form of malicious gossip. If fiction-making played a part in them (as it did), it was understood as part of an imaginative and dramatic process whereby we saw someone's character becoming more truly and distinctively itself, over time. It was a little like being in a repertory theater company. Everybody was a connoisseur and a prompter of everybody else's special parts and turns, and of course everybody was also a *player,* at least some of the time. A few were extroverted enough to play themselves to any gathering at the slightest cue, but even the shyest and most stolid could be roused into performance with a little adroit teasing: "Hey Fritz, I hear you're praying for Roosevelt these days . . . ." And the fulfillment of Republican Fritz as one of our dispensable character actors would advance a few more degrees, before our eyes.

Were these people really as colorful, as crotchety, as inexhaustibly interesting as they appeared to me as a child? Probably not, but they were all the human types we had; and what one of Dr. Johnson's friends said after his death, that no other man could ever remind him of the good Doctor, so unique was he, I would have to say about these characters out of my childhood. Perhaps that is just a facet of childhood, but the shared delight in personality that made them seem like *real characters* is lacking, at least in my experience, in big-city life. This is one of the prices we pay for our impersonalized and overpopulated urbanity, and it is a heavy one.

By the time the railroads came in 1910, life on the Plains had simplified and settled down to the mode into which I was born in

1937. Everybody had at least a half section of land; half of each farm was summer-fallowed each year, while the other half was cropped with hard winter wheat. In my time, the only strain of wheat was "Turkey Red," which was hardy enough for our climate, smut-resistant, and a good yielder. But my father and his friends never tired of exchanging horror stories about an earlier strain known as "Galgalis," which yielded bumper crops but produced a chaff so poisonously itchy that itinerant sack-sewers avoided fields of it like the plague, and hardy Missouri-bred farmers thought it no shame to come in and take baths at noon! True to form, the Ramseys were among the last to give it up . . . .

Farming then was not without its skills and tensions, but it was hardly agribusiness or the physically and economically frantic enterprise it became when irrigation arrived in the late 1940s. Horses, threshing machines, and wagons gave way to tractors, trucks, and combines in the 1920s, much to the relief of my father, who had wrangled, harnessed, and fed and watered enough horseflesh, he said, to operate the U.S. Cavalry for a month of Sundays. Nonetheless he sentimentally kept two old pensioners, Dix and Bess, for occasional haying and rock-hauling duties until they died of old age in my time.

What you did to be a wheat farmer was, first, in early spring, to look out your upstairs window for color in your fields, the most delicately beautiful green in the vegetable rainbow; it would appear overnight, in late March or early April. Then you prayed for spring rains which, if they came, also brought a fine crop of weeds on the summerfallow—Chinese lettuce, lamb's-quarters, mullein, several kinds of mustard, and the ubiquitous cheatgrass. So, not long after you finished plowing last year's stubble, you ventured out with a rod-weeder, which dragged an old spiketooth or springtooth harrow behind it to break up the clods if possible. Clods in bad years could become as big and dense as building blocks.

If I never have happier solitude than I've had in the seat of an old John Deere Model "G," weeding in late spring out on the rim, I'll not complain, dear Lord—the hypnotically regular twin-cylinder detonations of the tractor, to which songs could be shouted or even poems hollered with pleasing effect; the clear light, as yet without summer glare and dazzle; winter snow on the mountains still, but green on the foothills; the sense of power awakening in the earth and in me, rolling over it in third or fourth gear, the buried rod of the weeder roiling the moist soil and pulling up weeds as deftly as a florist's hand, while we charged around the field of last year's harvest, spiralling inward clockwise until at last, on the fourth day, we reached the invisible mysterious center of the land and finished. Then we would do it all over again, perhaps with a springtooth weeder, in a month or so. But I digress.

Through June and July, as the crop grew, headed, and began to "turn", there wasn't much to do with it, except for after-dinner excursions into the fields to see how the wheat was "stooling." As many as 20 or more stalks could "stool" out from one planted kernel, and this was the real basis of bumper crops. And in the horizontal light before sunset, we would "rogue" the tall rye-grass that always sprouted in the crop and could take over a field in a few years if not attended to.

By the end of July, when afternoon temperatures rose to 90 and big thunderheads began to float like ghost ships out of the southwest, you got ready for the one critical episode of the year, the Main Event—harvest. The big ungainly grasshopper-like combines—John Deeres, Internationals, Holts, and Olivers—were pulled out of their sheds, reassembled and groomed; harvest help was signed up off the street, or in the tavern, or sometimes out of the hobo jungles. For once in the simple year, with everything riding on the harvesting of one crop, life became urgent, agitated, combat-like, heroic. People yelled at each other; mistakes were dealt with summarily and without quarter. Life revolved around the pulsing, roaring, inhumanly dusty combines—factories on wheels—and around the hard coppery grain that somehow gushed out of their innards. The big Bemis and Chase wheat sacks, like cartoon money-bags, were jigged full, artfully sewn up from ear to ear by the sack-sewer, ignominiously dumped in bunches of seven or eight, and trucked off to the depot, day after day through August, field after field. My mother served up huge meals, noon and evening; sometimes, in the hottest weather, she angelically took out lemon-ade at midafternoon, when we were shut down for "greezin" or repairs.

This was the season when we *lived* one of my father's maxims: "Never get in the way of somebody at his work." This meant not talking silly on the job, or asking tomfool questions, or having to be told twice, or succumbing (as I often did) to a mysterious form of distraction known as lollygagging. In my father's world, the kind of person most likely to get in the way of one's work was a city-dweller, and I grew up believing that cities, even little burgs like Madras, were teeming with triflers and lollygaggers.

One afternoon, late in a difficult harvest, as we were just opening a field and therefore still close to the road, a man arrived in a shiny car. He got out, carrying a briefcase, and walked a few feet towards the lurching combine. He lifted his hand, a gesture half wave of greeting and half signal to stop. Oh-oh, I thought. My father nodded curtly from the tractor, and opened the throttle. Forty-five minutes later as we came round again, the man was still there, standing forlornly in the stubble now minus his briefcase. I was afraid that he might be foolish enough to try to stand his ground in front of the Caterpillar, but instead he scrambled in from the side. My father acknowledged his submission by slowing down slightly; as soon as the man was perched unsteadily on the drawbar behind the tractor seat, however, we resumed full speed ahead. It was an insurance salesman, and when he jumped off after a full round of shouting in my father's ear, his blue suit was golden with chaff. He didn't look back, poor man, probably not all the way over the mountains to Portland.

Breakdowns in harvest were inevitable given the pace, the rough ground, and the likelihood, in dry years of short stubble, of "harvesting" rocks. When they came, breakdowns dissipated some of the tensions in the field, for us kids at least, if not for our elders. On any afternoon, I could look from my perch on the "doghouse" of our combine and see which neighbors were broken down—no dust, a stopped combine, several pickups nosed in around it. You got so you could *hear* a breakdown about to occur; out of the normal roar and clatter, an odd syncopating thump or screech would appear. Then, generally before you could throw the main clutch out, it would grow into a terrible self-devouring clangor and the combine motor would stall. Silence, a whole field of it, broken only by my father's disgusted "*Shit!*" as he climbed off the tractor.

It could be a snapped draper belt or slat, or a broken elevator chain, or a bent sickle guide, or—worst of fates—a piece of rimrock through the cylinder, the whirling winnowing adjustable heart of the whole enterprise. *That* might take most of the day to uncover, and a day to repair, all in fiendishly awkward and knucklebusting confines in the bowels of the machine—if indeed the John Deere dealer had the parts you needed in stock, or could get them from The Dalles or Portland. Sometimes, carrying on a fine old American industrial tradition that must go back to Remington and Eli Whitney, the delivered parts wouldn't fit.

The most spectacular breakdowns I remember were a wheel breaking off our Oliver, pitching the whole machine over at a crazy angle, with me hanging on for dear life, and, another time, on my grandfather Mendenhall's antique wooden Holt "hillside" machine, the 20-foot counter-balanced wooden header boom snapping off, plunging the mighty header into the ground and catapulting me, the boy header-tender, ten feet in the air.

Finally unexpectedly to my hopeless young mind, we would be swathing down one final strip of wheat in the middle of the last field. Quite suddenly then, everything was stubble, and harvest was over. Time to cheer and toss our filthy straw hats into the header behind the last stalks of wheat. This ceremony my brother and I learned from an old sack-sewer; our father was never so demonstrative. He would already be calculating the yield, from the wheat haulers' tare-weight receipts at the depot. Twenty-five bushels per acre was a very good high average; and only once in what proved to be the last big year for dryland farming in our parts, 1948, did we hit 40 bushels. Ours were piker yields compared to what Umatilla and Palouse farmers got every year with far less trouble, but then they didn't have our scenery.

Harvest done, we turned to the next enterprise, hauling straw out of the now-cancelled fields. Two good compatible forkmen could pitch five acres of the big straw dumps an hour, as the truck started and stopped, crawling between the long rows of dumps, always on the downwind side, and the "tromper" up on the load reeled and staggered, trying to make each trip to the straw-stack "pay." At age nine I learned how to drive, after a fashion, pressed into service behind the wheel of an old Ford truck with a jack-rabbit clutch. First I threw the tromper, my brother, clear off the load with one of my wild starts; then in desperation I discovered that I could leave the truck in gear and secretly ride the clutch, then *ease* it out. In two hours, of course, I had developed a severe case of jitters and burnt the clutch out.

It may have been that same year, hauling straw one morning off a field south of our house, that Dad and one of our cousins killed seven sleeping rattlesnakes under seven consecutive dumps. After my brother had gamely tromped the straw into a load and they began to pitch it onto the stack, they discovered two more rattlers in the truck, by now no longer sleepy!

My father, never one to risk much time or money on the ingenious labor-saving devices that tempted other farmers, did install unloading derricks at our two main stackyards. The truck-loads were pitched on top of rope or cable nets, and then at the stackyards these nets, bulging with several tons of straw, were supposed to be drawn up out of the truck, positioned over the stack, and then dropped. This dramatic operation was performed by the man "building" the stack, who yanked on a trigger rope dangling beneath the load swaying over his head, and ran like hell as the straw tumbled down. Sometimes he didn't run fast enough, or stumbled, and we had to dig him out; sometimes he triggered the load prematurely, and it fell in the wrong place, or over the side. Occasionally the net rigging would foul or break, and the whole load would dangle in the air like a threat, or it would trip itself and fall back in the truck or onto the ground, to be pitched angrily and with twice the difficulty back onto the stack. My bachelor uncle Max, who was often a bemused participant in these labors, once tried to console my father after such a mishap: "Well, anyhow, Gus, it sure was spectacular!"

As I write this, I realize that one of the reasons I love William Faulkner is that, beyond any other writer, he knows and conveys the essential comic violence of farm life, as in that great Flem Snopes story "Spotted Horses." Faulkner helps me remember, from my farm-boy days, the wonderful violence of large animals, and of crude and unwieldy farm machines—and the often drastic behavior of men and women trying to manage either or both. My father was often an irascible and always an accident-prone man, who once broke his foot merely kicking the rump of a stubborn shoat pig. A degree of overt violence was universal in our lives, I think, beginning with the brutal extremes of the climate. But I remember it, despite the very real element of physical danger and fear, as often being very funny.

Rarely, thank God, did people go after each other physically, but language, generally flat and laconic amongst us, could rise to wonderful heights of magical abuse, and actions sometimes spoke more eloquently of exasperation than words. Once my father's dear cowboy friend Lloyd, a gentle and churchly man of Baptist persuasion, came upon me trying to get a balky pack mule to move. (We were on a pack-trip around Mt. Jefferson.) Its hooves were planted in the trail like plowshares. Lloyd, who was never heard to swear even mildly but who knew mules, tried a few whistles and chirps and Indian signals, tried his quirt, tried a pine-branch—and then removed a short length of chain from the mule's pack, and began to belabor the beast over the tail, all the while whistling "Onward Christian Soldiers" breathlessly, whanging out each triumphant note with the chain on the mule's rump. That mule marched all day like a good Christian.

But I was talking about straw-hauling after harvest. The great incentive to finish with the straw was that we could then take a vacation, generally a camping trip up in the Cascade forests, far from combines and chaff and straw piles. One afternoon in August 1945, as we were topping out one of the main stacks in front of our house, we heard the Warm Springs mill whistle hoot over and over again. Presently an endless line of cars appeared on the highway, heading for town, horns blaring. Somebody who knew us leaned out of his window and hollered, "THE WAR'S OVER—JAPS SURRENDERED—BIG SHINDIG IN TOWN TONIGHT!" We actually quit early, an unheard-of concession. I remember reflecting that if this had happened during harvest, we wouldn't have paid any attention, and a few days later, we'd have been up in the mountains. Excellent timing, General McArthur!

That night, we gathered in the Madras City Park to sing patriotic songs; the soldiers from the airbase had hoisted a piano onto a flatbed truck and then lifted up my mother to play it. Hoarded prewar booze was passed around, scandalously, in full view of the Methodist and Christian churches. Before the celebration divided between the sobersides and the revelers, talk ran through the crowd of the new-fangled bombs—just two of them— that had destroyed the two Japanese cities. Somebody joked about getting such a device war surplus to blow the rocks, once and for all, out of his west 40. But in church that Sunday, our stern preacher asked the question that still haunts our lives, mushroom-shaped. "The terrible war is over, thank God," she said, "But consider what new violence have we begun?"

But in that tumultuous year, as always, life did resume its simple rounds. After a week or so of camping, we came back home to perform the last laborious sacraments of dryland farming: burning what was left of the straw piles; carrying the burning straw in iron pitchforks from pile to pile until the whole field crackled and smothered in sweet white smoke; weeding and harrowing the fallow ground if need be; drilling next year's crop; and—a special local version of Farmer Adam's Curse—hauling rocks.

It is early November, the first snow is on the mountains, and I am too young yet to go to school. My dad has hitched old Dix and Bess to a stoneboat, and we have gone out to the rim to resume the farmer's perpetual war against the encroaching stony ballast of his land. Rocks of every size, shape, and color seemed to boil up each year out of some inexhaustible petrous nursery below to wear out plowshares, snag weeder-rods, and rattle through a combine's delicate innards like cannonballs. The south side of the field is bracketed with a double four-foot row of rocks, a monument to the fortitude (and hernias) of our predecessors. But for me it is a fine game to tramp afield with my dad, heft a good rock in each hand like a caveman, carry them back to the stoneboat, and lob them in, as he does.

Half an hour later, it is not so fine a game, and after an hour, I ask why we are doing this, anyway. He says, jesting, "Because the rocks don't look good in a field," and he invites me to build a little rock cairn so that we can see what ground we've covered. I am intrigued and set to work, as he goes on with the stoneboat. I learn much there about gravity, and balance, and the intransigence of irregular objects, and when he comes back, I have made us a man out of piled-up rocks, a man of many grating and unstable parts. My father admires him and then, before I can protest, dismantles him into the stoneboat. I squall, and he says, "Well, then, make another one, to mark this next row." And so I do, all day long across the field, making stone men to praise our work and assert our image.

These were, roughly speaking, the seasons of our farming work each year, until the coming of irrigation. They were what it was given us to do with our land, seemingly as fixed and irrevocable as the passage of winter into spring, and spring into summer and fall. Everything else—unseasonable weather, illness, injury, arrivals and departures, birth and death—seemed somehow incidental to the order of our accustomed work.

Soon after the end of the war, my father did impose another order upon the year, secondary to the farming and less complicated, but at times just as demanding. From his boyhood on, he'd wanted to be a stockman; no doubt this seemed to him like an appropriate second-generation fulfillment of the western dream that impelled his father to leave Missouri for Oregon in the first place. He'd kept good horses and a few Herefords for a number of years, affecting the style of a rancher more than most of his family and neighbors. But in 1945 he startled everybody by buying a rundown 1400-acre sheep ranch, a good hour's rough drive to the east, in the foothills of the Ochoco Mountains.

This place, which my mother named "The Sky Ranch" after the Sierra retreat of the Barber Family on radio, seemed to be in a different world than the "home place" on Agency Plains. It was high—over 4,000 feet, much of it—and hilly, sloping up to the east; the lower reaches were all juniper and sagebrush, giving way to pockets of Ponderosa pine and Douglas fir higher up. It had its own weather and was wet, at least by Agency Plains standards, with springs and creeks everywhere. It was remote and wild; deer and even elk grazed around the old farmhouse, coyotes skulked along the roads, and the fields, tiny and irregular by our standards, were already reverting to nature. It was and is a place of inexhaustible wonder.

The first year, we plowed the fields up—the soil black as coal—and planted a mixture of wheat and crested wheatgrass. The wheat was to serve as a harvestable covercrop for the grass, which would, once established, provide summer pasture for our future herd. It was an unusually rainy year. The wheat grew so tall that a grown man could walk into a field and disappear in green (small boys were afraid to), and some of it never did ripen. According to Dad's master plan, this was the only time we tried to crop it, but the wheatgrass established itself abundantly, and we were ready to go into the cow-and-calf business in earnest. Before very long we'd built up a herd of 75 to 80 Hereford cows—not registered breeding stock, but good solid animals.

The cowboy side of the year went something like this. In early spring, the cows would start calving in the feed lots in front of our house. Feeding them hay and straw morning and night, we kept an eye out for trouble, especially with the heifers. Sometimes we had to assist at breech births, and my mother thought nothing of boarding one or more half-frozen whiteface babies on the back porch, until they were able to stand up and nurse. Once we actually skinned a dead newborn calf and tied the hide on a poor little waif that had been abandoned by its mother. The bloody disguise kept sliding off, but it worked; within a day or two the waif and the bereaved cow were inseparably cow-and-calf. By the time the ground had thawed out and yellowbells were in bloom, the feed-lots would be alive with gangs of long-legged silly calves, all running and bucking in concert, tails in the air, as if possessed by the contrary winds of spring.

Good that they didn't know what was coming. Generally in May, when the winds had subsided and the ground was safely dry, we rounded them up for branding. Our brand, of which I was inordinately proud, was a very old design out of the High Desert— "Box-Dot" on the left rib, so: ⊡. If you hit just the right place on the calf's side, the brand would stretch equilaterally around the dot as the critter grew, until it looked at maturity like a square sign-board two feet across, with a cryptic dot in the center. We generally had outside help from Lloyd Luelling and others, at whose brandings we in turn would assist. The corral became a sort of gothic assembly line: somebody roping each calf, another catching its legs, a third tending the branding iron in the fire and giving vaccinations against blackleg and other dread diseases, a fourth, armed with a sharp knife, managing the earmarks (a notch over the left ear and one under the right) and castrating the poor bull calves.

The last operation always gave me the wim-wams, although in truth it seemed to hurt the young calves less than the earmarking and branding. Such an arbitrary meddling with destiny! We never dined on "Rocky Mountain oysters" in our household, but once on a neighbor's farm, I watched the mother and daughters gathering them out of the bloody dirt in dishpans with a peculiar glee that cost me my appetite that noon.

Then, in late spring, with the grass well-established at the Sky Ranch, came the move to summer pasture. Sometimes in company with neighbors and their herds, but more often alone, we simply rounded up the herd and started off cross country to the east. Like in the old days; like in the movies! Barring some serious misadventure, our drives took two nights and parts of three days. After a trip or two each way, the herd established its traveling leadership. Two or three older cows fought amongst themselves for pride of place, but together they led the whole dusty, bawling, unstable herd like prophets. The trouble generally came in the rear echelons. Calves stupidly would get inside fences, to straggle alongside the herd for miles; bulls would break out of the herd to fight other bulls at farms we were passing; on country roads, some impatient SOB out for a drive would try to force his car through the herd and spook it.

I remember three serious stampedes, each occurring on the drive home from the Sky Ranch in November, when dark skies and cold winds seemed to dispose the cows to spook easily. One ruckus came when we tried imprudently to force the herd right through the north end of Madras, and the lead cows balked at the freshly painted yellow lines on the streets, thinking them cattle-guards. Another happened as we trailed past an abandoned homestead, and an old windmill suddenly began to tear itself to pieces in the high winds. A third stampede—the worst—occurred when the first *Oregon Journal* helicopter discovered us and choppered right down to eyebrow level for some feature-page photography, scattering terrified cows and horses in every direction. It took hours to regroup after that one; my father muttered darkly about carrying a shotgun . . . .

The much more common problem was sheer dusty boredom and exasperation from trying to urge 200 lazy cows and skittish calves to walk 30 miles, browsing but not stopping, while staying out of wheat fields and going through the right gates. The first day out, we all had brave cries and catcalls to make them go; the next day, hoarse from yelling in the dust, I usually resorted to rattling a rock in a can or slapping my levis. The strain of maintaining and guiding brute inertia wore us down fast. I would dream of plodding hooves and dust and bellering for a week afterward, and I would be sore for days from unconsciously urging everything along from the saddle.

In truth, although my father became a successful stockman who knew his herd by heart and was always in control of it, and my older brother grew up as an expert horseman, I was no cowboy and I knew it. I was on reasonably good terms with our horses, but riding to me generally meant hard work and long hours, divided between boredom and fear. None of my best friends was a cowboy, either. I saw a horse slip and fall on my brother and break his leg as they were chasing a cow on a highway; I saw my father's tall horse step in a badger-hole at full gallop during a Sky Ranch roundup and cartwheel on and over him, breaking his leg in 13 places. I had my own share of minor horseback accidents and decided early on that for thrills, I'd stick to machines. On my 12th Christmas, in place of the young horse I should have wanted, my folks conceded and gave me a motor scooter.

The only times I truly relished my periodic service as reluctant cowpoke were when we were trailing the herd around Madras, or even through it. Then the boredoms and tensions of the job were offset by the prospect of being seen and wondered at by townspeople and friends, as we nudged the critters of the Box-Dot down side streets and across vacant lots. Then, full of the romance of it all, I sat very tall in the saddle. Once when I was about 13, I nearly ran down a man and his son on the sidewalk in front of the Post Office as my horse scrambled to bring a steer back into line. Far from being upset, the man told his little boy, "Look closely there, son, you're seeing a little bit of the real Old West!" And over my shoulder, insufferably, I said, "That's right, son."

As time went on, it grew more and more difficult to trail the herd to summer range and back. Around Madras suburbs sprang up on our routes, while out in the country irrigated farmers were tearing down the tight six-wire fences that the old ranchers had used, replacing them—if at all—with puny electric fences. We would soon start *trucking* the herd to and fro, a grueling two-day job that was much harder on men and cows than the drives. But there was one last memorable adventure before that part of our Old West faded away.

We were bringing home the cows; it was unseasonably hot for November. As we neared the eastern outskirts of Madras, my father cautioned us drovers about keeping the herd especially tight, because of the new houses and yards on our route. In particular, he said, watch out for open gates and doors! I was riding a rear point when suddenly I saw a heifer break off from the herd, followed by a couple of steers, heading for the open back-door of a new bungalow. I spurred to catch up and yelled, which only served to speed up the action. As if running on rails, the heifer galloped up to the door and through it, with the steers close behind.

Uncertain what to do now, I went around to the front door and waited discreetly. After what seemed like an eternity, I heard terrible noises from inside and then the heifer exploded through the screen door, something lacy caught on her horns, and skidded across the porch. She was closely followed, in eerie silence, by the lady of the house, with the steers right at her heels. The critters headed back towards the herd; I thought it impolitic to wait around for further developments, and got the hell out of there myself. I don't think my father ever knew what happened, but that was the last Box-Dot old-style wild West cattle-drive through town. I reckon there's an ordinance against such things now, in Madras.

And then, corresponding to the seasons of the year when we left our wheatfields to themselves, there was school. In my father's boyhood, with homesteads on every quarter-section, there were several one-room schools on and around the Plains. But by the time my brother and I started, there was just one, located opposite Hi Links's house on the north end, auspiciously known as "New Era School, No. 35." It was about three miles up the Market Road from our place; we were driven to it, or rode horseback, or bicycled.

The school sat back east of the road; it was a fine big squarish building, actually painted (white), with a portico on the southwest corner where the teacher stood and rang her handbell to call us in. Inside, there was a cloakroom leading through two doors to the big airy single classroom, with tall windows on the east and north sides and blackboards on the west. Behind a curtain in the southeast corner of the room was a cozy library with books to the ceiling—an irresistable place. The teacher's oak desk faced ours; we sat in four rows, very loosely ranked by age and size. I don't recall less than 12 pupils or more than 21; usually there was at least one from each grade, but little attention was paid to grade levels *per se.*

A huge old Waterbury stove sat in the back, with an iron shield and railing around it—good for drying mittens and caps in winter, and if you pressed crayons against the hot metal, they would bubble and run down in streaks of oil color. There was no electricity, no indoor plumbing, and no audiovisual aids, except for an old donated Victrola, on which we played huge Music Appreciation records featuring the Longines Symphonette, and sometimes, at noon, my brother's precious Harry James boogie-woogie records.

Here again I seem to have been bred more for the 19th century than for the 20th—but there are worse anachronisms, maybe. I know enough horror stories about one-room country schools to appreciate how lucky we were for teachers. My first (a pedagogical saint if there ever was one) was Mrs. Elva G. Hall, who as a young woman had taught my father at another school and later had taught college English. Now in her late 60s, widowed and unwell, Mrs. Hall was back where she began her career, in a one-room Central Oregon school, because the war had dispersed all the younger teachers.

Mrs. Hall lived in the little "teacherage" south of the school, and in my first year the school board built a wooden walk between the two buildings so that she could avoid the mud and snow. Alas, the boards iced over in January, and she fell and broke some ribs. My Aunt Lela came in as a substitute for a few weeks, putting my brother and me on the spot. We were also on the spot with my father's half-sister, Aunt Lily Watts, who was Jefferson County's first and only school superintendent; fortunately, she only visited school in the spring to administer the county achievement tests, and we tried to play like she wasn't kin.

We all mythify, I think, our first-grade teachers; no doubt it has something to do with the fact that they are the ones to unleash in us the awesome powers of written language and numbers. I thought that Mrs. Hall was in reality two witches; a good morning witch, clear-eyed, alert, and cheerful; and a bad afternoon witch, cranky, red-faced, wheezing, and much older. The pathetic fact was that she was suffering from hardening of the arteries and hypertension, which probably meant that after lunch and a nap, she felt miserable the rest of the afternoon. Soon after she retired and went to live with her son in Denver, she wrote to each of "her children" to tell us that she'd gone blind. Still she wrote us long wonderful letters, full of flattering questions about ourselves, her unguided script wavering bravely across the page. She was the first person I loved who died.

There was a certain imbalance in Mrs. Hall's teaching. She burned like a filament whenever we passed in our lessons through the realms of language, literature, history, and art; our forays into arithmetic and science were likely to be perfunctory, tentative, and brief. Or am I only remembering my own early affinities? Well, her school proved to be no nursery for mathematicians, or physicists, alas; I remain a booby at anything beyond simple-math. But often when I am working on a poem, or reading one, she is there somehow, in her good-witch guise, plump in one of her shapeless shiny brown dresses with a brooch at the neck, cheerfully urging me to claim yet more of the dictionary's gift of fine words.

When she had gone through the lessons our various grade levels demanded, she would read to us, at length and with great feeling. Never mind that her texts were of the order of *The Little Lame Prince* and *Toby Tyler;* or *Six Weeks with the Circus* and the poetry of Arthur Guiterman; never mind that an outsider might have found it strange that she often wept over such matter. Because we loved her, we wept too; it seemed the least we could do. Between our preacher's praying, my father's swearing, and Mrs. Hall's reading out loud with tears, language was strong stuff.

I used to ask cheekily whether the "new era" of our school had a name, and when it would grow into an old era. Mrs. Hall would smile indulgently and tell us that *we* were supposed to be the new era; I guess we believed her. But we were aware, too, that beyond the mountains over the ocean, men who'd once carved their initials on our desks were on jungly islands shooting and being shot at by the Japanese. We secretly hoped that before winning the war, the American forces would let themselves be pushed back as far as the Pacific states; we prepared ourselves accordingly.

By 1942 the Army airbase at the southern end of the Plains was in full operation; hotshot pilots were "wringing out" experimental fighter planes, and using our broken landscape, it was rumored, to train for secret missions overseas. B-17 bombers were always zooming out of our canyons at treetop height, pushing incredible waves of echoed sound before them. Once, two B-24 "Flying Fortresses" collided in formation over the Mutton Mountains north of the Plains and struggled right over our house, spewing flames and debris and parachutes. And one day after school, my dad and I watched a special clipped-wing Airacobra powerdive 30,000 feet into a plowed field just east of the school. The plane made a crater as deep and wide as a basement; the pilot, whose parachute didn't open, made his own crater a hundred yards away. We kids fancied that such important operations would surely draw the invaders our way; when a Japanese submarine shelled the Oregon coast in 1942, we assumed that the invasion of Agency Plains was imminent.

This collective fantasy, coupled with Mrs. Hall's utter indifference to formal recreation for her pupils, meant that we almost never played real games at noon or recess or before school, least of all games joining both sexes. No, we boys were digging in for battle! I think my brother Jimmie and his friend Gordon and some other kids started it in the summer of 1942. Beginning a half mile down the canyon below our house, they built a sequence of rimrock fortresses and lookout stations, in case the invading enemy came that way. It was agreed that we would make our last stand against General Tojo and his hordes, if it came to that, at New Era School.

That fall, what had begun as a little experimental foxhole in the soft dirt next to the road in front of school became a fine deep "pillbox" big enough to hold everybody, all the boys that is. With childish singleness of purpose, we soon roofed it, camouflaged the roof with sod, installed a periscope and a tin-can stove, brought in our toy guns and some foodstuffs, and became a military brotherhood—a guerilla band known as the "Red Moles." Gordon, who was artistic and clever, painted the flag. We had time, and mind, for nothing else.

The girls, feeling understandably jealous and neglected, mocked us and mounted one or two attacks, which were easily driven off with clods and verbal abuse. Poor things, they retreated to mope around the building and murmur threats about telling Mrs. Hall. For a week or two they tried to imitate our enterprise under a flag proclaiming themselves the "Red Ants," but without a fortress or hideout there was no romance in it; soon they returned to dolls and tag, and even took up our neglected game of snaring sagerats with string nooses.

Meanwhile, the grand excavations continued. The soil, unusually deep and loamy for the Plains, was irresistible for digging—dark, compact, lacking in rocks, and fragrant. First we tunnelled to the north about 20 feet, ending in a chamber; then we dug side tunnels, storage rooms, and an escape tunnel under the fence and into the borrow-pit by the road. At home, our parents were missing spade, trowels, and buckets; although we tried to wash away the evidence of our labors each day, our mothers were mystified by the chronic filthiness of our clothes and bodies. It was wonderful. Gordon and Jimmie dug a special sideroom, which they declared off-limits to us little kids; cigarettes and pin-up photos were suspected. No matter that I never learned to swing a baseball bat properly, or play jacks, or hopscotch, or marbles; it was enough to belong to the Red Moles, eating jelly sandwiches like K-rations in our candlelit earthworks, with someone on duty at the periscope, ready for all enemies!

In truth our enemies were all strangers. Our sociology, based on *fewness,* precluded playing war games in two or more opposing gangs, as children normally do; we wouldn't have thought of such formal playground warfare. And if the shunned girls had demanded admission with the magic words "We *really* mean it!" it would have been granted, not out of charity but to avoid strife. I think we feared internal strife and friction more than anything. In my five years at New Era, I do not recall a single fight or feud, or even a good name-calling argument at school. There were occasional punitive "dirty tricks," when after repeated warnings we took steps to correct various bad habits in our schoolmates, like tattling or trying to be "bossy." Some of these measures were pretty drastic, but the tattling or bossing generally did stop as a consequence, the offender/victim forgave and was forgiven, and we carried on together as before.

As I conjure up my childhood there, growing up with my tiny circle of playmates, which was everybody else's circle, I marvel at the sheer repressive tranquility of it all. Given the ways of the world at large, I'm not sure that it was good training in lifemanship, or even psychologically healthy. But we did manage to get along, less than siblings and somehow more than friends. Snooping in my brother's "Secret Diary", as I tried to do about once a month, I came upon this entry, which struck me as remarkable even then: "Friday. Today I *almost* got mad at Gordon . . . ."

Finally change invaded the Plains. The war ended, Gordon and Jimmie graduated, Mrs. Hall retired, and in the fall of 1945 a new teacher arrived to take her place. Mrs. Hering was young—my parents' age; in fact she and my father had been high school sweeties. She was, I already knew, red-haired and high-spirited. Any hopes we had of carrying on as postwar Red Moles were dashed the first morning of school. "Well, boys," Mrs. Hering announced brightly, "that was quite an underground fort you had out by the road. When I came by last month to look at the school, I fell through the tunnels and sprained my ankle. No more of that, boys. The war's over, but we'll have team sports instead!"

So we filled in our beloved tunnels and brooded on rebellion. By the end of the second week, we'd secretly excavated a new, bigger, and better pillbox in a different corner of the schoolground; she found *that* before we could even roof it and thanked us for digging such a fine big trashpit. We conceded defeat, returned our parents' long-lost digging tools, and resigned ourselves to learning the sissy sports of softball, soccer, and broom hockey.

So began the last new era of New Era School. Enrollment swelled, as whole neighborhoods from western Idaho moved to the Plains in advance of the North Unit Irrigation Project. Mrs. Hering, master teacher that she was, kept us hopping. One of us paid her the ultimate grudging tribute: "Good God, she sees everything!" At the furthest extreme from the furtive pleasures of the Red Mole campaign, she engineered an elaborate all-school musical pageant celebrating the Oregon Trail, with a real campfire on stage and a life-sized replica of a prairie schooner painted "Oregon or Bust," around which we rallied to sing "Old Dan Tucker" and "Sourwood Mountain" while on the Trail, and the Oregon state anthem, "Land of the Empire Builders," once we had reached the Promised Land.

Let no historian mock my fancy that with this childish pageant, our odd local extension of the Oregon Trail came to an end. We had done what we could with what was left of the frontier. Now the dryland fields were being leveled and subdivided for irrigation; rock-infested ground through which our grandfathers first drove a plow for free was selling for hundreds of dollars an acre. Outlanders who wore rubber boots and talked mysteriously about "headgates" and "subbing" and "ladino clover" were buying the land and renaming our old Market Road "Boise Drive."

People began to talk about a plan to consolidate New Era School with the Madras school system. Our parents fought it angrily, knowing that our little community, like many another, would lose its traditional center if the school closed. But when it came to a vote, the newcomers, who claimed to speak for the future in all things, won overwhelmingly. We would all go to town next fall, riding buses, to become "new kids" among strangers.

Near the end of school that spring, the principal from Madras paid our teacher a call. She had once taught under him, and she had confided in us that they were bitter enemies; it looked like he'd come out to rub salt in our wounds. It was afternoon recess, and he strutted right through our softball game "like a German general," somebody whispered. Mrs. Hering met him on the porch, blocking his entrance. What she said to him, glaring down on his Prussian head, we couldn't hear, but her hands were making fists and her red hair was tossing. Suddenly he turned and began to stalk back to his car. Mrs. Hering covered her face with her hands. We followed him silently through the yard, and as he drove off, we all threw rocks and gravel at his car until it was out of range, on the road back to town.

Oh memory, memory, to look into the upstairs dark and see the scattered farm-house lights of Agency Plains again, the lights I once thought permanent as stars! And if I could, I'd go down to the phone in the kitchen, and ring five *longs,* the never-used Emergency Number, and say to all my listeners and rubberers, "Hello, this is Jerry, I have an emergency. Don't do anything different; just go on being yourselves in the old way as long as you can; but hear this. Our world here is going to change; the big world has surely found us out. We are about to fly apart from each other like sparks. I love you all; so long for now."

Our Pleasant Condition, Surrounded by Fewer Acres of Clams

John M. McClelland, Jr.

Early Pacific Northwest writers produced a few primitive gems. The one I like best is "The Song of the Old Settler,"[1] by Francis Henry. The first several of his ten verses describe a pioneer's attempt to gain riches by digging for gold, and when that failed, by farming in the Puget Sound Country. Then he wrote:

> I arrived there flat broke in mid-winter
> > And found it enveloped in fog,
> And covered all over with timber,
> > Thick as hair on the back of a dog.
>
> I took up a claim in the forest
> > And sat myself down to hard toil.
> For two years I chopped and I niggered,
> > But I never got down to the soil.
>
> I tried to get out of the country,
> > But poverty forced me to stay
> Until I became an old settler,
> > Then nothing could drive me away.
>
> And now that I'm used to the climate,
> > I think that if man ever found
> A spot to live easy and happy
> > That Eden is on Puget Sound.
>
> No longer the slave of ambition,
> > I laugh at the world and its shams,
> As I think of my pleasant condition
> > Surrounded by acres of clams.

"The Song of the Old Settler" is a delightfully humorous description of life as it was for many of those settled in the

Northwest. The Old Settler had come west with high hopes and suffered severe disappointments. He endured these and persevered, making the best of what he found (mainly the bounty of nature, including clams), and he was, withal, reasonably content with his lot.

As we look back over the course of this region's early and recent history, a continuing pattern of confidence in the future can be seen. That confidence was bolstered, as the years went on, by what actually occurred. Realistic hopes were fulfilled, not always, but eventually. Expectations were met or even exceeded in due course if not right away. There were rich resources to be developed and exploited. Towns and cities had to be built and expanded. The need for railroads and wagon roads and then highways led inevitably into planning, and plans always were laid in the expectation that their fulfillment would constitute progress. If the Northwest had paused to devise a motto or slogan it might well have been "Onward—Ever Onward."

Successive generations believed that the Northwest's full potential was too great even to imagine. Its resources, especially timber, were usually described as inexhaustible or limitless. Opportunities were described with similar superlatives.

Throughout the 19th century and almost up to the present day, expectations of great things to come have probably provided more guidance and inspiration here than anywhere else in the nation. This would not be particularly noteworthy were it not for the events of the last 25 years, which have altered or even eliminated some circumstances and conditions on which these rosy views of the future were based. It is these circumstances, how they have changed and how they have affected current attitudes that I will examine here.

In any period, the attitudes of a people and its leaders toward the future influence what they do. When our hopes are high, we work hard to seek their fulfillment. If they are not high—if there are serious doubts that our efforts will be rewarded—we are not inclined to strive as diligently. In the Northwest, at least until recently, prospects for reward have been unfailingly good.

In the oldest part of the world, so overrun with people that hardly enough food can be extracted from the earth and its waters to satisfy basic needs, people can be concerned with little more than survival. I have seen these conditions in the back country of China, where there seem to be no birds and animals because they eat food needed by humans. The rural Chinese don't expect much of the future.

Those who came to the Pacific Northwest were not concerned with mere survival. They were moving to a land of opportunity, fully intending to become prosperous—perhaps wealthy. They knew what lay ahead, or thought they did. This was new country, virgin in all respects. What was here—land, water, timber, fish, grandeur, mild climate—so inspired those who first saw it that they were moved to describe it in extravagant terms.

Captain George Vancouver may have been looking up at the mountain he named Rainier when he recorded this observation:

> The serenity of the climate, the innumerable pleasing landscapes, and the abundant fertility that unassisted nature puts forth, require only to be enriched by the industry of man, with villages, mansions, cottages and other buildings, to render it the most lovely country that can be imagined, whilst the labor of the inhabitants would be abundantly rewarded in the bounties which nature seems ready to bestow on cultivation.[2]

Others, after Vancouver, were similarly inspired to use superlatives in reporting what they saw or heard about the Oregon Country. Much of this went into print. Lewis and Clark, Hall Jackson Kelly, Washington Irving and a number of others produced a body of literature early in the 19th century that stirred the imaginations and inspired the dreams of many young men who eventually were to seek the fulfillment of those dreams.

And so what came to be known as the Oregon Country developed a magnetic allure that brought on what was called "Oregon fever" in midcentury, leading to the rush to claim and hold free land. There developed a strongly held feeling, emphasized by promoters extolling the virtues and prospects of townsites where land was for sale, that the Northwest was an unexcelled land of opportunity.

The environment itself fostered positive feelings. No one can measure how much effect the pleasant elements of the Northwest environment—the green grandeur of the mountain ranges, the white peaks, the numerous rivers and streams, the lordly Columbia River, and the vast inland sea named Puget Sound—have had on the attitudes of the region's people through the decades. (And, we need to remember, this is one element that is little changed.) Descriptions of the region's natural wonders, widely published and reprinted in eastern newspapers, were read eagerly by the curious and adventurous. Here was new country waiting to be claimed, they read, with resources ready to be used, towns needing to be established, roads and railroads still to be built and riches everywhere to be gained. And the honor and distinction of doing it awaited those who were first.

The fur trade brought the first inhabitants. Next came the land-hungry, the adventurers, the missionaries, some fugitives, some escapees from slavery or its consequences, and those restless souls impelled by an undefinable magnetism to be found on all frontiers. The trickle across the plains in the early 1840s swelled to a stream after the treaty of 1846 was approved. One of those pioneers was James Clyman, a fur trapper and mountain man who kept a better-than-usual journal. "All ages and sects," he wrote, "are found to undertake this long tedious and even dangerous journey for some unknown object never to be realized even by the most fortunate. And why? Because the human mind can never be satisfied, never at rest, always on the stretch for something new."

The original immigrants could do little more than claim and clear land and struggle to make a living. But they succeeded well enough to cause them to write home to friends and relatives, urging that they too undertake the grand adventure. Thousands did. The pioneers were resourceful and ingenious. Little towns were started. Primitive sawmills and grist mills were established beside swift streams. Here and there a school house was built. Civilization sprouted in Eden. It grew and flourished.

It would be unreasonable to conclude that all or even most of the anticipations that inspired those settlers and early developers were realized. But hopes diminish only gradually in the face of disappointment, and often something unexpected causes them to be renewed. Fulfillment of hopes was often delayed, but hopes were seldom abandoned. Many of the journals and reminiscences of 19th century Northwest settlers reveal this. Some ambitious goals could not be reached. Projects undertaken could not all be realized. The prosperity that was to be the result of unceasing labor and sacrifice was sometimes elusive.

A recurring theme in the novels of H. L. Davis is the frontier struggle that did not quite work out. Davis wrote of what he knew best—the land along the upper Columbia where he was raised. Some of his characters were people who had left comfortable surroundings and circumstances to make the long journey west in pursuit of the commonly held frontier dream. James T. Potts, in a recent commentary,[3] notes that Davis's characters had great faith in people's ability to fulfill their early promise, yet they were often disappointed because so many of their dreams didn't materialize.

But disappointments were endured, and hopes that were shattered were soon replaced by new ones. Such was the general climate of buoyant expectancy prevailing in this favored land that disillusionment and defeatism were generally scorned. The bigness and richness of the land and its timber and its waters (and what was being done with them by those who did succeed) had a strong effect on those who faltered. It was hard to give up—to conclude, after failure, that a second try, or a third, would not succeed.

An almost insurmountable early obstacle was isolation. Markets for what could be produced were distant. Early California had a few centers of population where lumber, wheat, potatoes, oysters, and salmon could be marketed. Hawaii needed lumber. Ships were built as quickly as needed to carry all that could be shipped and sold. But what the Northwest really needed (a need recognized at the time the first settlers came) was a railroad, stretching eastward over those dry plains to connect with the river cities on the Mississippi and the Ohio.

The eventual certainty of a railroad sustained hopes for the future year after year. Isaac Stevens, on his way west to become the first Washington territorial governor, surveyed a route for a railroad. The survey results were published in a well-documented set of books, tangible proof that a railroad could be built and probably would be as soon as men with millions or the ability to raise millions could be induced to undertake what assuredly would be a profitable adventure.

The decade of the 1850s was marred by violence that sent the pioneers scurrying into hastily built blockhouses seeking safety. Stevens had to be an Indian fighter as well as an Indian treaty-maker and governor of the territory. But he was not the least discouraged. "Gather heart, fellow citizens," he exhorted in an early message. "Do not talk of leaving us in our hour of adversity but stay till the shade of gloom is lifted and await that destiny to be fulfilled." "I have an abiding confidence in the future destiny of our Territory," he said on another occasion. "Let us never lose sight of the resources, capacities and natural advantages of the Territory."[4] The hostility of the Indians—the bloodshed and the fear of more violence—darkened the prospects of the settlers, but there was never any doubt about the eventual outcome. The Indians who resisted being forced out of their homeland would be put down, and eventually they were.

The development of the Northwest was not greatly affected by the Civil War. During the 1860s population increased by 75 percent, although railroad plans had to be shelved because of the war. But by 1867 hopes of a railroad were revived. Governor Marshall F. Moore said this: "The grand enterprise of connecting Puget Sound by railroad with the upper Mississippi and the great Northern Lakes has at last assumed a tangible shape . . . This road will be built . . ." In 1871 construction on the long-awaited railroad finally was started. Rails were laid at Kalama and pushed northward toward Puget Sound. Then came a frustrating decade of waiting for construction to be completed as it was delayed by financial crises. Not until 1881 did the first boxcar of anything made or produced in the Northwest move to eastern markets.

The railroads did fulfill long-held hopes. Towns came into being along the route. Land values rose. And, best of all, more people poured in. The assurance that someday there would be a railroad had sustained hopes and schemes for a broadened and better future during the 30 years from 1852 to 1882. The actual advent of the Northern Pacific Line, (and later the Great Northern,

Union Pacific and Milwaukee lines) stimulated those hopes and turned them into great expectations. This wonderful country was linked at last with the populous East. Its time had come. Nothing could hold it back now.

Some of the towns that sprang up along the railroad route, such as Spokane, Yakima, Tacoma, and Seattle, were destined to grow into cities. (Portland preceeded the railroads, but it blossomed after their coming.) Urban enterprise thrived on the spirit of expectation created by the railroads. Cities made possible concentrations of people. The land in such places therefore was valuable. Bring in people and the land could be sold.

Some townsites were established on little but hopes and dreams and didn't develop at all. Others that expected to become metropolitan centers remained only towns. Port Townsend hoped to become the New York of the West, because its location where Puget Sound met the Strait of Juan de Fuca was convenient for sailing ships that could not easily navigate inland waters. The several elaborate stone business buildings along its main street, which make Port Townsend a quaint tourist center, now, are monuments to the unfulfilled dreams of the 1890s.

The metropolis, it turned out, was destined to be Seattle, inside Elliott Bay on Puget Sound. The original settlers wanted to call their settlement New York. They were sure that so favorably situated a place would grow eventually into a city of great size. The seal of Washington Territory, adopted in 1853, shows a Goddess of Hope seated with her right hand pointing to the word "Alki," meaning "by and by." A log cabin is in the foreground with the outline of a city in the background. The seal depicts the great dream—from log cabin to metropolis. Those who were to be Seattle's founders settled on Alki as the original name. By and by it might be New York. By and by a great future for everyone in the Northwest.

More than the chance for material gain motivated some settlers. There were those who reveled in the opportunity to become public leaders, write constitutions and laws, and found churches, schools and lodges. Judge Matthew P. Deady of Portland touched on this aspect of frontier allure in a speech in 1886:

The population of (Oregon) was not formed by the mere gradual . . . overflow of people from one longitude to another. Unlike colonies on the Atlantic seaboard . . . it was from the beginning a distinct settlement of self-governing and directing people separated from their point of migration by thousands of miles of uninhabited country; that, while the Atlantic colonies were generally planted and watered by some powerful company or proprietor in England, and largely aided and directed thereby, the Oregon colony was emphatically a popular political movement, conducted by private persons, without any recognized head or concerted plan. It was one of those singular movements of the human race in which numbers of people, without preconcert or purpose, are moved by some common controlling purpose to transplant themselves to some unknown and remote region, and, having done so proceed at once by a political habit or instinct, to unite together in a civil society and found a state upon whose escutcheon they might well inscribe 'Alis volat propriis' (She flies with her own wings.)[5]

By 1889, when Washington achieved statehood, its population had increased in ten years, as a result of railroad expansion, from 75,000 to 300,000. In 1879 even Seattle did not have 5,000 inhabitants. Ten years later three cities had more than 25,000. "Truly the recent past," wrote Governor Ferry, "gives promise of a future which will realize our most sanguine anticipation . . . the citizen of Washington can look upon his state with pride and anticipation which cannot be too great."[6] Governors and other speakers often could not resist being carried away, so enthused were they about the future. They may not even have noticed in the 1890s when a government agency, noting the extent of development in the West, declared the American frontier officially closed. It was then that Frederick Jackson Turner wrote his famous piece about the significance of the frontier in the historical American scheme of things.

The frontier may have been closed, but in the mid-1890s the Northern Pacific was still distributing elaborate promotional literature aimed at luring more people into the Northwest to claim free land or buy cheap land. Maps showed the ownership of every square mile, so that those to whom land meant wealth could see where they could claim 160 acres of free land under the Homestead Act, and where Civil War veterans could collect a bonus in land,

and where timber and stone lands (judged unfit for homesteading) could be purchased for $2.50 an acre. "In this prosperous country," said the Northern Pacific literature, "with its varied resources and healthful climate there is ample room for millions of settlers to secure comfortable homes and become independent."[7]

The Northwest was reaching the height of its railroad development potential about the time gold was discovered in Alaska in 1898. Seattle became the gateway to the North and the recipient of much of the wealth that was found there. The gold rush inspired the Alaska-Yukon-Pacific Exposition, bringing west large numbers of Americans who came to see, not to stay. But many did come back, entranced by the natural beauty and convinced that here was a good place for one to make a fortune.

Another exposition of world's fair proportions was held in Portland. The Lewis and Clark Centennial Exposition had promotional value for Oregon similar to that of the AYP for Washington. Both fairs said to the world: "Look at what the Pacific Northwest offers! Opportunity, wealth, grandeur. Come, be a part of this promised land." That phrase—"Promised Land"—was to become the title of a book by Richard Neuberger in the 1930s. In it he extolled the accomplishments of the public power era and mustered his most eloquent language to describe the possibilities of the future. What Neuberger and others foresaw 40 years ago was not disputed. The Northwest then was still a land of promise and opportunity.

During the second decade of the 20th century, World War I had to be endured, and regional concerns were put aside while the nation struggled to prevail and survive. When victory was won and the troops came home, a new era began. It was expected to be a satisfying one, with new opportunities.

In the post-World War I decade, the means for taking full advantage of the Northwest's abundant resources at last were available. Logging was emerging from the steam-donkey era. Paved highways and trucks were making river steamers obsolete. Irrigation in eastern Washington and Oregon brought orchards to barren hillsides, and some visionaries in Ephrata and Wenatchee conceived the idea of damming the Columbia River to irrigate the

Columbia Basin. In this period the Long-Bell Lumber Company, which had cut out in the South, came to Washington. Long-Bell came to buy old-growth fir, to build what it claimed to be the world's largest sawmills, and, partly as an afterthought, to found a model city—Longview.

The Long-Bell executives were cautious. What were the prospects of this unfamiliar region? Their engineers made studies and wrote reports. Soon the city founders were as enthusiastic about the Northwest's prospects as Hall Jackson Kelly had been nearly a century earlier. The slogan adopted for Longview, which had a population of 3,700 in the year of its founding, 1923, was "50,000 by 1930." It had not reached that ambitious goal 59 years later. The timber Long-Bell had bought, originally part of the Northern Pacific land grant, was expected to supply the mills for 50 years. It didn't. The big sawmills had to be closed in the mid-1950s.

But the Weyerhaeuser Company's timber was more abundant, and its mills in Longview and elsewhere could carry on. In the 1930s, Weyerhaeuser and other timber firms offered new slogans to provide assurance that the Northwest's forest resource would not suffer the same fate that befell the forests of the lake and southern states. "Timber is a crop," proclaimed the major operators, pointing to their reforestation efforts. What was left after logging crews had clearcut the old growth was not simply cut-over land, but tree farms where seeding and planting would provide new crops of timber.

Development came to a halt in 1930, but, despite the Depression, people in the Northwest did not lose confidence in the future. The bottom had been hit, but there would be a recovery. The government at last was doing something about bank failures, unemployment, low wages and poverty. Social conditions improved even when economic conditions did not. Collective bargaining became legal, and unions thrived. The outlook was uncertain for many years, but it was nevertheless promising, as it always had been.

Depression ended abruptly with the outbreak of war in Europe in 1939. By then the early power dams on the Columbia River—Bonneville and Grand Coulee—had begun producing the cheapest power in the nation. That brought to the Northwest its first major industry not dependent on the forests or the land—aluminum. The dams were expected to help the Northwest as much as the railroads did. Here was power in unlimited amounts. Surely it would cause new industry to migrate west just as the people had, lured by opportunity.

And nothing was considered quite as desirable in the post-Depression years as more industry, providing permanent employment. Up-and-coming chambers of commerce hired salesmen and printed brochures, competing with one another for industrial prospects. They were mainly disappointed, especially the smaller cities in the hinterland. But that did not mean the small cities gave up hope of growing bigger and richer.

In the first part of the 1940s, the push to move on to greater heights remained strong. This was recognized even by scholars. The late Professor Charles Gates, a respected historian, wrote this in 1940:

> It is true that some of the goals to which the pioneers aspired have now been reached . . . [but] we still have something of the pioneering outlook on life. We look forward to the future now with anticipation, as men did a half century ago. The Pacific Northwest is today (as it was then) a place where dreams are cherished and where the hope of great achievement lures us on. Rich resources are yet waiting to be exploited. There are industries to be established and cities to be improved.[8]

But there appeared also, as early as 1940, some early expressions of doubt that the Pacific Northwest could or should go on as it always had, aspiring for more development, hoping for growth, and trusting in a bountiful future. The anonymous authors of the book *Oregon* (part of the federally sponsored American Guide Series) were professional writers in Portland, poor and eager to work at the end of the Depression. They included this in their preface:

> Oregon is still the most unspoiled and uncluttered spot in America—and partly because the gold rushes of California and Alaska left it undisturbed. Soon, perhaps, it will be changed by the coming of Power, the inrolling of immigration from the dust bowl, the devastation of timber cutting and forest fires, and the boosting activities of chambers of commerce.

It may be regrettable to see this peaceful, beautiful land transformed into a network of highways, clogged with cars and defaced with hot dog stands, the groves littered with tin cans and papers, the hills pock-marked with stumps, and the cities cursed with the slums that seem to accompany industrial progress.[9]

These apprehensions came in time to be shared by enough others to prevent some of the worst fears from being realized. And they led to gradually changing public attitudes about the Northwest and the way its resources were being used and its environment altered.

These changes resulted from the realization that the adjectives "limitless" and "inexhaustible" could no longer properly be applied to the Northwest. Surpluses of power and water and timber and places to camp or build houses with a view of the water had come to an end. The change in attitudes was also encouraged by the realization that the world was more limited than past generations thought. Pictures of it could be taken from outer space. There was our world, hanging there—a mere sphere and not a particularly big one.

The successor to transportation as a prime sustainer of hopes and expectations in the Northwest was electric power. Electricity was produced in superabundance as one dam after another was completed. A high voltage intertie line was built through Oregon so that excess energy could be sold in California. Then hydro electric energy went rather suddenly from abundance to scarcity, and resort was made to a new method of power production—thermonuclear. But nuclear energy, however common it may become eventually, could hardly buoy hopes and expectations because of its exorbitant cost. As this is written, increases of 50 percent in power rates to consumers are being proposed merely to pay the interest on nuclear plant bonds in Washington.

Population growth had always been a prime regional objective. More people had always been needed to fill in the great gaps and to turn villages into towns and towns into cities. But in the 1960s, it began to appear as if unlimited population growth was no longer desirable. Those who had been in southern California saw the consequences of crowding and congestion. The end of the hydro power surplus was a consequence of population growth, and it startled some. People were using the additional power, not new industry.

And if more people were not desired, what reason was there to promote new industry? There developed then a climate of opposition to any new "dirty" industrial enterprise, and demands grew that existing enterprises cease polluting the water and air. The aluminum and pulp-and-paper industries complied under serious protest because clean-up was expensive. The lumber industry fortunately had already scrapped its waste burners, because wood of any kind had become too valuable to waste.

In the late 1960s there was still enough electric power left for one more aluminum smelter. Promoters announced that they wanted to build their plant on Guemes Island near Bellingham. The resulting uproar of objection to an invasion by industry of that unspoiled sanctuary soon had the smelter developers in retreat. Although they would have been welcome in Longview, which already had one aluminum plant that was struggling to filter the fluorides from its smoke, the developers chose a site near Astoria. But they delayed, and in the meantime even Astoria, down greatly in population from its heyday because of declines in its lumber and fishing industries, decided it didn't want a dirty industry either. Some wondered what John Jacob Astor, the fur trader entrepreneur, would think of the town bearing his name deciding that clear air and a waterfront unmarred by industrial ugliness were better than payrolls.

During this last quarter century, the Northwest has seen a marked change in advocacy. Instead of all-out efforts to grow and expand, this new advocacy calls for restraint, conservation, and the imposition of limits and quotas. Don't ask for more, take less. Stem the western movement; it has run its course. The old growth forests are nearly gone, so stop cutting trees. The canneries are closed and the price of fresh salmon is up to $8.00 a pound, so stop catching fish. The hydro energy is all being used, so conserve and don't allow any more uses for energy to develop.

Such feelings are not universally shared or accepted by any means. In the Seattle area, the Council for Economic Development, which was born of panic during the Boeing depression of the early 1970s, carries on its effort to make the Puget Sound area less dependent on one big industry. Chambers of commerce and port districts in Portland, Tacoma, Longview, and elsewhere have not abandoned their promotional efforts. But they operate quietly, trying not to attract public attention.

As the 20th century wore on, observant persons began to contemplate what had been occurring. The region's transportation system at last had been completed. The railroads, finished building a half century ago, were abandoning some lines. Good roads associations, formed long ago to lobby for new highway and bridge construction, were content to concentrate on road maintenance and improvement. The rivers had been dammed in so many places that no prime hydro sites remained. Some grandiose schemes, such as a canal to connect Puget Sound with Willapa Bay and the Columbia estuary, were abandoned without objection.

Two of the region's prime natural resources—fish and timber— were in a discouraging state of decline. Towns whose economy was based on salmon canning or lumber had declined or disappeared. Astoria once had 24 canneries; now it has 2. Sawmills and logging operations once were located every few miles along the lower Columbia; less than a half dozen remained by 1981. The lower Columbia has become a rusting, decaying museum of a dying era. Ghost towns abound—Mayger, Stella, Eagle Cliff, Waterford, Warrenton, Skamakawa, Brookfield, Pillar Rock, Altoona, Deep River, Grays River, Wauna, Cementville, Knappton. Among the inlets and islands of Puget Sound, one sees many other remnants of once-prosperous towns.

Until fairly recently, the people who came to the Oregon country had similar reasons for coming and similar motivations for what they undertook once they arrived. What needed to be done usually could be rather clearly envisioned. There was always something to look forward to. This sustained sense of expectancy—of great things to come—helped make the Northwest a desirable and exciting place to be.

Is it still such a place? What present expectations or hopes can compare with what was achieved in the past? It is a difficult question. Objectives and needs cannot be as clearly defined now as in other times. Newspapers of the region for many years published annually what they called "progress editions." The word "progress" is not used commonly anymore. Growth in some areas is no longer an objective; it is a problem.

Fortunately, the Northwest's resources are not entirely used up but merely depleted. Renewal of the fish runs and forests are objectives of growing importance. Attracting new industry not dependent on the natural resources is still considered desirable. What every town wants is a "footloose" industry of considerable size, such as Hewlett-Packard (building near Everett) or Fairchild Instruments (locating near Puyallup). Such clean industries that can go anywhere are locating in the Northwest, because there is room and because competition for trained workers is not yet intense.

Some have contended that the Northwest should now concentrate on improving, polishing and refining what was first produced in rough form. The region needs more or better facilities for health care, education, power generation, and recreation. It also needs to raise more state and local tax funds to make up for the curtailed westward flow of money from the federal treasury (which for many years has been faster than the flow of federal tax money eastward).

Do any great public works remain to be undertaken? An oil pipeline across Washington might be one, but that idea is about as popular as the scheme to divert water from the Columbia River to arid parts of California. No, the big building period in the Northwest appears to be over for as far ahead as anyone can see.

As for population growth, that is impossible to foretell. Asa Mercer, Washington's pioneer educator, was one of the early boosters of the Northwest. He predicted in the 1850s (to the amusement of many) that the Territory of Washington, which then stretched from the Pacific to the Rocky Mountains, would increase in population from 15,000 to 3,000,000. It took just a century for that prediction to come true.

What does the Northwest's future look like now to those facing it? I asked that question of several Northwest newspaper editors. Here are some replies:

Robert Chandler, Bend: Bend's growth surge has ended. The end of the boom has focused attention on our basics—lumber and tourism with a little agriculture thrown in. Lumber is in bad shape. Tourism will improve. Attitudes are changing.

Eric Allen, Jr., Medford: The decline of both agriculture and wood products argue against continued growth in southern Oregon. The new Urban Growth Boundaries will enhance city growth and discourage rural growth.

Tom Koenninger, Vancouver: Three new electronics firms assure Clark county of continued growth. Within a few years we should have a new community approaching 40,000 people, developed by the Genstar Corp., called Cascade Villages. It is patterned after the much-acclaimed Irvine, Calif., development. The new I-205 bridge over the Columbia will launch a new wave of residential and business growth in 1983. We do have as much to look forward to as past generations if, in our greed and lust to develop, we can manage and maintain the land and the natural resources properly.''

Ned Thomas, Port Angeles, Charles Wanninger, Bellingham, and *Glenn Lee, Pasco* all said they were watching changes in their communities with some apprehension, but did not expect adversity.

Wilford Woods, Wenatchee and *Glenn Cushman, Albany* made the point that public attitudes will have much to do with shaping future events in the Northwest. "Progress," noted Woods, whose father was one of the pioneers who conceived the Grand Coulee-Columbia Basin projects, "has to be accompanied by a political process that must have the approval of the public to become reality. The public changes. The Northwest, no longer young, has an increasingly large number of older citizens who make our demographics far different from those of earlier decades." Cushman said future opportunities depend greatly on public attitudes: "For example, if we really want more power we can have it. But we have to want it first. We don't seem to want it now."

Is the future of the Northwest perceived now to be any different from that of the nation as a whole? Probably not, because all parts of the nation are affected by the same economic and political forces that are responsible for the Northwest's current adversity. More than 1,000 widely scattered Stanford University alumni responded to a questionnaire which contained this question:

When we enter the 21st century, what would you expect to find?
Things better than now? (25.1%)
Things about the same as now? (23.8%)
Things worse than now? (37.1%)
Don't know. (24%)

Such answers never would have been given by Northwesterners in the 19th century, nor in the first half of the 20th century.

Hopes commonly expressed in the intensely developed parts of the Northwest are not necessarily shared by those in less-developed areas. Nor is there unanimity in any locality on the matter of growth and development. My company has newspapers in three Washington cities. Two of these cities would like very much to grow. The other is plagued with problems relating to growth.

Port Angeles is an old lumber and logging town in a county where Social Security is now the biggest payroll. Its best hope for the future lies in more persons choosing that area as a place to live out their last years. Port Angeles might become an oil terminus, and that would improve its economy. But most Port Angeles residents oppose the oil-port proposal for environmental reasons. Longview is a planned city designed to house a population of 100,000 or more, but it has not yet attained 40,000. Its forest products-based economy is not likely to expand. Bellevue, on the other hand, was incorporated only 30 years ago, yet it is now Washington's fourth largest city. Its main problem for years has been the control and regulation of growth. Other Northwest cities have struggled for decades to attain what Bellevue has had thrust upon it, almost unwillingly, in just a few years.

The growth pattern in the Northwest has been too uneven. Both eastern Washington and Oregon are thinly populated, while too many people are concentrated at the mouth of the Willamette River and on the east shore of Puget Sound. A regional objective might well be to better disperse population and industry.

In defining objectives for the years ahead, however, it is difficult to find ones that are not mundane. They seem solid and quite necessary but not very exciting. The sense of anticipation that we can expect to experience in striving to attain such objectives can hardly compare with that experienced by early builders with mud on their shoes. The Northwest was a special place as long as it was on the rise, climbing toward its almost utopian potential. It is not such a special place any more. It has entered into the inevitable period of maturity and left its youth behind.

Is this maturity something to be regretted? Are the fun and romance and adventure gone? Is the incentive to strive for more lacking? Is the future likely to produce fewer changes? Will the renewable resources—fish and timber—ever be satisfactorily renewed? The future cannot be foretold, of course. But it is quite evident that maturity has brought changes in public attitudes, especially about the environment. The course of future development will differ markedly from what has gone before.

My principal concern is whether the advancement of our region will be hampered or delayed because the Northwest is no more of a promised land or a future Eden than any other favored part of the nation. Over the years our Northwest states have attracted several million persons who were confident that in this prospering and developing region they would surely share in much that was good and wonderful. There was a certain mystique about this far corner that had enduring appeal to those looking westward. The Northwest could no longer be called the frontier, but it was where the frontier was last seen (and maybe some remnants were left). I know a newspaperman in Oklahoma who bought the weekly newspaper in Twisp, Washington, simply because he yearned for a Northwest connection.

There may still be some illusions remaining about this region offering opportunities superior to those elsewhere, but they are fading rapidly. Is our region likely to become like New England, which is noted more now for its luminous fall foliage and picturesque countryside than for its textile mills and fisheries? Will the Northwest become better known for its volcano and mild summers than for Weyerhaeuser, Boeing, and Grand Coulee dam?

But what difference does it make, if the Northwest seems to have more of a past than a future? What we have been talking about is simply historical development. These things occurred. Our region has come of age. What's wrong with that? Really not much if the momentum is not all lost. What we enjoy now is an accumulation of accomplishments of epic proportions handed down by the highly motivated generations of the past. Our concern now must be with the possibility that diminished motivations will fail to inspire accomplishments of equal worth for the benefit of those who come later.

The vitality is not gone from the Northwest, but it seems to be diminished and in need of renewal. Maturity may be a comfortable state, but we could become too comfortable. Remembering the Old Settler, we can say that it is no longer necessary to be the slave of ambition. And we can laugh at the world and its shams. But beware of our pleasant condition, for there are fewer acres of clams.

NOTES

[1] Francis Henry, "The Song of the Old Settler," in *Washington Pioneer Association Transactions, 1883-89*, comp. Charles Prosch (Seattle: 1894), 150.

[2] George Vancouver, quoted in *Boston Recorder,* 20 August 1822.

[3] James T. Potts, "H. L. Davis' View: Reclaiming and Recovering the Land," *Oregon Historical Quarterly* 82, no. 2.

[4] Charles M. Gates, *Messages of the Governors of the Territory of Washington, 1854-89* (Seattle: University of Washington Press, 1940), 14.

[5] Matthew P. Deady, quoted in speech by H. G. Struve, in *Washington Pioneer Association Transactions,* 1883-89, 74.

[6] Gates, *Messages of Governors,* 205.

[7] *Washington the Evergreen State* (Northern Pacific Railroad, 1894)

[8] Gates, *Messages of Governors,* xix

[9] W.P.A. Writers' Program, *Oregon, End of the Trail,* American Guide Series (Portland: Binfords and Mort, 1940)

Regionalism, Tending toward Sectionalism

David Sarasohn

In geographic terms, there is a relatively slight difference between "region" and "section." In historical terms, there has been a substantial difference between the use of "regionalism" and "sectionalism." Regionalism, to use a classification developed by the comedian Shelley Berman, is a Clean; sectionalism is a Dirty. Examples of each make the distinction clear: regionalism is Robert Penn Warren; sectionalism is John C. Calhoun.

Despite predictions that network television would eventually efface all geographic differences, sectionalism has clearly been on the rise lately. The emerging distinctions between Sun Belt and Frost Belt states, and the related division between energy-producing and energy-importing states, has clearly deepened sectional resentments, with the formation of antagonistic congressional caucuses and popular battle cries. The most popular bumper sticker in Texas several years ago was not an endorsement of the Dallas Cowboys, but a strip reading "Let the Yankee Bastards Freeze in the Dark." Meanwhile, Frost Belt senators such as Daniel Moynihan of New York complain of federal encouragement for the population shift toward the Sun Belt, sounding like William Seward lamenting the pre-Civil War "slavocracy's" control of the Buchanan administration. The 1970s were viewed in some circles as the second coming of the 1950s; the 1980s may yet prove to be a rerun of the 1850s.

The postures of Texas and New York in the new alignment could be anticipated, but Oregon's attitude toward itself and the rest of the country—and whether that attitude qualifies as regionalism or sectionalism—is less evident. Oregon, like the other states of

223

the West and South, is gaining population and congressional representation and clearly has a different set of problems and attitudes than the older areas of the Frost Belt. But it is at least meteorologically implausible to see Oregon as part of the Sun Belt. Moreover, Oregon (and the Pacific Northwest as a whole) is distinct in politics and self-perception from the tanned states that stretch between California and Carolina, or even from the equally booming Rocky Mountain region. The differences derive not only from contrasts in climate and location, but from both early and recent settlement patterns.

The result is a state of mind recognizably different than the one that prevails in the Sun Belt; the Pacific Northwest might well constitute a third force called the Rain Belt. But this image of something between Frost and Sun Belts should not be taken to indicate moderation. The feelings of Oregonians toward people outside the Rain Belt are easily as intense as those of Texans or New Yorkers, reflecting an attitude that may once have been regionalism, but is not more accurately described as sectionalism. Oregon's suspicions, however, are directed most strongly not toward the other side of the country, but elsewhere within the West. There is suspicion of Washington for being too fond of nuclear power and not fond enough of the Columbia River Gorge. "We used to speak of the Great Northwest," noted *Oregon Times* magazine in 1974, "but today no genuine Oregonian would tolerate Walla Wallans or Yakimanians standing in the family ranks." There is suspicion of Nevada and the rest of the West for wanting to grab Columbia River water, and above all there is suspicion of California for being California, and wanting us to be the same way. The greatest state folk hero of the last five years has been the television commercial border guard who keeps out-of-state beer out of Oregon.

Within Oregon, there have been two major and related manifestations of this sensibility: the cry to Pull Up the Drawbridge and the Cult of Livability. Both of these feelings could be accurately described as sectional; they are based upon a commitment to preserve local patterns of behavior and thought and a concern that outsiders, either by entering the area or by distant manipulation, are trying to alter those patterns to their own undesirable models.

The major difference between this attitude and other American sectionalism is crucial and largely self-defeating. Unlike colonial New England or the antebellum South or the turn-of-the-century Midwest, Oregon feels itself endangered not by a larger society which rejects its values, but by the far more lethal threat of a larger society which admires them.

In its earliest years, Oregon was settled largely by New Englanders, perhaps to a greater degree than any other western state. No subsequent influx has greatly broadened the original population mix. One effect of this, as Kevin Phillips pointed out in *The Emerging Republican Majority,* is that Oregon voting tends to parallel New England rather than the state's western neighbors. Oregon's voting history frequently makes it a regional anomaly; it was the only state in the West to reject Woodrow Wilson in 1916 and Harry Truman in 1948, and it came within one-fifth of one percent of being the only one to vote for Jimmy Carter in 1976. Only Oregon, Maine and Vermont maintained two Republican senators throughout the New Deal. Oregon's presidential primary choices have also differed from the regional consensus, from Woodrow Wilson's victory in 1912 to Eugene McCarthy's triumph over Robert Kennedy in 1968 (which led Kennedy staffers to label the state a giant suburb). Looking at the voting patterns differently, one might call Oregon a giant Vermont.

This New England connection, virtually unique among states thought of as Sun Belt components, extends into behavior other than voting. Oregon's bottle bill, which has become in the last ten years a major element in its self-image, has counterparts in four other states, including Connecticut, Maine, and Vermont. An editor of *Time,* ruminating in print about an impulse to simplify his life by moving to Medford to become a copywriter for the Harry and David fruit company, remembers hearing that Oregonians were a lot like New Englanders: politically liberal but personally conservative.

There has also been a persistent note of Yankee skepticism and restraint about the state, at sharp variance with the effervescent Sun Belt boosterism and fascination with size. E. Kimbark MacColl quotes a Ford Motor Company executive who told the Portland

Chamber of Commerce in 1928 that "Portland is a quiet, delightful place to live in, when one desires peace and complete rest, but it is not a center of business." Carl Abbott, in his new book *The New Urban America,* points out that for much of the 20th century the Portland city fathers regarded the major tool of urban aggrandizement, annexation, as too much trouble. Only when the 1960 census showed that the city had actually lost population did they recommence, in a very limited way, pushing out the city's boundaries. Similar instances of doubt about change and growth led Gordon Dodds to entitle the last chapter of his Bicentennial history of the state, "The Struggle Against Modern Life."

Now that modern life has gotten itself a pretty bad name everywhere, it is precisely that sense of rejection that lures people to Oregon and the Pacific Northwest in numbers that many claim will overcome the very characteristics that attracted them. This concern underlies much of Oregon's sectionalism and its eagerness to pull up the drawbridge; those most eager to pull it up have often just galloped across it into Oregon. "There is nothing more typical," observed Ron Abell, then editor of *Oregon Magazine,* "than the newcomer to Oregon who, as soon as he's comfortably ensconced, wants to shut the gates behind him and keep other people from coming in and ruining things."

To see why this is true, and why Oregon is someplace apart from the Sun Belt, we have to look at not only the old settlers but the new ones. From a map of population increases and congressional reapportionment according to the 1980 census, it would seem that Oregon's gains are in line with the overall population shift to the Sun Belt. But a closer examination suggests that the Rain Belt and the Sun Belt are growing to differing rhythms. Oregon, it seems, is riding a different population wave than the one on which southern California has long been surfing.

The really explosive growth of the Sun Belt came, of course, before anybody realized that a Sun Belt was emerging. During the decade from 1950 to 1960, California's population increased 48.5 percent and Florida's by 78.7 percent, against a national gain of 18.5 percent. But during that decade, Oregon actually grew at a slightly slower rate than the nation as a whole, 16.3 percent. By the next census in 1970, Oregon was growing marginally faster than the national average but still more slowly than California, 18.2 percent to 27 percent. Only during the 1970s did Oregon's growth greatly exceed that of the nation, bringing it an extra congressman. During that decade the state also, for the first time, grew faster than California, whose growth appears to be levelling off. From 1970 through 1979, Oregon's population increased at an average annual rate of 2.6 percent against California's 1.7 percent. From these figures, the growth of the Rain Belt looks like a separate second stage of the Sun Belt migration.

Moreover, the immigrants are coming from different places. The additional inhabitants of California and Florida are mostly still brushing the snow from their hair; when the New York Mets play at Dodger Stadium, it seems that all of Queens has settled on the third base line. The new Oregonians, by contrast, have left the areas to which other people are moving. A study of the one-quarter million people who moved into the state between 1965 and 1970 has shown that 83 percent came from the South and West. And, in general, the darkest apprehensions of Oregonians are confirmed; the newcomers do come largely from California. It is as though the demographic wave broke on the West Coast and the runoff headed north.

Oddly, the new migration seems to deepen rather than mitigate Oregon's sectionalism. The individual wearing a T-shirt reading "Oregon Is A State of Mind" has quite possibly just arrived from San Jose. Those who talk most insistently about Oregon's uniqueness, and most vociferously about the dangers of growth and development, are not always native Oregonians; the natives sometimes see growth as a way to gain urban amenities such as sewers, or to replace vanished logging and sawmill jobs. Very often the strongest language comes from the newer arrivals, who maintain that they don't want to see again what they've experienced elsewhere.

"For a number of years my family lived in Florida," began Eugene science fiction novelist Kate Wilhelm, responding to a question about what "livability" meant. "We were there when it changed. We saw the invasion of the concrete trucks, the swarms of development contractors and the results of their labors—endless condominiums . . . . We saw our beach change from a place where we could walk for miles, until we were exhausted, to a place where to walk at all became difficult. We had to walk at low tide, or else wade or clamber over the sea walls erected by resort hotel owners.''

The struggles to prevent this state of affairs are largely local battles, but as in most local battles, there is a sense that outside forces are involved, seeking to pervert and overcome the wishes of residents. For most of the Sun Belt, the role of malignant outsider has been filled by Washington, D.C.—a perception exploited with enormous profit by southern and western politicians. There is far less of that attitude in Oregon; although the federal government owns half of the state, Oregon has shown little interest in the Sagebrush Rebellion. Oregon's sectionalism is directed at the root of the problem: California.

It is not unusual for a smaller state to feel itself dominated by a larger neighbor; there is a New Mexico saying that laments the state's location, so far from Heaven and so close to Texas. But Oregon's objections to California are not a matter of size and power. Instead, California serves as that vital tool of mothers and economists, the bad example. It is perceived as overdeveloped and uninhabitable, the product of an unhealthy way of thinking. Opponents of an Oregon development project will denounce it as the product of a "California mentality"—or, if they wish to be really nasty, a "southern California mentality."

The bitterness of this feeling is difficult to overstate. The author of a recent essay in *Earthwatch Oregon,* the magazine of the Oregon Environmental Council, argued, "I don't want Oregon to be just a better L.A.," and went on to raise the California spectre no fewer than five times in a one-page article. A letter-writer to the Portland *Oregonian* last year defined the California mentality crisply as "eyesore condominiums, numerous fast-food franchises and ugly shopping centers." Opponents of a tax-cutting initiative in 1978 argued effectively that the measure was just a northern version of California's Proposition 13. Oregonians have even managed to put a variation on one of the oldest of American battle cries. "We know this is God's country," an official of a small Willamette

Valley town told *Willamette Week* earlier this year. "People in this town are not afraid to tell you to go back *down* where you came from."

Unfortunately, it seems clear that they will not; they will, instead, keep coming. A part of the bitterness of Oregon sectionalism is the feeling of some state residents (similar to a feeling held by other encircled regions) that the battle may already have been lost. Oregonians have seen the future and it looks like Orange County. One science fiction writer from Eugene has declared that area lost and has moved to less-settled Jackson County. A Portland outdoor writer says that British Columbia is now the Oregonian's Oregon.

But for the rest of the country, Oregon retains a powerful mystique, which has kept people moving in even as the economy has declined. "People in California look to Oregon as salvation," says a real estate agent from Grants Pass. "Oregon is the last hope of many people, including many who'll never actually get up here." Joel Garreau, in his book *The Nine Nations of North America,* gives most of his nations names like "The Foundry," "The Breadbasket," or "The Empty Quarter." But a wide strip running along the Pacific Coast from San Francisco to British Columbia is designated "Ecotopia." The chapter on that region begins on top of a mountain in Oregon, where Garreau explains what paradise smells like.

But if Ecotopia had a motto, Garreau notes, it would be "Leave. Me. Alone." The name itself comes from a novel by a Berkeley author advocating secession of the region (a proposal also made by *Oregon Times* in 1976). While residents along the entire coastal strip might be interested, Oregon would likely provide the secession movement's fire-eaters. Washington State relies too heavily on federal military contracts to really want to be left alone, and both Seattle and San Francisco are too cosmopolitan and wired into the rest of the country to be truly isolationist. But Oregon, with a strong sense both of its own uniqueness and of encroaching external corruption, might at this point seriously consider going into business with its own postage stamps.

There are already some indications that Oregonians feel that their destiny is somewhat apart from that of the country as a whole.

A poll taken in 1981 by Northwest Attitudes found that Oregonians were more pessimistic about whether the United States was headed in the "right direction" than were residents of Idaho or Washington. But 39 percent of Oregonians (a higher percentage than for the other two states) thought that their state would be a better place to live in the future.

One major component lies at the core of both Oregon's sectionalism and the immigration that largely provokes it—the collection of conditions and attitudes that make up Oregon's peculiar institution, "livability." The word "livability" is barely used outside Oregon; an Oregonian might suggest that this is because the condition doesn't exist outside the state either. But within the state, the notion of livability has achieved totem-like proportions. Cities sprout Committees for Livable Neighborhoods, politicians campaign on the issue, and the debate over any proposed public or private project is likely to rage over whether it will enhance or diminish the area's livability. When the city of Eugene passed a special tax levy in 1980 to restore Sunday library openings, street cleaning, and several park, swimming pool and fire-fighting positions, the proposal passed during a tax-cutting time partly because it was labelled the "livability levy." According to Carl Abbott, the word was pervasive in Portland politics of the 1970s: "Every candidate for commissioner advocated 'livable neighborhoods' or 'citizen organizations to keep neighborhoods livable' . . . ." The concept has been enshrined among the state's treasures, along with Mt. Hood and the Portland Trailblazers. "Oregon's livability," declared a letter in the *Oregonian,* "is why we're all here anyway."

Exactly what is meant by livability, however, is not entirely clear. The most immediate, emotional definition usually has to do with fresh air; a founder of the Cascade Run-Off road run in Portland once said, "Livability means being able to breathe without thinking about it." But Portland now has the 11th-worst air in the country among metropolitan areas, and to stand on a hill in Jacksonville and look toward Medford, the destination of many Californians, is to suspect that the newcomers brought the Los Angeles basin with them. Frequently, the mention of livability evokes descriptions of Oregon's natural attributes—the coastline, the Cascades, and the unseen desert that covers most of the state. But there are other places that go down to the ocean, and Oregonians tend to be fairly disdainful of many of them.

If livability has any definition, if there is some least common denominator to its persistent use in debate, it is related to the idea of limits. In its most sharply etched form, such as disputes over coastal development in Depoe Bay or Newport, livability appears as the limitation on what can be done to the environment for profit, a sentiment uncomplicated enough to be expressed on a T-shirt. In urban neighborhoods, the cry can apply to anything from noise control to limiting a municipal impulse to put a freeway through several hundred Portland living rooms. But often it seems to involve a limitation on people themselves (usually other people). It sometimes appears, with a certain irony, as though the fewer people inhabit an area, the more livable it is.

This aspect of livability was expessed by former Governor Tom McCall's famous statement, "Visit our state of enchantment— but for heaven's sake, don't stay!" Although McCall's position was, in I-dare-you fashion, counterproductive (the ensuing decade was the period of the state's most explosive population growth), it was immediately adopted by his constituents. Jim Cloutier of Eugene designed the Oregon Ungreeting Card, proclaiming on the outside, "Governor Tom McCall of Oregon invites you to visit," and on the inside, "California, Washington, Idaho, Arizona, and Wyoming."

Although tourism is the third largest industry in the state, it can even seem as though visitors aren't welcome; Oregon campgrounds have a surcharge for cars with out-of-state license plates. (The response was predictable: Idaho now puts a surcharge on cars with Oregon plates, and Washington, with Olympian subtlety, levies a surcharge on cars from states that levy a surcharge on Washington cars.) If Ecotopia had a motto, it would be Leave. Me. Alone.

Oregon is not, of course, the only state to react strongly to increased immigration. Colorado is perhaps its closest present analogue, both in internal reaction and external perception. That State is more directly in the mainstream of Sun Belt migration patterns than Oregon and is growing even faster, with its own natural attractions augmented by energy deposits and the songs of

John Denver. But the image of a beautiful, almost otherworldly refuge is common to both places. According to an admissions counselor at the University of Oregon, eastern students coming out to look at the U. of O. are usually, on the same trip, also visiting the University of Colorado.

Probably as a result of its own population influx, Colorado has also become interested in the area of limits. Voters there cancelled plans to hold the 1976 Winter Olympics in Denver, and the last gubernatorial election was a contest over who could control growth more tightly. And recently, a "Native-Born" Coloradan movement has emerged, with people who qualify displaying signs on their automobiles, in an implicit objection to the new arrivals (who sport their own signs).

There are at least two apparent differences between the situations of Oregon and Colorado. First, as noted earlier, the staunchest opponents of new immigration to Oregon are likely to be recent arrivals, who would rather turn in their Nikes than sport a bumper sticker labelling themselves newcomers. And despite the intermittent resentment directed at new arrivals, Oregon's quarrel is fundamentally with the rest of the world, not with itself.

The second, more crucial difference involves what is being defended. Coloradans talk angrily of the encroachments of excess population on the Rockies and the canyons, but livability in the Oregon sense has less to do with natural attributes than with a perceived way of life. And while Oregon, with an ocean next door, has perhaps greater geographic diversity than Colorado, one component of its way of life is a strikingly homogeneous population.

In the late 19th century, the Northern Pacific Railroad sought to populate the Northwest by sending 632,000 pieces of promotional literature to Britain, Sweden, Denmark, Holland, Switzerland and Germany, essentially anticipating the later ethnic calculations of the Immigration Act of 1924. The resulting immigration, added to the earlier New England roots, produced a heavily Anglo-Saxon population base. The most frequently noted aspect of this near uniformity is the state's small black population, but Oregon is also among the states lowest in percentage of Catholics and of residents with a mother tongue other than English. In these categories,

Oregon is among the least diverse of all states outside the South. It was this situation that caused organizers of Robert Kennedy's 1968 campaign to complain that Oregon was a giant suburb. This homogeniety also has a perceptible narrowing effect on the way of life that livability is intended to defend. Portland is a textbook example of Calvin Trillin's dictum that one should never eat ravioli anyplace where Italians are not at least a strong minority of the City Council.

It would be unfair to state flatly that ethnic uniformity is an unmentioned element in livability. Many of livability's most fervent advocates do not fit the prevailing pattern. But livability, like the environmental movement in general, is essentially a white middle-class concept and concern. There is also a perceptible suggestion that livability has something to do with ideas of comfort and security, conditions which Oregon is considered to possess in greater measure than some more diversely populated places that Oregonians regard as unlivable.

It seems clear, at any rate, that the concept of livability, as used and admired by Oregonians, does not include any assumption that demographic diversity is desirable or helps to make a society interesting or challenging. "I am very concerned that these 'planned communities,' with their food and energy production, their bike paths and their sandal shops, will all look and live alike," wrote Carlotta Collette in Portland's environmentally impeccable *Rain* magazine recently. "They'll all be little Eugene, Oregons and Boulder, Colorados with their shopping malls and oh-so-white homogeneity. The dreams are good, the plans careful and often very creative, but they leave out a large portion of our people and our country."

Avoiding this result will likely require ways of thinking that have not been prominent in livability considerations up to now. "While a general concern for Oregon's livability must be ongoing," E. Kimbark MacColl has written, "we should continually ask for whom the environment is being preserved or improved. We should be wary of self-congratulation and smugness, because we have been unusually fortunate. We have yet to experience the really painful population pressures that await us."

The prospects of dealing with these pressures, however, are somewhat clouded by the sectionalist intensity with which Oregonians view themselves and their lifestyle. Oregonians believe that they live in a unique commonwealth, and they have even managed (in a major strategic error) to persuade the rest of the country of it. To preserve this uniqueness they, bolstered by the stream of new arrivals, have developed a suspicion of the outside world and a distrust of agents of change. Admittedly, anyone operating on a policy of resolute opposition to external trends and developments is likely to be more often right than wrong, and both the impulse to pull up the drawbridge and the vague battle cry of livability represent understandable and frequently shrewd motivations. But there is also a tendency for these attitudes to turn into isolation and complacency; given the depth of feeling involved, it seems that Oregon is an active element in a rising wave of sectionalism in America.

A look at two different groups of Oregonians, at opposite ends of the state, may suggest something of the emotions involved. Manzanita is a small coastal community about ten miles south of Cannon Beach. Like much of the area on the west side of the Coast Range, it seems not quite in the mainstream of the state; Craig Smith, who managed Senator Packwood's reelection campaign last year, commented afterward that "Fishermen think of Salem much the way the Scots feel about London." But like much of the rest of Oregon, Manzanita has ambiguous feelings about development and outsiders. The coastal areas of north Tillamook County, from Garibaldi to Manzanita, have banded together to encourage tourism by retaining a Portland advertising firm, which has printed brochures dubbing the area "The Treasure Coast." On the other hand, there is opposition to any road improvement that would make Manzanita more directly accessible from Portland and the Willamette Valley. Within the polished-wood-and-stash-tea atmosphere of the Manzanita Inn, it is said that some people would open fire on the road crew.

Admittedly, there is a substantial degree of hyperbole to this, although the arc of the hyperbole is revealing in itself. But the language doesn't sound too different from that used by another group at the other end of the state, around Medford and Grants Pass. The survivalists—people who are moving to Oregon in expectation of the impending collapse of American civilization—have generally been regarded as fanatics with incomprehensible mental processes. But their way of thinking and attitude toward Oregon is really only a somewhat exaggerated version of the state's prevailing ideology. As words, after all, survivalism and livability are not that far apart.

According to the late Mel Tappan of Rogue River, Oregon, author of *Survival Guns,* the first commandment for survivalists is "You've got to get away from a city. It will be crazy." An Oregon advocate of livability might disagree only over the use of the future tense. Survivalists are interested in clean water and air and are opposed to military encampments in the areas where they propose to retreat. And they tend to fit the same white middle-class pattern apparent in the Oregon livability movement. Mel Tappan once complained that the "awareness of the need for retreating" was striking "too many doctors and lawyers . . . and not enough plumbers, electricians, or carpenters."

The essence of survivalism, by definition, is a search for safety, which often comes to mean security before as well as after the disaster. And the survivalists' ideas of what constitues security tends to reflect their backgrounds. "There are no large cities," says Bill Pier, a Los Angeles survivalist entrepreneur, explaining why he proposes to move to southern Oregon. "There 's no major minority population." It might be difficult, in fact, to distinguish too sharply between the motivations of those who come to Oregon in search of survival and those who come in search of livability. Moreover, the canned-goods Calvinism of the survivalists—their sense that salvation is not for everyone—is largely a somewhat exaggerated version of the exclusionist tendencies implicit in livability.

The obvious difference, of course, is the intensity of response. Oregonians may hope that fewer people come into the state, but most don't plan to greet them with automatic weapons. But as the anxiety level of the average Oregonian rises, that of the survivalists, after they have been in Oregon for a few years, declines; western civilization doesn't seem so precarious in Medford as it did in Los Angeles. After a while, survivalists may become not much more suspicious and exclusionist than the rest of the Oregon population; reaching that level may not require them to calm down much at all.

Several years after a carefully calculated move to Oregon, survivalists slowly turn into Oregonians. Unfortunately, they are emerging from their retreats to find that Oregonians, under the banner of livability, are slowly turning into survivalists.

CONTRIBUTORS

Judith Austin was born in San Diego, grew up in New York City, and then moved West to accept a position with the Idaho Historical Society. She is Editor of *Idaho Yesterdays* and coordinator of publications for the Idaho Historical Society.

Edwin R. Bingham is a native Californian who received a Ph.D. in history from UCLA and has taught for many years at the University of Oregon. He is the editor, with Glen Love, of the recent book *Northwest Perspectives: Essays on the Culture of the Pacific Northwest.*

David Brauner is a native Oregonian and holds a Ph.D. in anthropology from Washington State University. He is a professional archeologist at Oregon State University and has authored several reports on his archeological work.

Richard Maxwell Brown is Beekman Professor of Pacific and Northwest History and department chairman at the University of Oregon. He has published books and articles on violence in American history and is now working on a booklength manuscript tentatively titled, "The Great Raincoast of North America."

Robert Frank is a native of North Dakota, received a Ph.D. in English from the University of Minnesota, and is currently chairman of the English department at Oregon State University. He is author of *Don't Call Me Gentle Charles: A Reading of Lamb's Essays of Elia.*

John McClelland, Jr., a graduate of Stanford University, has edited and published newspapers in Washington since 1939. He is the author of *R. A. Long's Planned City—The Story of Longview* and *Cowlitz Corridor,* a history of transportation in the Cowlitz Valley.

Jarold Ramsey was raised in the sagebrush country of eastern Oregon near the Warm Springs Indian Reservation. He has a Ph.D. in English and teaches at the University of Rochester in New York. He is the author of several articles, poems, and a popular book on Northwest Indian legends, *Coyote Was Going There.*

William Robbins is a native of Connecticut, received a Ph.D. in history from the University of Oregon, and teaches history at Oregon State University. He is the author of *Lumberjacks and Legislators: Political Economy of the Lumber Industry, 1890-1941.*

Richard Ross was raised in several places in the American West and earned a Ph.D. in anthropology from Washington State University. Ross teaches at Oregon State University and is recognized as an authority on the archeology of the Oregon coast.

David Sarasohn was born in New York City, completed graduate work in history at UCLA, and then taught at Reed College. He is a former senior editor of *Oregon* magazine and now writes for *New Jersey* magazine.

Richard White was raised in California and received a Ph.D. in history from the University of Washington. He presently teaches at Michigan State University and is the author of the award-winning book, *Land Use, Environment, and Social Change.*

Robin Winks is master of Berkeley College, Yale University, and is the author of books on American foreign policy, detective fiction, the history of Canada's black population, and other subjects.

INDEX